PLURALISM AND UNITY?

THE INTERNATIONAL PSYCHOANALYSIS LIBRARY

General Editor: Emma Piccioli

Violence or Dialogue? Psychoanalytic Insights on Terror and Terrorism
edited by Sverre Varvin & Vamik D. Volkan

PLURALISM AND UNITY?

Methods of Research in Psychoanalysis

Edited by

Marianne Leuzinger-Bohleber,

Anna Ursula Dreher, & Jorge Canestri

Foreword by

Daniel H. Widlöcher

International
Psychoanalytical
Association

LONDON

First published in 2003 by
The International Psychoanalytical Association
Broomhills
Woodside Lane
London N12 8UD
United Kingdom

British Library Cataloguing in Publication Data

A C.I.P. for this book is available from the British Library

ISBN: 0-9523905-3-1

10 9 8 7 6 5 4 3 2 1

Produced for the IPA by Communication Crafts

Printed in Great Britain

www.ipa.org.uk

CONTENTS

THE INTERNATIONAL PSYCHOANALYSIS LIBRARY
IPA Publications Committee ix

ACKNOWLEDGEMENTS xi

EDITORS AND CONTRIBUTORS xiii

FOREWORD
Daniel H. Widlöcher xix

1 Pluralism and unity in psychoanalytic research: some introductory remarks
Marianne Leuzinger-Bohleber & Dieter Bürgin 1

2 The pluralism of sciences and psychoanalytic thinking
André Green 26

3 Plurality of sciences and the unity of reason
Michael Hampe 45

4 Between hermeneutics and natural science: some focal points in the development of psychoanalytic clinical theory in Germany after 1945
Werner Bohleber 63

5 Freud and psychoanalytic research: a brief historical overview
Alain de Mijolla 81

6 What are we looking for? How?
Roger Perron 97

7 What does conceptual research have to offer?
Anna Ursula Dreher 109

8 What kind of evidence makes the analyst change his or her theoretical and technical ideas?
Ricardo Bernardi 125

9 The logic of psychoanalytic research
Jorge Canestri 137

10 Attachment theory and long-term psychoanalytic outcome: are insecure attachment narratives less accurate?
Mary Target & Peter Fonagy 149

11 Psychotherapy with a victim of extreme violence: clinical case report and qualitative analysis
Sverre Varvin 168

12 Preliminaries for an integration of psychoanalysis and neuroscience
Mark Solms 184

13 Two pathways towards knowing psychoanalytic process
Norbert Freedman, Richard Lasky, & Marvin Hurvich 207

14 Psychoanalysis and science:
some remarks on demarcation and legitimation
Folkert Beenen 222

APPENDIX
Summary of additional studies presented at
the Pluralism of Sciences Conference 231

REFERENCES AND BIBLIOGRAPHY 239

INDEX 261

THE INTERNATIONAL PSYCHOANALYSIS LIBRARY

IPA Publications Committee

The International Psychoanalysis Library, published under the aegis of the International Psychoanalytical Association, is the product of the editorial policy of the IPA Publications Committee: to serve the interests of the membership and increase the awareness of the relevance of the discipline in related professional and academic circles, and to do so through a continuity of publications so that the benefits of psychoanalytic research can be shared across a wide audience.

The focus of the Library is on the scientific developments of today throughout the IPA, with an emphasis within the discipline on clinical, technical, and theoretical advances; empirical, conceptual, and historical research projects; the outcome of investigations conducted by IPA committees and working parties; selected material arising from conferences and meetings; and investigations at the interface with social and cultural expressions.

This second volume of the International Psychoanalysis Library originates from the IPA Conceptual Research Subcommittee's conference "Pluralism of Sciences: the Psychoanalytic Method between Clinical, Conceptual and Empirical Research", held in Frankfurt am Main in September 2002.

Emma Piccioli
Chair, IPA Publications Committee

ACKNOWLEDGEMENTS

We are indebted to the many colleagues who have given us support and helpful critique in writing and publishing this book: Cesare Sacerdoti and Emma Piccioli from the Publications Committee of the International Psychoanalytical Association, and Klara and Eric King of Communication Crafts; they have been the most important persons in this context. Without their competence, tolerance, and enormous work and engagement—in spite of the time pressure—this book would not have been published. We are also grateful to Ute Ochtendung, University of Kassel, who carefully edited the first versions of the manuscripts.

The contributions of this book are modified papers that were given at an International Conference, "Pluralism of Sciences: The Psychoanalytic Method between Clinical, Conceptual and Empirical Research" in Frankfurt am Main in September 2002. This conference meant an enormous investment of work and time on the part of many colleagues in the Sigmund-Freud-Institute (particularly Renate Stebahne, Marion Ebert-Saleh, Irma Ellersdorfer, Axel Scharfenberg, Herbert Bareuther, Werner Häcker, Oliver Glindemann, and Bernhard Chlopek, as well as the scientific staff, particularly Heinrich Deserno, Stephan Hau, Wolfgang Leuschner, and Tamara

Fischmann). Their extraordinary support created an atmosphere that contributed to the fruitful scientific exchange between researchers from different research cultures within the IPA. Again: many thanks!

Marianne Leuzinger-Bohleber, Anna Ursula Dreher, & Jorge Canestri

EDITORS AND CONTRIBUTORS

Folkert Beenen* (Amsterdam) is a psychoanalyst in private practice and former Head of the Research & Quality Control Department of the Dutch Psychoanalytic Institute. His special field of interest is integrating clinical work and scientific attitude/research in psychoanalysis.

Ricardo Bernardi* (Montevideo) is a training analyst of the Uruguayan Psychoanalytical Association, Professor and Head of the Department of Medical Psychology of the School of Medicine and on the Area of Research of the Faculty of Psychology (Universidad de la República, Uruguay), co-author of the National Program for Mental Health in Uruguay, and Chair of the Scientific Programme Committee of the 43rd International Psychoanalytical Congress. His special fields of interest are epistemology and philosophy of science; theory and history of psychology; psychoanalysis and society.

Werner Bohleber (Frankfurt a/M) is a psychoanalyst in private practice and a training and supervising analyst, vice-president of the

* Member of the Research Subcommittee for Conceptual Research of the International Psychoanalytical Association (Chair: Marianne Leuzinger-Bohleber).

German Psychoanalytical Association, and Editor of the journal *Psyche*. He is also Co-Chair for Europe of the Research Advisory Board of the IPA and member of the Working Party on Theoretical Issues of the EPF. His main research subjects include trauma; the psychoanalytic investigation of National Socialism; adolescence and identity; and nationalism, xenophobia, and anti-Semitism.

Dieter Bürgin* (Basel) is a training analyst of the Swiss Psychoanalytic Society (Basel Seminar), and head of the Department for Child and Adolescent Psychiatry, University of Basel, Switzerland. His research fields include infant development and psychoanalytic technique; development of triadic relationships in individuals and families; psychosomatics; psycho-oncology; and psychoanalytic psychotherapy with children and adolescents.

Jorge Canestri* (Rome) is psychiatrist and training and supervising analyst for the Associazione Italiana di Psicoanalisi and for the Asociación Psicoanalítica Argentina; Chair of the Ethics Committee of the IPA, of the Working Party on Theoretical Issues of the EPF, and of the 42nd Congress of the International Psychoanalytical Association in Nice (2001). Having specialized in linguistics and epistemology, he has published numerous psychoanalytic papers in books and reviews in this field.

Anna Ursula Dreher* (Frankfurt a/M) is a psychoanalyst and supervisor in private practice; she trained in the German Psychoanalytic Association, and she has publications on the foundations of research in psychoanalysis, on conceptual research, and on basic psychoanalytic concepts.

Peter Fonagy (London) is Freud Memorial Professor of Psychoanalysis and Director of the Sub-Department of Clinical Health Psychology at University College London, Director of the Child and Family Centre at the Menninger Foundation, Kansas, Director of Research at the Anna Freud Centre, London, a clinical psychologist, a training and supervising analyst in the British Psychoanalytical Society in child and adult analysis, and Chair of the Research Subcommittee for Empirical Research of the IPA. His numerous publications include the fields of developmental research, psychoanalysis and attachment theory, mentalization, and affect regulation.

Norbert Freedman* (New York) is Professor Emeritus at the State University of New York's Downstate Medical Center, and a faculty member and Director of the Program of Research in Psychoanalysis and a training analyst in IPTAR. His major area of interest is the study of symbolization and de-symbolization in the quantitative and qualitative study of the psychoanalytic process.

André Green (Paris) is a member of the Paris Psychoanalytic Society, former Vice-President of the IPA, a former professor at University College, London; and Honorary Professor at Buenos Aires University. His fields of research include borderline personality disorders; narcissism; language; affect; the work of the negative; time; and applied psychoanalysis.

Michael Hampe (Bamberg) is professor of philosophy at Bamberg University. His main fields of interest are contemporary metaphysics and the philosophical problems in biology and psychology, and he has numerous publications and books in this field.

Marvin Hurvich (New York) is a professor at Long Island University; clinical professor in the New York University Postdoctoral Program in Psychoanalysis; a training analyst at IPTAR and at the New York Freudian Society. His major area of interest is the clinical, theoretical, and empirical aspects of annihilation anxiety.

Richard Lasky (New York) is a clinical professor in the New York University Postdoctoral Program in Psychoanalysis, and a faculty member and training analyst in the Program of Research in Psychoanalysis in IPTAR. His major areas of interest are the dynamics of development in the analytic process, and multiple personality and the related dissociative disorders.

Marianne Leuzinger-Bohleber* (Frankfurt a/M) is a training analyst in the German Psychoanalytical Association, a member of the Swiss Psychoanalytical Society, professor for psychoanalytical psychology at the University of Kassel, and head of the Department for Basic Research at the Sigmund-Freud-Institute, Frankfurt. Her main research fields include epistemology and methods of clinical and empirical research in psychoanalysis; interdisciplinary discourse with embodied cognitive science; and modern German literature.

Alain de Mijolla* (Paris) is a training analyst, a member of the Psychoanalytic Society of Paris; Founder and President of the International Association for the History of Psychoanalysis; Editor of the *Dictionnaire International de la Psychanalyse*; and the author of many papers in the field of the history of Sigmund Freud and of the psychoanalytic movement, especially in France.

Roger Perron* (Paris) is training analyst of the Société Psychanalytique de Paris and Honorary Director of research at the Centre National de la Récherche Scientifique. He received his PhD from the Paris University. His main interests include child autisms, thought processes, symbolization in the analytic process, and he has published numerous publications in these fields.

Mark Solms* (London) is Honorary Professor of Neuropsychology at the University of Cape Town, Director of the Neuro-Psychoanalysis Center of the New York Psychoanalytic Institute, a consultant neuropsychologist at the Anna Freud Centre, London, lecturer in psychology at University College London, an associate member of the British Psychoanalytical Society, and a member of the British Neuropsychological Society. He is the main founder of the journal *Neuro-Psychoanalysis* and of the Society for Neuro-Psychoanalysis, and he has published widely in both neuroscientific and psychoanalytic journals.

Mary Target* (London) is a clinical psychologist and psychoanalyst in the British Psychoanalytical Society and a senior lecturer at University College London, organizing a Masters course in Psychoanalytic Theory. She is also Deputy Director of Research at the Anna Freud Centre, conducts research on attachment and personality development and on psychoanalytic and psychotherapy outcomes, is involved in systematic reviews of the efficacy of child mental health treatments, and also studies models of psychoanalytic education and chairs a Working Party on this for the European Psychoanalytic Federation. She has a half-time psychoanalytic practice.

Sverre Varvin* (Oslo) works in private practice and is senior psychiatric consultant at the Psychosocial Centre for Refugees, University of Oslo. He is a member of the Norwegian Psychoanalytic Society, a training analyst, and vice-president of the International Psychoanalytic Association, and he chairs the IPA Working Group on Terror and Terrorism. His research interests include traumatization, psychotherapy with traumatized patients, process-outcome research in psychoanalysis, and qualitative research,

Daniel H. Widlöcher (Paris) is Professor Emeritus of psychiatry at the University Pierre and Marie Curie and Head of the Psychiatric Department at the Salpêtrière Hospital, where he heads the centre for psychoanalytic and psychotherapy training. He trained in the French Psychoanalytical Society and is a training analyst of the French Psychoanalytical Association. He organized the International Psychoanalytical Association Congress in Paris (1975). He is currently President of the International Psychoanalytical Association. His numerous publications include different therapeutic techniques in working with children, psychoanalytic theories of change, metapsychology, historical papers on psychoanalysis in France, identity, depression, and psychopharmacological treatments.

FOREWORD

Daniel H. Widlöcher

We are all aware of the fact that psychoanalysis is a discipline that is in constant progress; proving it is another matter. How can it be visibly demonstrated to the cultural and scientific world? Let us discuss here our own representation of it and the way in which we seize the theoretical and clinical developments that are at work and that we favour with our own contribution.

Psychoanalysts and their institutions spend a considerable amount of time and energy on activities—conferences and publications—known as scientific. An important proportion of the budget of our institutions is allocated to these activities. What part of our investment results in an advance in our knowledge and practices?

It is true that these activities have a particular finality, of a repetitive nature, which keeps psychoanalysis alive by enabling what I would refer to as "generalized supervision"—that is to say, to develop our permanent capacity to transmit our psychoanalytic listening to a third party. Communicating our experience, testifying about our practice to other psychoanalysts, is a constant necessity for this practice. It legitimizes the very existence of our institutions.

But to this circular process, which constitutes a permanent characteristic of our institutions, one needs to add a linear process, an axis of progression, on the basis of which psychoanalysis evolves and progresses. It is this axis that requires better emphasis, to others and to ourselves.

Without necessarily disputing the value of psychoanalytic discoveries, contemporary culture is more interested in its future than in its past. Should we not leave to other methods and other sciences the task of widening the knowledge within the domain in which it previously worked so successfully? Such is the challenge of the current debate.

Certain psychoanalysts do not want to take up this challenge: the discovery handed down to them by Freud and his successors suffices for them to renew the experience themselves in each of the individual situations they are called upon to treat. At the extreme opposite, others have hardly any confidence left in the clinical: they feel that naturalist methods will take over in the widening of psychoanalytic discovery. A debate has ensued. In order to keep this debate at the serious level it deserves, it seems to me that it is necessary to place it in a position where it can, and should, retain the clinical process. For this, it is necessary to clearly oppose a process that considers psychoanalysis as a research tool with one that considers it as an object of research.

Psychoanalysis as an object of research

The opposition between quantitative and qualitative methods, between objective and subjective research, does not entirely take this distinction into account.

Quantitative research is undertaken mainly when we consider psychoanalysis as an object of knowledge. This is thus submitted to verification and interdisciplinary confrontation, which are at once both the practice of psychoanalysis and the empirical knowledge collected by it. It is the psychoanalytic method itself as a tool of knowledge and transformation that is explored by this way and that becomes the object of research. Psychoanalysis is no longer held to be a tool of discovery—it is considered an object of knowledge. Much writing has been dedicated to this naturalist approach (cf. IPA, *An Open Door Review of Outcome Studies in Psychoanalysis,* edited by Peter Fonagy, 1999). It has already given rise to numerous debates and to many books, thanks to the International Psychoanalytical Association's voluntarist policy, which has been in place for many years now, particularly via the activities of its Research Committee and its Research Advisory Board, with the view of financing psychoanalytic research programmes.

Cross-disciplinary dialogue is necessary if we wish to avoid a growing gap between our knowledge of mental activity and that provided by the related scientific disciplines.

Psychoanalysis is often questioned about its relationship with neurobiology. Given the considerable progress accomplished in the knowledge of the brain, there is some surprise as to why psychoanalysts have not made better use of this knowledge. I do not believe this question to be very relevant at this point. We study mental activity at a level of complexity that would be oversimplified by any comparison. The links that can be established in the area of memory or the emotions, for instance, are still very partial. The "real" question, at the present time, lies in the source of mental disorders and in the comparison of the action of medication and of psychotherapy. This is the area in which we need to conduct research, and which should lead to a certain consensus: by dismissing oversimplified schemes (such as opposing symptom and cause, or benign disorders and serious disorders) and coming back, perhaps, to the distinction between processes (such as the depressive or anxious response, or psychotic disorganization) that are accessible to medication acting on diffuse neuronic structures on the one hand and personality changes caused by complex psycho-physiological mechanisms on the other.

We are facing, with contemporary science of the mind, two intimately related phenomena. The first is the consequence of what has been called the cognitive revolution, and it has freed science of the mind from the behaviourist tyranny. For a great many years, psychoanalysis had constituted the only scientific approach to mental activity. It had done so with its method, which was clinical psychopathology—hence the gap with contemporary cognitive science, which is founded on the experimental method and artificial intelligence simulation. The second phenomenon has to do with the way this cognitive revolution has federated a whole set of scientific domains (psychology, linguistics, artificial intelligence, logic, etc.). Psychoanalysts had, from the start, established links with one or the other of these domains (such as, with linguistics, from Freud to Lacan; Lagache, Rapaport, or G. Klein with psychology; Eliott Jacques with social psychology; Spitz and Bowlby with ethology; and so forth).

Today, discussion needs to be opened with a "common market" of cognitive science, and psychoanalysts have some apprehensions in doing so, especially as the reduction of complex thinking operations to several elementary mechanisms takes different paths, depending on whether it is confined to the psychoanalytic approach (as with Bion, for instance) or is seeking to establish some compatibility with other cognitive models.

During the whole of my university career I was interested in the relationships between psychoanalysis and the cognitive sciences. I was already teaching the place of psychoanalysis against that of psychology when cognitive methods and studies were being developed. I have always considered that the confrontation between these two sciences of the mind could actually be of benefit to them. Whereas cognitive science has upheld affective and emotional variables as constant, psychoanalysis offers a complementary approach that addresses an area that cannot be excluded from a global view of the mind. As for psychoanalysts, I have often regretted their lack of interest—their hostility even—to studies that would enlighten, in a new way, their clinical experience and the use they make of exterior concepts that lie outside methodology but are present within their comprehension of thought, such as language or memory.

Approaches such as these aim not at advancing psychoanalysis, but at showing that the complex thinking processes to which its study is devoted are based on elementary operations identical to those on which language or communication science is based. The models and the use of these models differ, of course, but the mental activity to which they refer is one and the same. This is the condition under which psychoanalysis can, and should, maintain a dialogue with other domains. Marking the differences and the originality of the approach should not also mark a narcissistic and paranoid withdrawal but lead to dialogue and exchange.

This is how we can get out of the misdirected debate on the legitimacy of psychoanalysis. The scientific value of psychoanalysis will not be demonstrated by any experimental confirmation, but by showing how it contributes to the knowledge of mental activity through its own, specific approach, which should be seen as a contribution to related branches of the science of the mind.

In the report he presented in 1912, with a view to creating the International Psychoanalytical Association, Ferenczi struck this optimistic note: "If we compare the scientific stagnation of current psychology and psychiatry and the sterility of anatomical research in the last few decades to the dynamism and vitality of our work . . . we shall quickly perceive that we have no reason to envy our clinical colleagues . . ."[1] (Ferenczi, 1964, p. 286; translated for this edition). Such an observation was still well founded for those of my generation who were embarking on psychoanalysis during the 1950s. Admittedly, this is no longer the case today, when, rather than the one identified by Freud, the challenge is the following: in a scientific and cultural field that is expanding on all sides, how much development is taking place in psychoanalysis? It is really the question of progress that is at issue. "What is new in psychoanalysis?" is a question we are asked not only by the media, but also by clinicians and scientists.

Psychoanalysis as research

Psychoanalysts would be mistaken to rely solely on empirical research in answering this question. To be sure, this research is necessary to achieve numerous objectives: evaluation of care, the development and studies of personality, process studies during treatment, and so on. But this is not enough. To base everything on such research would imply that our clinical practice and the theories it inspires are merely naive approximations of reality, without an objective foundation. In which case, psychoanalysis would be no more than one practice among others. But how can we reply to this question about progress in our clinical practice if we lack the means first of all to discuss it among ourselves before doing so with others? This is a question that is posed very forcibly today. Our presence within contemporary culture depends on how we reply.

Today, it is a matter of giving new impetus to our research policy by launching a programme of activities within the area of conceptual research—that which relates to knowledge linked to our clinical practice. Psychoanalysis has its place in a vast conceptual movement that has marked, throughout the past fifty years, the human and social sciences, which have the mission to structure knowledge emanating from social practices based on communication between men, such as pedagogy and the economic and political sciences.

As for any practice of human action, psychoanalysis in general, and the particular approaches that characterize its different schools, depends on models that articulate theory, technique, and the objects of knowledge. While distinct models were developing (and this is already true in the evolution of Freud's thought itself), the method appeared as an ensemble of models that more or less fit into each other. The current pluralism is a pluralism of theories, techniques, and grids of clinical listening. These models have added themselves one to another, at times assuming a predominant position or even the monopoly but without ever rendering the previous model null and void.

Different axes of research—historical, epistemological, and methodological approaches, and so on—belong within this domain. We need to carry out critical research on the concepts and develop systematic clinical studies. In brief, we need to complement traditional clinical debate with planned research. As with any research programme, these programmes need to be developed by defining their objectives beforehand, to expose themselves to a refutation of hypotheses, and to lend themselves to a more precise definition of their methods and validation. We can expect from this area of research not only a better knowledge of our practice, but also a better quality in our scientific exchange and greater rigour within our psychoanalytic thought.

In September 2002, a colloquium on this issue of articulation between the various forms of psychoanalytic research was held in Frankfurt, and the discussions were based on research work and epistemological thought. The present publication resumes the major part of these contributions, and the International Psychoanalytical Association, which supported this colloquium, can today be proud to count this work among its publications.

Pluralism and Unity? Methods of Research in Psychoanalysis is both a report and a manifesto for the future of the spirit of research within the international psychoanalytic community.

NOTE

1. Although this comment was in the original German and French editions, it did not appear in the English edition.

PLURALISM AND UNITY?

1

Pluralism and unity in psychoanalytic research: some introductory remarks

Marianne Leuzinger-Bohleber & Dieter Bürgin

Psychoanalytic research in times of globalization: uniformism versus multitude?

At the beginning of the twenty-first century, the world of sciences—including the world of psychoanalysis and all kinds of psychotherapy research—is determined by a global network. As a consequence, new possibilities are created, which is as true for psychoanalytic research as for other fields. In science an easy exchange of knowledge, research methods, and results has, of course, many advantages: a Korean analyst is able to discuss her research project with the most able members of the International Psychoanalytical Association's Research Committee—no matter whether they are located in London, Denver, or Santiago de Chile. However, it is a known fact that globalism has negative aspects as well: distinct local features, cultural multiplicity, and the charm of diverse traditions are

Part of this introductory chapter is a modified version of papers given by M. Leuzinger-Bohleber at the EPF Congress in Prague, April 2002, and at the 62nd Congress of French-Speaking Analysts in Brussels, 11 May 2002 (see Leuzinger-Bohleber, 2002b).

endangered through having to adopt a uniformity—or they may even disappear.

A similar danger can also exist for an internationally linked psychoanalytic research community. An epistemologically outdated, uniform understanding of science in the sense of "*Einheitswissenschaft*" [unity of science] presumes to become the dominating or even exclusive definition of "science", simply because it claims to have apparently global and universally valid criteria of scientific quality. Such a uniform understanding of science destroys the richness and variety of attempts to research unconscious phantasies and conflicts, a research subject characterized by the fact that it is not observable directly, as well as by its complexity and its ambiguousness.

In contrast to a uniform view of science, in this volume the editors would like to make visible some of the variety and diversity of psychoanalytic research cultures in different psychoanalytic societies and their shared commonalities. It is our hope that the diverse approaches to the search for insight become apparent in this collection. The great respect and curiosity for the Other, for locally grown perspectives, could even guarantee a creative and innovative development in worldwide psychoanalytic research, as we would like to outline in this introduction.

We found a fascinating promotion for diversities and contradictory views in the first part of the well-known, provocative book *Empire: The New World Order* (2000) co-authored by Michael Hardt, a scientist in literary studies, and the political scientist Antonio Negri. In the book, which was recently released in German, the authors ask themselves which movements lead to new developments in times of globalization—that is, developments that are based on the local, diverse, and plural but where nevertheless a global perspective always emerges. Their thesis is that intellectuals in different countries will form a kind of intuitive, not strategically planned resistance. This occurs as soon as mighty, destructive globalized tendencies and strategies (on the part of any kind of "empire") start to dominate and threaten local traditions and value systems. Hardt and Negri use the term "multitude" for such innovative and creative movements and describe it as "the various amounts of productive and creative individuals in globalisation, which has learnt to sail this huge ocean. Always moving, they form the constellations of singularities and events; they continuously and globally force the system to reconfigure . . ." (Hardt & Negri, 2000, p. 71).

It seems to us that this thesis also has relevance to current psychoanalytic research. Productive globalized discourses on research in psychoanalysis probably also rely on the critique of the multitude. This means that intellectually and psychoanalytically active members of the different psychoanalytic societies criticize the uniforming of science and globalizing movements in order to "continuously and globally force" international research institutions "to reconfigure" in the wake of contradictions that manifest themselves locally, in the diverse psychoanalytic cultures. These protests and critical reflections—in the sense of a "multitude"—are not planned or coordinated. Nevertheless, they can form a common force—for example, by remembering the specific quality of psychoanalysis as a science of the unconscious, which cannot be studied through seemingly globally "true, effective, and objective" research strategies that have been postulated worldwide.

Let us briefly remember why the myths of science, of "objectively measuring" psychoanalytic processes and therapy outcomes, seem to dominate a certain international Zeitgeist: during the last two decades, the health-care systems of many countries have put pressure on psychoanalysis as a way of treatment. Psychoanalysis should show in an "objective" way that the results of treatment are effective, efficient, and cost-effective. The psychoanalytic communities have tried to take up this challenge in many different ways: the IPA presidents Joseph Sandler, Robert Wallerstein, and Otto Kernberg made great efforts to strengthen research in psychoanalysis by creating the annual Research Conference in London, the Research Advisory Board, and the Research Committee chaired by Peter Fonagy. In 1985 Horst Kächele and Helmut Thomä organized a pre-conference on empirical research in Ulm, separately from the IPA conference in Hamburg. In contrast, such pre-conferences took place right before the main conference in Santiago de Chile in 1999 and in Nice in 2001.

The stronger direct contact, especially with quantitative–empirical research approaches in psychoanalysis, has enabled many members of the IPA to participate actively in a critical discussion on research in psychoanalysis. Representatives of most different, locally conceived traditions in research are in a position to express their standpoints. To name just one example: the connection between psychoanalytic research and philosophy, literature, and art is a great deal more important to French and German colleagues than empirical–psychoanalytic research based in psychiatry and academic psychology (see the contributions of André Green and Roger Perron in this volume). Some believe that trying to prove the results of psychoanalytic treatment in an empiricist–objective way is a gesture of exaggerated adjustment to the above-mentioned Zeitgeist, which uses the "myth of science" to disregard feelings of impotence and helplessness while one is confronted with the complex and often hidden determinants of psychic suffering in human beings. Instead, these colleagues plead for an intensive reflection of this Zeitgeist, applying the Freudian tradition of cultural criticism ["*Freud'sche Kulturkritik*"] in order to try to understand the unconscious roots of idealized terms of science like "objectivity" and "efficiency".

These manifold discussions on psychoanalytic research may have been one of the reasons why the current president of the IPA, Daniel Widlöcher, wanted to underline the breadth of possible research areas in psychoanalysis by creating a second Research Subcommittee for Conceptual, Clinical, Epistemological and Historical Research. Within this body, the plurality and variety of psychoanalytic research is to be considered, and contradictions and controversies, freed from the hidden resistance against quantitative–empirical research, are to be brought to the surface. Of course, with the existence of two different subcommittees, some danger of reciprocal projections could arise and support polarizations that are in reality non-existent. We, however, hypothesize that the multitude of different research traditions could push ahead the psychoanalytic research fleet on this globalized ocean and clamour for a change of direction wherever necessary and wherever rationally justified.

Such unavoidable corrections of mainstream positions and political decisions within the IPA research culture may be based on scientific discourses, including the critical reflections of different research traditions and diverse epistemological backgrounds. Therefore we would like to sketch some of these discourses and reflections in the early parts of our introductory remarks, illustrating some of the roots of the current pluralism of science. We then try to contribute to a more precise definition of clinical, conceptual, and empirical research in psychoanalysis while at the same time introducing the different contributions of this volume. The chapter concludes with a brief report we have added on the International Conference held in Frankfurt in September 2002—"Pluralism of Sciences and the Psychoanalytic Method between Clinical, Conceptual and Empirical Research"—which was organized by the new Research Subcommittee and at which the papers that make up this book were originally presented.

Clinical psychoanalytic research and "Freud-bashing"

According to Freud and many contemporary psychoanalysts, clinical experience and research cannot be separated. Insight is followed by the curing of the patient and simultaneously supports research. However, in the age of worldwide "Freud-bashing" (see, e.g., Lear, 1995), there is more and more criticism of this "*Junktim*" of research and curing (Freud, 1926e). With this criticism, the understanding of science as described above is once again radically questioned: it is claimed that this psychoanalytic understanding of science does not correspond to "science" (as, for example, applied in experimental, controlled studies). These claims are often based on a naive but powerful idealization of natural science, whose triumph over the human and social sciences is celebrated. What epistemological arguments and points as regards content can be put forward to counter these attacks against psychoanalysis, which stem from the current natural–scientific positivist research paradigm? How can it be justified that even if not every clinician is devoted to research, clinical–psychoanalytic everyday experience is still the indispensable "field-research" for psychoanalysis? Are genuinely psychoanalytic or extra-clinical "objective" criteria decisive for clarifying whether insights are limited to a specific clinical situation, to a single case, or whether they contribute generally in the "scientific" sense to a knowledge that is "universally valid"? Are there differences between "healing" insights in the psychoanalytic situation and "research"—and if so, what differences?

These questions lead us right to the centre of the epistemological, methodological, and clinical discourse of today's psychoanalysis. Therefore, only some of the above-mentioned aspects are discussed in this introduction in order to contribute to a current discussion that already fills entire libraries.

The understanding of psychoanalytic research and its criteria is influenced not only by scientific theory, but also by specific cultural phenomena: consider, for instance, the corresponding discourses in the Anglo-Saxon compared with the European continental (e.g. French and German) culture (see, e.g., Werner Bohleber's contribution in this volume). When it comes to ourselves, we are most familiar with research traditions in Switzerland and Germany. The following thoughts are based mainly on these traditions. We take them as a contribution to the current effort, concerned with intensifying the dialogue between psychoanalysts and researchers who belong to these different research cultures.

Some remarks on the history of science: "unified science" and the "pluralism of sciences"

Since resources in the German health sector have become tighter, the "scientific nature", "efficiency", and "effectiveness" of psychoanalytic treatment have once again come into doubt. In the wake of these debates it is claimed time and again that psychoanalysts need to subject their work to so-called controlled studies, apparently forgetful of the fact that discussion concerning these studies has gone on for decades (cf., inter alia, Kächele, 1992).

Political motives apart, a historically outdated "model of unified science" ["*einheitswissenschaftliches Modell*"] is declared the yardstick for quality and forms the basis for these claims. According to this standard, for example, the natural scientific ideal of the controlled, "prospective–empirical" double-blind trials (Randomized Controlled Trials: RCTs) is considered the most important scientific hallmark. Hardly anyone remembers, however, the fact that RCTs were originally used in pharmacology in order to test "blindly" the effect of a new medication in comparison to a control group, who were given placebos, and that this research strategy cannot simply be taken out of its context and transferred to other disciplines. It certainly cannot be denied that research based on this paradigm boasts striking successes in medicine, and an idealization of the scientific paradigm of pharmaceutical medicine seems therefore understandable. However, it is impossible to equate the success of a psychotherapy with the success of a medication. Evaluation of the first is far more complex: each patient's and his or her therapist's idiosyncrasies have to be taken into account; moreover, the large variety of therapeutic dyads cannot be ignored. On the other hand, psychoanalysis cannot escape from proving its efficiency. It is impossible to avoid this responsibility by pointing to the speciality of the science if we want to stick to our demands that psychoanalysis remain a cure financed by public means. Above all, it would be problematic for us psychoanalysts to retreat to a psychoanalytic ivory tower, as this might mean that eventually our science's creative and innovative potential could run out. We know from chaos theory that each shielding of a system means that its liveliness and creativity dries out. Thus, according to our experience as clinicians and researchers, we have to come to terms with a characteristic area of conflict: on the one hand, there is the danger of over-adjustment to an understanding of research that is inadequate for psychoanalysts; on the other hand, there are the perils of refusing a scientific discourse by a self-absorbed retreat to an exclusive discussion within our psychoanalytic ivory tower. This is an area of conflict that we have to be able to bear and to reflect on critically if we are to prevent the future of our discipline being seriously threatened. If psychoanalysis sacrifices its autonomy as scientific discipline and clinical–therapeutic method, it will lose its "thorn Freud" and, as Freud (1926e) feared, become just another partial discipline in medicine. He writes in *The Question of Lay Analysis*:

> Yes indeed. I wanted to bring up a third interest—the interest of science. What I have to say about that will concern you little; but, by comparison, it is of all the more importance to me.
>
> For we do not consider it at all desirable for psycho-analysis to be swallowed up by medicine and to find its last resting-place in a text-book of psychiatry under the heading "Methods of Treatment", alongside of procedures such as hypnotic suggestion, autosuggestion, and persuasion, which, born from our ignorance, have to thank the laziness and cowardice of mankind for their short-lived effects. It deserves a better fate and, it may be hoped, will meet with one. As a "depth-psychology", a theory of the mental unconscious, it can become indispensable to all the sciences which are concerned with the evolution of human civilization and its major institutions such as art, religion and the social order. It has already, in my opinion, afforded these sciences considerable help in solving their problems. But these are only small contributions compared with what might be achieved if historians of civilization, psychologists of religion, philologists and so on would agree themselves to handle the new instrument

> of research which is at their service. The use of analysis for the treatment of the neuroses is only one of its applications; the future will perhaps show that it is not the most important one. In any case it would be wrong to sacrifice all the other applications to this single one, just because it touches on the circle of medical interests [Freud, 1926e, p. 248]

However, if psychoanalysis refrains from the critical dialogue with other sciences and the public, it will not only sacrifice its potential as far as critique of culture is concerned but also its innovative, creative new findings and developments in its own discipline.

As far as philosophy of science is concerned, we suppose that there are some parallels to dealing with this area of conflict, in the above-mentioned paradigm of unified science. "Scientific objectivity" and "unambiguous truths" are idealized, whereas epistemological differences between the various scientific disciplines are denied. [The idea of the "megalomania of being able to achieve and control everything" included in this concept is a related subject, with which Devereux (1967) dealt intelligently in the area of research; a more recent brilliant analysis of the same issue was published by Holzhey (2001).] We want to address this point briefly. (See also Michael Hampe's contribution in this volume.)

Hampe and Lotter recently (2000) demonstrated the historical roots of this paradigm. Bacon and Descartes were the first to compare "naturalistic experience" with scientific knowledge. Thus, they stood out against scholastic science, in which, rather than new knowledge being generated, it was well-known experience that was to be discussed and reasoned. Bacon and Descartes explained—in contrast to the latter assumption—that the discovery of until then unknown fields of reality was the real aim of the new sciences in the seventeenth century. According to their findings, new discoveries can only be made by means of a methodical and controlled experience, whereas everyday experience rather dulls people's minds instead of brightening them. Interestingly, this important role of methodologically controlled experience was increasingly forgotten in the nineteenth century, and it was not until much later that it turned up again in an idealized form—in combination with the way scientific experiments are conducted nowadays. The physics experiment, which examines quantitative dependencies between exactly defined entities in artificially generated systems (cf. controlled double-blind trials), became the paradigm of scientific experience for a long time.

In the opinion of Bacon, Bachelard, and Popper, scientific experience is opposed to everyday life. According to them, "empirically based" means the "result of a certain measurement" that is not based on everyday experience but—if it is scientifically interesting—produces new knowledge that does not correspond to the usual way of thinking—that is, everyday experience—and is independent of the respective researcher conducting the experiment. Karl Popper describes science as a generator of hypotheses that are all the better the more improbable they seem to be in the light of everyday experience (and predominating scientific assumptions). Scientific experience should approach truth in a completely negative way by "falsifying" hypotheses.

This contrast between scientific and personal experience proved to be crucial: everyday and life experience can never be simply repeated, and they are neither independent of the situation, nor can they be separated from practical issues, as is the case with experiments. Moreover, we learn "by experience"—that is, we attribute to experience importance, its own activity and creativity—in contrast to the empiricists, who consider a researcher's subjective experience during an experiment a source of distortion.

After intensive discussions of these issues, Popper's view of suddenly newly emerging scientific discoveries by experimentally revolutionary individual works has meanwhile been modified. As early as 1935, Ludwig Fleck pointed to the fact that experiments that are the basis for truly new scientific findings are usually unclear and incomplete and are marked by the fact that their result cannot be reproduced. Therefore, discoveries may by no means be considered as unique perceptions of the unexpected as found in a "clean experiment". On the contrary, they are based on a lengthy research process. In this, perceptions that seemed at first unfamiliar and thereby constituted in the beginning unnoticed "anomalies" become challenging new insights if they are discerned as such in a specific historical context of discovery [*"Verweisungszusammenhänge"*] (cf. Kuhn, 1977). These insights in a special context of discovery always have a social context. Thus, experience is not "objective" or "neutral" but "makes sense according to one's style of thinking" (Fleck, 1935).

In the history of psychoanalysis, there are many examples for the social and cultural context of scientific discoveries: even Freud himself modified his discoveries and theories by conversing with Fliess and with the members of the *"Mittwochsgesellschaft"* ["Wednesday Meetings"], and also by the impressions that social and societal events made on him (cf., e.g., the influence of the First World War on his writings on clinical phenomena and cultural theory: Federn, 2001; Grubrich-Simitis, 1981; Mijolla, 2003; Perron, 1999; Sandler & Dreher, 1996; Steiner, 1994; or, related to the history of science, Wallerstein, 2001, and others).

Due to the reflections outlined above, the impact of the researcher's personal and social experience on his research process has been successively released from the empiricist's deprecation. Moreover, it has increasingly been discussed that the "object or subject of experience" is different in the individual sciences of experience. During the past 50 years these discussions have led to a modern understanding among German scientific theoreticians of the pluralism of scientific experience, method, and "truth" (cf. below), even if, despite this specification of the sciences as "joint possession", there is still an insight into the blurred difference between scientific experience and other kinds of experience (cf., inter alia, Kurthen, 1998).

> As soon as we understand scientific experience in Bacon's sense as the discovery of something new (and not only as the basis of discovery in a special context), the typical aspects of everyday and life experience become relevant for the scientific concept of experience whereas the "empiristic" thought is reduced to a mere reception of facts. This applies to the practical as well as the social and the negative side of experience. For activities such as practising the conduction of experiments, handling equipment etc. are all part of science itself. It is only by experience that the scientist learns to perceive the details which make a phenomenon so particular. Therefore, it is just as impossible to consider observation during an experiment simply an information which is clear and definite enough to be repeated any time as it is impossible to come across this kind of information in real life. An inexperienced medic is unable to see the same things under the microscope as the experienced one, an inexperienced ethologist is unable to distinguish the socially relevant movements in a pack of wolves. [Hampe & Lotter, 2000, p. 14]

Of course, this problem is especially explosive in an area such as psychotherapy and psychoanalytic research: only the experience gained in a psychoanalysis and a long psychoanalytic training as well as during a professional life gives psychoanalysts the ability to recognize independently and actively as well as to observe systematically the patients' unconscious processes.

It is interesting that we have had an analogous debate in psychoanalysis for years. To mention just one example: Bornstein (1989) stated in a summary of a special volume of the *Psychoanalytic Inquiry on Methodology in Psychoanalytic Research*: "However, the epistemology of science has changed. Logical positivism no longer reflects the standard of scientific theory. Science has entered a postmodern era (Toulmin, 1986) wherein relativity and subjectivity are recognized as intrinsic to scientific investigation" (Bornstein, 1989, p. 166). However, it is explained that even if the concept of the "pluralism of sciences" is, indeed, concerned with postmodern liberation of the myths of uniformity (Kiesler, 1966), it simultaneously deals with the specificity of the research methods and quality criteria in different scientific disciplines, which can by no means be equated with the postmodernist "anything goes" (see also Rubovits-Seitz, 2001).

To return to the debates in the history of science: the specification of the sciences and the emphasis on the pluralism of sciences also applies to another assumption that was common in the nineteenth century and is still widespread: the schematic difference between the so-called natural sciences ["*Naturwissenschaften*"], on the one hand, and the humanities ["*Geisteswissenschaften*"], on the other. According to this, individuals are considered cases corresponding to a general rule in the natural sciences, whereas in the human and social sciences the focus is on the understanding of "the phenomenon itself in its unique and historical concretion" (Gadamer, 1960, p. 2). The authenticity of the historical experience is presumed to be another reason for this categorical difference. Moreover, the latter refers to the supposedly artificial character of (natural) scientific experience, in contrast to the historical event of human and social experiences that are based on traditions, existing artefacts, texts, and so on. Therefore, seen in the light of history, this sharp differentiation cannot be held on to, as the natural scientific experiments can also not be considered to be independent of the social context in which they take place, and they are "theory- as well as experience-based". On the other hand, it is also important that attempts are made to test assertions by referring to intersubjectivity in the human sciences. These assertions, too, have to be general; they cannot simply be based on single events. Therefore, if the differences between natural sciences and the humanities are carefully scrutinized, it can be noted that they vanish more and more—which is one reason why the current discourse in the philosophy of science is centred, above all, around the understanding of the respective specific experience, methods, and quality criteria, both in the various natural sciences and in the individual humanities—that is, the debate is centred around a systematic comparison of concepts of experience in the individual sciences the members of which should preserve their own values ["*Werthaltigkeit*"] and communicate them among themselves.

Psychoanalytic research in the age of the "pluralism of science"

In our opinion, the consequences of these reflections in the field of the philosophy of science are that modern psychoanalysis should neither feel obliged to adapt to the criteria of "science" in terms of a unified science characterized by the natural sciences, as some—mainly Anglo-American—therapy researchers claim, nor should psychoanalysts define their profession in the state of suspense between the arts and the sciences, as some German psychoanalysts would have it (e.g. Lorenzer, 1985). Instead, psychoanalysis may vigorously defend its specific psychoanalytic concept of experience and its specific "test and truth criteria" in line with other, equally specific sciences. In view of the pluralism of the sciences stemming from the various concepts of experience, psychoanalysis is—by positioning itself in this way—by no means isolated but has concerns similar to those of other contemporary sciences, which all attempt to explain to each other the special character of their discipline, to start a dialogue, and, at their best, to promote an interdisciplinary cooperation—a cooperation that takes place despite the different angles from which each discipline approaches the same subject of research (cf., inter alia, Leuzinger-Bohleber, 1995, 2002b). The idea of a unified science, as—full of enthusiasm and persuasive power—it was first proclaimed during the era of German idealism and later in a different form during that of logical empiricism, has not turned out to be tenable. "Like all euphorias, the notion of a philosophical unified science was not a permanent one, it passed. At this point I only want to state that I do not know of any serious representative of philosophy of science who still cultivates the notion that a phenomenon such as a unified science exists" (Hampe, 2000, p. 28). The sciences have, rather, become more subtly diversified. The differentiation between the natural sciences and the humanities as proclaimed by Dilthey at the end of the nineteenth century can no longer adequately depict the diversity of the various scientific disciplines with which we deal today (cf. Follesdal, 1999). Thus, it has become increasingly obvious that it is no longer possible to conceive of a unified theoretical concept for all these sciences. There is no form of scientific theory that could be applied equally to mathematics, physics, biology, psychology, sociology, archaeology, history, and philology, let alone to medicine, jurisprudence, and theology. We are, indeed, in a state of the "pluralism of the sciences": first of all, pluralism of sciences means not only pluralism of subjects, but, second, also of scientific forms of theories; third, these different forms of theories produce a pluralism of scientific experience, which is made possible by trying to discipline our everyday experience. Quality of experience, its importance with respect to precision, completeness, and so on are thus declared values. In the individual sciences the pluralism of these different epistemic values is realized in different ways, and in each science special methods have been developed in order to ensure that the precision, completeness, level of contrast, and so forth, which are defined by each science in a unique way, could be developed step by step. Therefore, the pluralism of sciences means, first of all, a pluralism of "theories, secondly of experience, thirdly of epistemic values ["*Erkenntniswerte*"] and fourthly a pluralism of methods" (Hampe, 2000, p. 33).

In psychoanalysis it is considered especially important that these reflections result in the necessary detachment from a unified theoretical concept and also from the notion—represented by the logical empiricists—that theory and experience could be separated (cf. Figure 1.1). The scientist's process of insight does not consist of two completely separate steps: his experience and its subsequent conversion into a theory. As illustrated by the use of a microscope, a theory not only uses past experience but makes this experience happen at the same time. Thus—as already mentioned—the difference between scientific and everyday experience is reduced.

The precise differentiation between an analyst who considers himself a practitioner and not a scientist is more difficult, as, in our opinion, clinical practice cannot be separated from a research attitude. However, we find contradictory opinions on these issues in the discussions about the "Junktim research" ["*Junktim-Forschung*"] on this point. Thomä (1981), for instance, pleads for a separation of therapy and research. We do not agree, because we think that the analyst's therapeutic stance cannot be separated from the desire to discover new insights into unconscious connections, which is, in other words, a research intention, independent of the question of whether or not the insights gained from the psychoanalytic process are subsequently scientifically communicated. Moreover, the truthfulness of interpretations can only be investigated by patient and analyst in a common process of searching for shared insight, which means with the intention of attaining an intersubjective agreement.

As it is essential to distinguish science from the practical application of knowledge—for instance, a baker's or a fruit gardener's skills—and from ideologies and religious dogmas, what common defining characteristics of science can be found despite its pluralism? What is the "unity" of sciences compared with practical knowledge transfer or belief systems like religions, and so on? According to Hampe (2000), distinguishing traits would be "the disciplining of experience" or the systematic use of methods. An Anglophile is likely to read English literature and a musicologist to listen to Bach in a more sophisticated way than would a lay person. A chemist will perceive smells and tastes differently, and a psychoanalyst will react to an analysand's dreams in a more specific way than would someone who is untrained. Therefore, scientific experience is not simply a quantitative increase in everyday experience: it is more precise, more complete, and more representative, and its level of contrast is higher, full of self-criticism concerning the necessity to reflect on the possible subjectivity of one's experiences. Moreover, the scientist is different from the practitioner who applies knowledge, in the sense that the former considers such above-mentioned criteria as precision and the extension of his knowledge as the ultimate goal, whereas a baker or a fruit gardener, for example, invariably has to make economic use of his knowledge as his efforts determine his standard of living. Thus, sciences can be distinguished from other forms of life such as dogmas, ideologies, practical skills and truisms, and so forth by the fact that they are less characterized by shared modalities of thinking, experience, or methods than by the willingness for and ability of intersubjectivity, which enables the communication of the different methods, modalities of thinking, and experience involving a simultaneous abandonment of the idea of charismatic initiation as a precondition of this intersubjectivity.

Thus, it is finally the "unity of reason" (Hampe), the striving for insight as a value in itself, by which the sciences are related or even united. The willingness to and the ability of intersubjectivity is considered a consequence of this stance, a stance that also characterizes psychoanalytic research. Hampe illustrates this "unity of sciences" with the following example. If an observer watches different forms of life from a distance, science will be discernible as one single "unified" entity. It is the great distance that enables us to see the sciences as one entity—as, for example, from an aeroplane the woods seem to be one single entity alongside cities and lakes, even if for pedestrians each tree remains a single plant.

The striving for intersubjectivity in psychoanalytic research

Which possibilities for achieving "intersubjectivity" in psychoanalysis have been developed as a yardstick for scientific quality? From Figure 1.1 (a modified version of a chart by Ulrich Moser, 1992) it can be discussed whether the genuinely psychoanalytic research method can only be used during the psychoanalytic situation in a professionally described framework with the aim of gaining "new insights" into unconscious processes that come to light in transference and countertransference, dreams, slips of the tongue, acting out, and so on. The above-mentioned "Junktim research" is based on the use of this method, psychoanalytic clinical research (Figure 1.1). We owe almost all of our considerable insights into unconscious processes to this kind of "clinical psychoanalytic research". In an effort "to be intersubjective" and to establish a dialogue with other scientific disciplines, other "extra-clinical" research strategies have also been developed in the course of the 100 years of the existence of psychoanalysis (Figure 1.1).

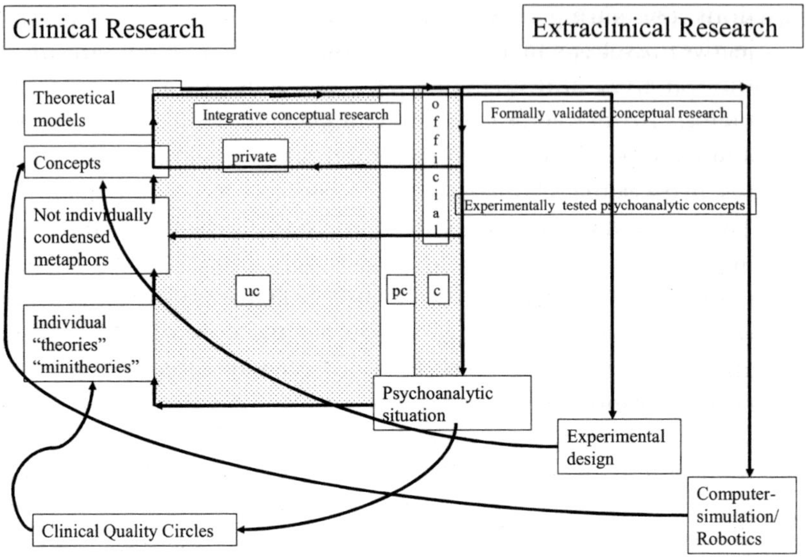

Figure 1.1 Psychoanalytic research

Clinical and extra-clinical research in psychoanalysis

1. The left-hand side of Figure 1.1 shows an illustration of the specific research method in psychoanalysis, the so-called "Junktim research": the intensive clinical experiences with individual patients are the fundamental basis of our successive clinical and theoretical understanding of unconscious processes arrived at by applying specific psychoanalytic research methodology. Moreover, the circular process of scientific discovery (a process in time sequences!) illustrates the above-mentioned falsification of the paradigm of logical empiricism: theory and empirical observation cannot be separated but always determine each other.
2. Discoveries and hypotheses collected in the psychoanalytic situation can later become the subject of clinical or extra-clinical research, thus aiming at achieving intersubjectivity of one's own personal observations and interpretations of clinical data. Clinicians who want to do clinical research, the clinical researchers, have to think systematically and self-critically about their clinical observations, testing them again and again in new clinical situa-

tions, comparing them with others described in the (intersubjective) psychoanalytic literature, and, finally, writing them down transparently and critically. The extra-clinical researchers use material from the clinical situation (reports of the patient or the analyst, tapes, videos, etc.) for this circle of research and again in the process that starts when the session is over.

3. The processes of discovery and of gaining a deeper understanding—in other words, the successive steps of generalization—are more or less the same for both the clinical and the extra-clinical researcher. Both can try to "discipline" their experiences systematically, aiming at being precise, complete, representative, transparent for independent observers and thus "intersubjective", and so on, with respect to their observations, their theorizing, and their systematic testing of their hypotheses. The difference is not mainly a one in quality but a difference in the procedures used in testing the hypotheses. The extra-clinical researcher uses criteria from empirical research in order to test his hypotheses. The clinical researcher has a whole range of different methods at his disposal with which to deal with some of the limitations of his research methods, such as blind spots within his own subjective observations and reasonings: super- and intervisions, interdisciplinary research groups on clinical issues, operative groups, qualitative research, and so on (see, e.g., the contributions of Jorge Canestri and Roger Perron in this volume).

It should be mentioned that the scientific quality of psychoanalytic research does not depend mainly on the choice of the method for testing hypotheses: clinical as well as extra-clinical (empirical) research can be of high or low quality. In clinical and extra-clinical research we find "believers" side by side with self-critical scientists who are aiming at collecting precise, complete, representative, transparent, self-critical, and intersubjective observations, discoveries, and insights. [These processes can themselves be subject to psychoanalytic research: Jorge Canestri, Peter Fonagy, and Werner Bohleber reported on their investigations into these processes in a working party of the European Psychoanalytical Federation (EPF) in Sorrento in 2003 (see also Canestri, 1999; Horowitz, 1981). They are studying how the minds of the analysts work in the clinical situation and how theoretical concepts are applied. Haydée Faimberg studies the same issue from another perspective and also presented her findings in Sorrento.] Both clinical (on-line) and extra-clinical (off-line) research may contribute to a scientific stance that is concerned with intersubjectivity in communicating experiences, methods, and results from research. Leuzinger-Bohleber (1995) discussed some strategies developed in clinical–psychoanalytic research in order to ensure their "scientific value" or the quality of clinical–psychoanalytic research. The criteria for defining the quality of clinical research are known to be far more difficult to grasp than are those of extra-clinical, empirical research. As already mentioned, this is the subject of intensive current discussions in the second Research Subcommittee (see Leuzinger-Bohleber, 2003). [But, of course, Peter Fonagy is right in pointing out that these epistemological arguments will not mean that every practising analyst is automatically a researcher. Wallerstein (2001) differentiates between "search" and "research" in the clinical situation. Every analyst is searching, but for that search to become research, a certain formalization and systematic categorization of the data have to be undertaken (see also Killingmo, 1992, p. 37; Taylor, 2003, p. 3). How, then, can we characterize the multitude of different possibilities of doing research in psychoanalysis?]

When it comes to quality criteria of extra-clinical research, which are easier to describe, it is important in our context that extra-clinical, psychoanalytic research is based on the processes connected with theory formation in the psychoanalytic situation and is closely intertwined with the classical "Junktim research" in psychoanalysis.

Incidentally, Freedman, Lasky, and Hurvich (2000) report on long discussions on this point in the House of Delegates of the IPA, in which it was also demanded that empirical psychoanalytic research (e.g. via tape recordings) should be built on clinical psychoanalytic research instead of taking its place.

> After lengthy debate, a compromise, indeed a reasonably synthesis, was arrived at. What at first seemed to be incompatible views, were reshaped into a position statement that included four points: (1) any effort at validation must be rooted in the history of psychoanalytic clinical thought, (2) the evaluation of process should originate in the subjective and intuitive judgement of the engaged and experienced analyst, (3) evaluation should be corroborated by consultants using the time honoured methods of

> peer review and supervision, and (4) only then would these essentially clinical procedures receive external validity though the study of recorded texts. This ideal prescription was accepted by the house and was communicated as a news release and was sent to all IPA Societies in the three regions. [Freedman, Lasky, & Hurvich, 2000, pp. 2–3]

Theories or models that are then tested extra-clinically (experimentally) have always been generated in the clinical situation: they are therefore based on clinical research. Not many members of the psychoanalytic community know how many experimentally tested psychoanalytic concepts exist today (cf., inter alia, Bachrach, Galatzer-Levy, Skolnikoff, & Waldron, 1991; Leuzinger-Bohleber & Stuhr, 1997; Leuzinger-Bohleber & Target, 2002; open door reviews by Fonagy, 1999; etc.) and how many interesting experiments and empirical studies are being conducted at the moment. We can only mention some of the areas in which an expanding experimental and empirical research activity can be observed here at the moment: projects dealing with the investigation of mentalizing processes, self-reflecting functions, or attachment patterns conducted by Peter Fonagy, Mary Target, and their research team (see their contribution in this volume); the investigation of transference processes by means of analysing mimicked exchange processes in therapeutic interactions conducted by Rainer Krause and his team in Saarbrücken, Germany; the investigation of the Freudian dream theory by means of PET and fMRI studies, which are in progress at the Sigmund-Freud-Institut in Frankfurt in cooperation with Mark Solms (see his contribution in this volume), as well as the large number of psychotherapy outcome and process studies (see, e.g., the contribution of Norbert Freedman and his group in this volume; for the research group working with the Analytic Process Scale in New York, see Waldron et al., 2001; for the large number of studies applying Q-sort techniques, see Jones, 2001, and Albani, Blaser, Jones, Thomä, & Kächele, 2001; and for the Ulm research team, see Kächele, 1992). Other psychoanalytically conceptualized experiments are concerned with developmental psychology and brain research. To give, again, just one example: for about the last 10 years, Bürgin and colleagues (Bürgin & von Klitzing, 1995; von Klitzing, Simoni, & Bürgin, 1999) have performed a series of infant studies on the concept of triangulation.

In all these different areas, central parts of psychoanalytic developmental and memory theories as well as theories of change are investigated systematically, either experimentally or empirically. The quality criteria of such studies are described quite precisely and are concerned with objectivity, reliability and validity, methodical stringency, precision and outcome relevance, and so on. Moreover, it is relevant for psychoanalytic projects if the insights that are gained find their way back to clinical psychoanalytic research and clinical practice and have a stimulating effect there (cf. feedback in Figure 1.1).

Equally clear quality criteria exist in the second extra-clinical area of psychoanalytic research: the not very popular possibility of examining complex psychoanalytic theories as regards their inner logic and terminological and conceptual precision by means of computer simulations (e.g. Colby & Stoller, 1988; Moser, von Zeppelin, & Schneider, 1991; see below).

Clinical, conceptual, and empirical research in psychoanalysis

Let us just add a few remarks on the possible differences between *clinical, conceptual, and empirical research* because often these different forms of psychoanalytic research seem not to have been specified clearly enough. *Clinical psychoanalytic research,* as described above, may be characterized by the circular process of recognition and generating insights and knowledge—comparing clinical material again and again with theoretical concepts and models. Clinical psychoanalytic research leads to a constant revival and "re-discovery" of psychoanalytic concepts on the one hand and to the development of new concepts and models on the other. Sverre Varvin illustrates this kind of research in his contribution to this volume. The intention of this kind of research is to understand unconscious fantasies and conflicts of a certain patient or a specific group of patients. Concepts are one tool: an instrument for gaining knowledge, not the subject of the research itself.

This is one of the main differences between clinical and *conceptual research* in psychoanalysis that has been very much in vogue during the last years. Anna Ursula Dreher, who—in intensive cooperation with Joseph Sandler—has been involved with psychoanalytic concept research for years, elaborated this issue in her contribution in this volume:

> Conceptual research defines itself by its subject matter: namely, psychoanalytic concepts, those tools of language by which we attempt to grasp empirical phenomena—especially clinical phenomena—theoretically. As a working definition, I would put it this way: conceptual research is concerned with the *systematic* investigation of the meanings and uses of psychoanalytic concepts, including their changes, in relation to both clinical *and* extra-clinical contexts. Now, one might ask: what could possibly be so problematic about concepts that it is of interest to make them even the *subject* of research? [pp. 109–110]

According to her understanding, conceptual research is not defined by a certain research method but by the subject of research. It may be illustrated by the line on the top of the left part of Figure 1.1.

Process A: integrative conceptual research

Dreher discusses various strategies for studying psychoanalytic concepts clinically, empirically, and theoretically in the psychoanalytic literature dealing with the history and current discourses of the concepts, such as psychoanalytic textbooks or dictionaries (e.g. Laplanche & Pontalis, 1973, or, recently, Mijolla, 2002), expert validation, the integration of new clinical data and observations, the results of empirical and interdisciplinary studies, and so on (for a comprehensive discussion of conceptual research, see also Dreher, 2000). Hugo Bleichmar (2003) presented an impressive example of such an integrative conceptual research on depression at the last Joseph Sandler Conference in London. His conceptual research is grounded in years of clinical experience and in his integration of theoretical and empirically based knowledge. Ricardo Bernardi reports on another study in conceptual research in this volume. He investigated how—facilitated by certain historical circumstances—concepts are implemented in psychoanalytic societies and how they are integrated with former theoretical orientations of psychoanalytic groups afterwards.

Process B: formally validated psychoanalytic concepts

Another form of conceptual research in the basic sciences is not very well known: a formally validated psychoanalytic concept research has been developed since the 1960s by the research team based around Ulrich Moser and Ilka von Zeppelin in Zurich. They have applied modern techniques, such as computer simulation, in order to test systematically and externally the inner consistency, the logical and terminological precision, and the lack of contradiction within complex psychoanalytic concepts like dream theory and the psychoanalytic model of defence. Rolf Pfeifer and I have taken up this tradition in several papers on memory, recalling and working through in the psychoanalytic situation while taking into account newer developments in the so-called embodied cognitive science (Leuzinger-Bohleber & Pfeifer, 2002).

Process C: experimentally tested psychoanalytic concepts

Finally, psychoanalytic concepts may be tested experimentally. As mentioned above, we find many impressive examples of this kind of conceptual research in the psychoanalytic literature. We cannot think of any empirical or experimental researcher who would deny that sophisticated concepts are always the presupposition for interesting and productive empirical or experimental studies. One can find no empirical or experimental study without a theoretical conceptualization—a framework for designing, planning, and pursuing the study as well as for interpreting possible results.

However, it has to be remembered that there exist fundamentally different epistemological positions concerning the relationship between clinical, conceptual, and empirical research. For some researchers (who identify with an understanding of a "unified science"), clinical psychoanalytic research is only capable of generating hypotheses or developing preliminary concepts that have to be "tested" empirically or experimentally in order to acquire a "scientific quality". For others, clinical—or conceptual—research is a specific scientific discipline, with its own research methods and strategies, quality criteria, and so on, as mentioned above. We find these two positions within the IPA research culture, often more or less separated from each other, with no productive interchanges or controversial discussions. Many contributions to this book aim to participate in such a discourse, elaborating possible differences as well as possible commonalties (see, e.g., the contributions of Anna Ursula Dreher, André Green, Roger Perron, and that of Mary Target and Peter Fonagy).

Another issue should be mentioned in this context, as, among others, Folkert Beenen discusses in his contribution in this volume: the transfer of empirically based knowledge to the clinical situation remains a relevant problem. Modified concepts have to enter the circular process of clinical recognition and understanding mentioned above. The clinical attitude of free-floating attention or, as Bion described, starting every new analytic situation with an attitude of "no memory and no desire"—in order to be open to unexpected new perspectives on the idiosyncratic patient and the specific analytic situation—remains a supposition for any helpful psychoanalytic clinical work. Psychoanalysis has often been described as a unique science in which the tension between "knowing" and "not-knowing" is not denied but is understood as an essential, even a constituting element. Schneider (2003) defines psychoanalysis as an "atopical" science that offers an idiosyncratic culture of "how to deal with a state of not knowing", of uncertainties and ambiguities. Curiosity about future discoveries, open-mindedness, a professional way of listening to the conscious and unconscious communications of the patient in the psychoanalytic situation and of dealing with our own anxieties and tensions when faced with the not-yet-understandable are well-known core parts of our professional attitude, our psychoanalytic identity.

In this sense psychoanalytic concepts might be a help as well as a potential danger for the process of gaining insights into unconscious conflicts and phantasies in the analytic situation. We all know that we cannot understand without differentiated, precise, flexible, elastic, and innovative theoretical concepts at the backs of our minds. At the same time we also know that concepts and theories can be "misused" for personal defensive purposes and—in this case—for narrowing instead of enlarging insights and discoveries. Therefore, on the one hand, the quality of concepts is an essential determinant for such a productive—respectively, unproductive—application in the clinical situation (as discussed elsewhere—see Leuzinger-Bohleber, 1998), while, on the other, a creative and critical reflection of the above-mentioned oscillation between understanding and "not understanding" in the psychoanalytic situation means a continuous struggle towards an adequate psychoanalytic attitude: one core trait of our psychoanalytic profession. This might be one reason for the extensive culture of super- and intervisions within all the psychoanalytic communities of the IPA.

To summarize: concepts—whether experimentally tested or not—have to be rediscovered and constantly adapted carefully and self-critically to new clinical situations (see also Edelson, 1995; Fischer, 1995). Therefore a direct feedback line from the experimental to the clinical situation is missing in Figure 1.1.

Pluralism of sciences: the psychoanalytic method between clinical, conceptual, and empirical research

In order to intensify the dialogue on these issues within the IPA, the Research Subcommittee on Conceptual, Clinical, Epistemological and Historical organized an International Conference in Frankfurt (26–29 September 2002). The Sigmund-Freud-Institut took the lead in organizing this congress. André Green passionately elaborated his view of psychoanalytic research. His lecture is published in this volume in the original version. The main papers of the conference were given by members of the Conceptual Subcommittee and are published in slightly modified form here. The conference covered five headings:

1. general introduction;
2. Anglo-Saxon and continental research traditions;
3. clinical and conceptual research;
4. psychotherapy outcome and process research;
5. neuropsychoanalysis: a new interdisciplinary enterprise—relevant for future psychoanalytic psychotherapy research?

Unfortunately, in the limited framework of this English publication we are not able to include the other papers presented at the conference. All the papers will be published in German (Leuzinger-Bohleber, Deserno, & Hau, in press), and they are available in English at the Sigmund-Freud-Institut in Frankfurt or from the contributors themselves. One aim of this presentation was to build a bridge between the more theoretical main papers of the conference and the concrete research practice, and most of the participants tried to discuss the relevance of the theoretical and epistemological considerations of the main speakers to the planning, conceptualization, and carrying out of their current research projects. We have therefore included a short overview of the presented studies in the Appendix of this book in order to give an impression of the multitude and variety of current psychoanalytic research, even in a relatively small section of a psychoanalytic research community (most of the studies were performed at the Sigmund-Freud-Institut in Frankfurt). By presenting some of the research being carried out at the Institute, we also hoped that an open, critical, interdisciplinary, and international wind might blow through our psychoanalytic research institute in the future. In this sense we counted on the multitude of locally interwoven individual researchers in a globally connected psychoanalytic world.

Thus we are very grateful to all the members of the IPA Research Subcommittee for elaborating their thoughts on psychoanalytic research in this book. We hope to contribute to a critical reflection on the role of international psychoanalytic research in our modern times and therefore to a creative and innovative research culture within the International Psychoanalytical Association.

2

The pluralism of sciences and psychoanalytic thinking

André Green

It is a great honour for me to have been asked to give a public lecture for this exceptional and outstanding conference on the Pluralism of Sciences, at which, as a researcher, I could not help noticing some details. On the one hand, I am granted the exceptional position of being the first and only speaker—as if a message were expected from me—on the eve of the Symposium proper, which starts on the following day. On the other hand, the announcement of my lecture is just in front of a photograph of Freud. Some people may think that it is my portrait that is in front of my name—or, if Freud is identified, that we have exchanged our names!

This is only half joking. When I tried to understand how it is that I was granted such an honour, I may have given the impression that my position reflected more or less what could have been Freud's if one could ask him his opinion and get an answer from his grave—wishful thinking.

I could not resist opening Volume 24 of the *Standard Edition,* at the General Subject Index. The result was not a surprise for me. There is no mention, in that scanning of Freud's work, of the term "Research". Two answers came to my mind, the first of them by far the most important: Freud did not mention research, because he was pretty sure that all his work was a matter of research, not the slightest part of it escaping this label. He felt no need to apply another method for his investigation. So I am not surprised by the title of Alain de Mijolla's paper: "Freud and Psychoanalytic Research." The second possible answer is that such research on psychic activity was practically non-existent in Freud's time. Let us open the *Outline*:

> We know two kind of things about what we call our psyche (our mental life): firstly, its bodily organ and scene of action, the brain (or nervous system) and, on the other hand, our acts of consciousness which are immediate data and cannot be further explained by any sort of description. Everything that lies between is unknown to us and the data do not include any direct relation between these two terminal points of our knowledge. [Freud, 1940a [1938], p. 144]

When the *Outline* was first published, both in German and in English, it was accompanied by extracts from Freud's contemporary fragments: "Some Elementary Lessons in Psychoanalysis." Mentioning, in this writing, that the science of psychoanalysis involves a number of hypotheses, he adds: "*It is hard to say whether they should be regarded as postulates or as products of our researches.*" This observation is still of great value today. The word Freud uses for "postulates" is *Voraussetzungen,* translated as hypothesis or supposition or condition. The *Oxford Compact Dictionary* gives the following definition for "hypothesis": "(1) A proposition made as a basis for reasoning. (2) A supposition made as a starting point for further investigation from known fact. (3) A groundless assumption [from Greek: *hypothesis* foundation]." Hypothesis is linked to conjecture, deduction, induction, themata. This last, rather unusual word needs to be defined. The *Dictionnaire d'Histoire et de Philosophie des Sciences* starts like this: "For some years it has been more and more accepted that presuppositions, which owe nothing to phenomena and which are at the start neither demonstrable nor falsifiable, play a determinant role in the preparatory phase in the research in experimental or human sciences" ("Themata", Gerald Holton). Such has been Albert Einstein's position, and also Heisenberg's and Schröder's. We can also find it in Kepler, Newton, Bohr, or Steven Wainberg. Listening to what Einstein said—namely, that his convictions were stronger than the results of the science of his time—we can easily put the same words into Freud's mouth, even to the point of refusing to acknowledge some other results in physics that run against his theory.

In the first lines of the "Papers on Metapsychology", Freud wrote:

> We have often heard it maintained that science should be built on clear and sharply defined basic concepts. In actual fact no science, not even the most exact, begins with such definitions. . . . Even at the stage of description, it is not possible to avoid applying certain abstract ideas to the material in hand, ideas derived from somewhere or other but certainly not from the new observations alone. Such ideas which will later become the basic concept of the science are still more indispensable as the material is further worked over. They must, at first, possess some degree of indefiniteness. There can be no clear delimitation of their content; so long as they remain in this condition, we come to an understanding about their meaning by making repeated references to the material of observation from which they appear to have been derived, but upon which, in fact, they have been imposed. . . . The advance of knowledge, however, does not tolerate any rigidity in definition. [Freud, 1915c, p. 117]

The richness of language is unmatchable, and psychoanalysts can only agree on that. The word "hypothesis" can have different uses: proposition, supposition, groundless assumption. Here, we find the whole range of the debate. On the one hand, psychoanalysts consider that they need basic statements, which cannot themselves be proven, suppositions as starting points for the development of investigation, as their opponents consider that they stand on groundless foundations. In fact, what is presently the subject of debate is the value of clinical research, considered as the only reliable basis, "again and again". We are asked to prove our hypotheses, our conceptualizations, and the outcome of treatment.

I have defended a different point of view. I have tried to introduce the concept of "clinical thought" (*La pensée clinique*). In my opinion, it was wrong to consider the clinical as just a kind of application of other basic factors that could be scientifically investigated and could reach a theoretical status, but that the word coming from medicine needed to be reconsidered when we were speaking of psychoanalysis. To summarize: I thought that there was a specific kind of *causality* in clinical thought, which could not be reduced to other modes of thought that were more closely linked to science. The type of development of clinical symptoms, configured in psychoanalytic constellations, indicated a kind of rationality and development of its own. This rationality was at the basis of the communication between psychoanalysts sharing a same experience and sharing, also, the conviction that so-called objective scientific reasoning was not quite appropriate for the understanding of the genesis, development, outcome, complications, and complexities of what we label, in other terms, neurosis, psychosis, perversion, depression, and so on. Clinical thought creates concepts that deal with the reasons of the unconscious and their parameters, the diversity of the answers that are called by them, their extensions, their transformations, their rationalization, under the influence of the counter-cathexis that, in certain instances, induces decathexis. One of the main characteristics of clinical thought is that it is *dialogic*—that is, it deals not only with the patient who suffers, but also with the one—the analyst—who has the task of listening to the suffering in the couple they form, thanks to a very special type of listening and empathy. We know today that it is impossible to deal with the questions related to transference without considering countertransference—that is what, in their own contexts, object-relations theory and intersubjectivity say.

Moreover, no matter how great the diversity and depth of the answers we can give to clinical questions and enigmas, there will always remain a "*practical–theoretical gap*" (*écart théorico-pratique*, Donnet), which is a source of difficulty. What I mean is that, according to our experience, no theory will ever be able to cover all of the field of psychoanalytic practice, and no psychoanalytic practice will fit totally and exactly within the limits of the field of any existent theory. These remarks find their cause in the nature of psychic activity. "Limits of the soul: You would not be able to go and find them, how far the road may get you into them. It includes such a deep Logos" (Heraclitus, Bichs, Vol. 45). They are accepted limitations of our discipline, and they further our need to know more about it.

It may be that many of the problems that we confront suffer from a certain degree of confusion. Psychoanalysis was discovered within the field of medicine. A doctor, who had also had an advanced scientific training discovered the unconscious—and he discovered it because the teachings of science were disappointing and the clinical thought constraining. All psychoanalysts know about Freud's first attempt to integrate biological thinking in the Draft (1950 [1892–1899]), which he wrote (mostly on a train!) to help Fliess to understand what he meant, in his language, because he felt how reticent he was. And how his next move was to deny his own writing (we know he was opposed to its publication). He turned his back on the Draft and, a few years later, wrote *The Interpretation of Dreams* (1900a), the book that reflected his true analytic thinking. Even until today, many scientists say how much they regret Freud's moving from physiology to psychology. They wish us to correct this error, and to come back to the 1895 inspiration of the Draft. They are unable to see the difference between the Draft and the work on dreams. Moreover, they criticize Freud's ideas on dreams (Allan Hobson, M. Jouvet). Happily enough, other scientists are better able to understand what Freud meant (Kustadt, 2001). But for psychoanalysts, *The Interpretation of Dreams* is the first, and perhaps the most important, of Freud's books.

But the more he advanced and the more the discipline progressed after his death, the more did a growing awareness take place that psychoanalysts had to be severed from medicine: even though psychoanalysis was a therapy, it needed to be defined on its own. Medicine, obviously, relies on scientific progress. The question of whether psychoanalysis is also dependent on scientific progress deserves to be raised. Some major writers in psychoanalytic literature (Bion, Winnicott, Lacan) have questioned the adequacy of the medical models in psychoanalysis.

Following Freud, psychoanalysts are frequently proud to call themselves "scientists". This reminds me of an anecdote about a man who pretended that he was going to get married to a daughter of the Royal Family, and that it was nearly half done. When asked what he meant, he replied: "I have already convinced *my* family, I just need now to convince *hers*!"—because as far as I know, not much has been heard about scientists thinking that psychoanalysts could be considered their peers: most of the time, they wish to keep clear of any contact with them. Even under the best possible circumstances, there is a pluralism of sciences. We have clinical, conceptual, and empirical research. The question is whether these different disciplines, if they are not sciences, are considered on a par with them or whether some psychoanalysts secretly distinguish between the true science, empirical research, and the others—clinical and perhaps also conceptual research—which are just chat.

When we consider Freud's case, it seems obvious to me, as Jean Starobinski showed long ago, that psychoanalysis is a kind of two-headed eagle, with one of its heads born from medicine, psychiatry, science, while the other was rooted in culture: in literature, art, the history of civilization, and so on. Let us remember that the discovery of the Oedipus complex was due as much to the patients whom Freud analysed as to his profound knowledge of Greek tragedy and his familiarity with Sophocles and then with Shakespeare. In today's terms, this distinction could be labelled as the complementarity within the psychoanalytic approach of exact sciences and human sciences. The matter is very complex, and the problem needs to be sorted out. The first conclusion we can reach from these observations—and this is the meaning of our Symposium—is that we are in great need of a *research on research*! It is important for us not to duplicate in our discipline the anecdote of the man trying to find his lost keys under the gaslight on one side of the street, "because at least there is some light in this place", though he knew he had lost them on the opposite, dark side, where it was useless to search for them because there was no light at all there.

In order to present some working hypotheses, we must ask some preliminary questions.

1. Is it so certain that psychoanalysis is a science?
2. If not, to what group of disciplines does it belong?
3. What are the kinds of findings made by science that can be integrated into psychoanalysis?
4. If some advances in science suggest that some psychoanalytic concepts are unproven or even false, is this a sufficient condition to reject and discard these concepts?
5. What sciences may serve as models for psychoanalysis?
6. What is the relationship between clinical psychoanalysis and other applications of psychoanalysis?
7. How do we deal with the multiplicity of theories that have proliferated since Freud's death?
8. What profit can we draw from the conceptions of epistemology?
9. What is the place of psychoanalysis in the present state of knowledge?

I am fairly sure that all these questions are legitimate. But you will agree with me that today's "*ouverture*" cannot cover all the fields opened by them.

In September 1997 a conference was held at University College London, chaired by Joseph Sandler; during this conference Daniel Stern and I presented our views on clinical and observational psychoanalytic research. When Joseph Sandler decided to publish a monograph in order to relate our controversy (Sandler, Sandler, & Davies, 2000), he also included in the volume another controversy, which I had had previously with Robert Wallerstein in the *Newsletter* of the International Psychoanalytical Association (Green & Wallerstein, 1996). I suppose that it is my contributions to these two controversies that may explain my presence here. I shall not come back to them in detail, as they are supposed to be known, and I have not changed my mind and I maintain my views. At the 1997 conference at University College, Peter Fonagy, the "flying Englishman", was away and could not attend. This time, he is with us, and he will be able to say how much he disagrees with me, as he did in earlier circumstances. But last week we were together in Munich and, very surprisingly, we were almost in agreement—almost!

From the nine points I have enumerated, I shall only take a few, trying to answer them to the best of my knowledge.

The authors of the introduction to this conference rightly observe that the topics we are discussing are largely the result of a Zeitgeist. The eighteenth century, of which Freud can be considered an inheritor, was called the Age of Enlightenment. It is possible that in the future the twentieth century will be called the Age of Science. It would be preposterous to question the benefits mankind has obtained from the progress of science, even if we have also suffered from its shortcomings. But this is not enough. We have to be aware that the scientists are not always very neat in their positions. They frequently play a double game, and there is a special settling of scores towards psychoanalysis: many of them consider that psychoanalysts are crooks, and that Freud deserves the Honour Award among them. (They share the views of M. Borch-Jacobsen, Frederick Crews, Peter Swales.) Why do I speak of a double game? On the one hand, scientists are perfectly happy to admit that science cannot cover the whole field of what has to be investigated and that science applies to a very limited portion of reality. But even when they hold this view, they consider, on the other hand, that in fact there is no other way of knowing except through the scientific method. In other words, all that is left is considered as sheer ignorance. And, of course, for them, psychoanalysis is, at best, the illusion of knowing something trying to mask its real ignorance. Another of their strategies is to admit that, for the present time, what we know for certain is what sciences know now, and the rest is waiting to be discovered in the future. But when the future does not bring any additional knowledge in some fields, very frequently the reaction of the scientist is to say that what is ignored is unimportant and can be neglected. So one can speak of an illegitimate pretension on the part of science to monopolize such knowledge, considered as certain. We remember Karl Popper's *The Logic of Scientific Discovery* (1934), and his comments on falsifiability. Three facts are to be recalled. (1) After Popper's statement that psychoanalysis was not falsifiable, Grünbaum pretended that in fact it was and, moreover, that it was false! Grünbaum was hailed by scientists and also by a number of psychoanalysts who shared his criticisms, though everything he writes about psychoanalysis shows a blatant misunderstanding of what I call the psychoanalytic mode of thought. (2) The reaction of some scientists was striking. Kuhn, Lakatos, and Feyerabend discussed Popper's views, arguing that, in fact, scientists did not work this way. Everybody remembers Feyerabend's provocative statement: "*anything goes*" (1975). (3) We must distinguish between the different procedures: the thinking of discovery, the thinking of demonstration, and the thinking of verification. A psychological analysis shows significant differences in the three types. In any case, there is a widespread conviction that the only worthwhile knowledge is the knowledge of science. Forget Art!

The idea that different types of knowledge can coexist is not accepted. All the knowledge drawn from culture is considered as amusing or diverting, but unreliable. If you really want to know something about the mind, the reading of Shakespeare is useless, whereas reading works about artificial intelligence is always useful. I am quite aware that my view can be considered exaggerated, but I am not sure that, in the end, this is not really what scientists believe.

In a previous work (Green, 1991), published in a book containing the contributions to a Symposium on the Unconscious and Science held in 1988 at UNESCO, I proposed a distinction between the subject of science and the subject of psyche. The subject of science is the subject that can be found in the scientific method. Lacan said that the subject of science could be dated with Descartes.

The subject of psyche contains what belongs to the subject of science and also includes what cannot be the subject of science. If we have a scientist who can be awarded a Nobel Prize and he believes, in his private life, in religion (any religion), then the task of the subject of the psyche is to understand how both aspects, the scientific and the non-scientific, can coexist in the same person and be part of his personality structure. I was struck by the fact that many neuroscientists referred to the works of William James, for which they had the greatest respect. But no one remembered that the author of *The Stream of Consciousness* and of *The Psycho-Physiological Parallelism* was also the one who wrote *Memories of an Occultist,* about communicating with ghosts through mediums sitting around tables in the dark. His brother, Henry, the novelist, was rather sceptical. This, for me, does not invalidate William James's interesting views on consciousness. But as a psychoanalyst I cannot avoid putting together these two aspects of the philosopher who first supported Freud but finally concluded with the poor remark that Freud was sexually obsessed.

A comment by Bion comes to my mind. On 28 February 1960 he wrote:

> The scientist's mistrust of human intellectual effort tends to make him look longingly at the machine that can so often be made to appear the ideal recording instrument, a matter of rigid scales, pointers, unchanging weights, and so on. This attitude, which has something to commend it, yields matter for speculation if one considers it as betraying suspicion of anything that possesses life. How are we to find the truth, to gain knowledge, if facts can be recorded only by an object incapable of judgement or anything we regard as thought on the one hand, and on the other if thought is possible only by an object incapable of recording facts?
>
> The difficulty may not be real in any significant way, but seems so because the method of formulation, in terms of knowledge, truth, and reality, leads to fallacious exaggeration of some elements of the problem, to the exclusion of others. Progress is less impeded if we consider "know" to refer to a relationship, and reality and truth to refer to qualities of mental phenomena necessary to sustain mental health. [Bion, 1992, p. 146]

The authority of Bion, however unquestionable, is not enough for a scientist. The latter would only observe that I quote him because we share the same ideology. But scientists do not seem to be aware that they also share an ideology.

Fortunately, not all scientists are narrow-minded with respect to psychoanalysis. For instance, Gerald Edelman, a Nobel Prize winner, in his book dedicated to Darwin and Freud, *Bright Air, Brilliant Fire*, the title of which refers to a verse by Empedocles, tries to spell out the assumptions underlying any proposed theory. He considers the physics assumption, the evolutionary assumption, and what he calls the *qualia* assumption. I have to quote him at length because his remarks are important:

> Qualia constitute the collection of personal or subjective experiences, feelings, and sensations that accompany awareness. They are phenomenal states—"how things seem to us" as human beings. For example, the "redness" of a red object is a quale. Qualia are discriminable parts of a mental scene that nonetheless has an overall unity. They may range in intensity and clarity from "raw feels" to highly refined discriminanda. These sensations may be very precise when they accompany perceptual experiences; in the absence of perception, they may be more or less diffuse but nonetheless discernible as "visual", "auditory", and so on. In general, in the normal waking state, qualia are accompanied by a sense of spatiotemporal continuity. Often, the phenomenal scene is accompanied by feelings or emotions, however faint. Yet the actual *sequence* of qualia is highly individual, resting on a series of occasions in one's own personal history or immediate experience. Given the fact that qualia are experienced directly only by single individuals, our methodological difficulty becomes obvious. *We cannot construct a phenomenal psychology that can be shared in the same way as a physics can be shared.* What is directly experienced as qualia by one individual cannot be fully shared by another individual as an observer. An individual can report his or her experience to an observer, but that report must always be partial, imprecise, and relative to his or her own personal context. Not only are qualia fleeting, but interventions designed to probe them may change them in unforeseen ways. Furthermore, many conscious and non-conscious processes simultaneously affect each person's subjective experience. Individuals may have their own private theories of the totality of their *individual* conscious experiences, but these can never be scientific theories. This is because other observers do not have adequate experimental controls available to them. The paradox is a poignant one: To do physics, I employ my conscious life, perceptions, and qualia. But in my intersubjective communication, I leave them out of my description, assured that fellow observers with their own indi-

> vidual conscious lives can carry out the prescribed manipulations and achieve comparable experimental results. When for some reason qualia do affect interpretations, the experimental design is modified to exclude such effects; the mind is removed from nature. But in investigating consciousness, we cannot ignore qualia. [Edelman, 1992, p. 114]

These ideas are absolutely capital for the orientation of psychoanalytic research. One can say that the qualia assumption is exemplified, in its purest form, by the analytic situation. Even more, as psychoanalysts, we can go beyond Edelman's observations, as we are interested not only in a phenomenal psychology, but in unconscious psychic activity. In order to understand a fourth assumption (which is ours)—I mean the *unconscious assumption*—the analyst must rely not only on what he can deduce from the unconscious of the patient, but also on his own in relation to that of the patient. So it is clear now that quantitative research is very far from being adequate to the investigation of the psychic unconscious. We do not imply that quantitative research must be abandoned, as far as psychoanalysis is concerned. We are just saying that it is peripheral and of little meaning, the central core of the research being about the unconscious. On the other hand, we can say that only the analytic experience—and, more specifically, the analytic session (Green et al., 1997)—is the indispensable condition of the study of the unconscious. It is in that way that we can say that the whole of analytic practice is permanent research, though this type of research does not fit in with the usual criteria of the scientific method.

We know that this position is not shared by Peter Fonagy, President of the Standing Research Committee of the IPA. More specifically, he does not agree with me and with others who claim that any research has to take into account the specificity of the analytic method (Fonagy, 2001). It is often said that science is characterized by its method, not by its target. Would it not be logical to confront the scientific method with the psychoanalytic method before deciding whether they are compatible?

In my controversy with Robert Wallerstein, I emphasized that what was most important in psychoanalytic research was what I call the psychoanalytic mode of thought. Some people have asked what I was trying to say with that expression. Without pretending that I can define it in a short statement, I will refer to the experience of every psychoanalyst's mind, listening to a patient free-associating and trying to understand through the analytic method what he or she wishes to convey. The analyst, thanks to free-floating attention, disregards the manifest content (which I will equate to an observable content), on the one hand establishing in his mind links between the elements of the material inside the communication labelled as intrapsychic latent content, and, on the other hand, examining the communications labelled as intersubjective between the patient and the analyst. Moreover, through the material, the analyst is able to refer what he listens to, what he thinks, what he feels, and what moves in from inside to establish the connections and relationships between different areas—language, memory, phantasies (conscious and unconscious), affects, bodily states, enactments and acting outs, somatizations, and so forth. When Fonagy says, "The mind remains the mind, whether on the couch or in a laboratory", I will ask him why the discovery of the unconscious was not made—and could never have been made—in a laboratory. The mind in the laboratory is essentially different from the mind on the couch, just as the mind on the couch is different from the mind in art, science, philosophy, religion, and so on. This position is consistent with Bion's hypothesis of the vertices.

Up to now, we will have to admit that psychoanalysts have been helped, in their work and in the understanding and treatment of patients, by the writings of the major authors of psychoanalytic literature: just to name a few of them, apart from Freud, we can still read Abraham, Ferenczi, Melanie Klein, Anna Freud, Bion, Winnicott, Marion Milner, Piera Aulagnier, Jacques Lacan—to limit myself to those who are no longer living. On the other hand, research, which has developed on a great scale recently, has not contributed in any significant way to psychoanalytic practice or theory. If you do not agree with me about this last fact, then there is a very simple way of testing my statement. Take, for instance, the lists of references of the papers of the last 10 years in the *International Journal of Psycho-Analysis* and make the following quantitative research: try to count how many times works of psychoanalytic research are quoted by authors. Conversely, how many papers on research do we find in psychoanalytic journals: where do they appear, who reads them, with what consequences? The question is not deciding whether we should or should not have psychoanalytic research. The answer is obvious. It is: *What type of research should we have? What method should we promote in order to match scientific and psychoanalytic research?* One conclusion seems to be unavoidable: *There is no unique answer, because there is a pluralism of the sciences. To my mind, this pluralism is not only about clinical, conceptual, and empirical research. It encompasses other disciplines.*

Let us start with *clinical research.* Instead of pleading for the primacy of this type of research, I shall now relate the experience of a research group of the IPA, which I have led for the past two years, on the topic of countertransference in borderline personality disorders. In order to have a broad view of the question, the group included two North-American colleagues, Otto Kernberg and William Grossman, two from Latin America, Jaime Lutenberg and Fernando Urribarri, two from the United Kingdom, Elizabeth Spillius and Gregorio Kohon, and, finally, two French analysts, Jean-Claude Rolland and myself. On purpose, in order to have the widest possible communication, the group included people who were experts in the psychoanalytic treatment of borderline personality disorders, some working with institutionalized patients, others in private practice, yet others more focused on neuroses, some having an experience of child analysis and some not. We usually met twice a year for a whole weekend, listening, at each meeting, to a case presentation, having beforehand read a paper written by the presenter. The members of the group included Kleinians, members of the Independent Group of the British Society, people related to object-relations theory, ego-psychology, French Freudians, and so on. There was a wide range of opinions. Very soon after our exchanges started, we realized that significant disagreements divided us. Some were in favour of an early diagnosis in order to make a prognosis and confirm that psychoanalytic treatment was indicated, while others thought that it was preferable to start the treatment and see how we could understand the patients' problematics before developing any preconceived ideas. While discussing each other's material, though, frequently we could broadly agree on the technical attitude adopted by the analyst, both in many other instances we had very great difficulties in understanding the grounds for the interpretation of the material by the analyst and how he/she handled the case. We each had the opportunity to explain the background of our thoughts, and it was obvious that this could only be understood via an examination of the psychoanalytic traditions of the Society to which each of us belonged. Though being citizens of the same country, analysts were also different in their approaches, according not only to their own personalities but also to the way they had been trained and had learned how to think of the problems with which they were confronted. Some considered that it was very urgent to reach a consensus, whereas others felt, on the contrary, that we should not do so too soon. In the end, I will say that the Research Group turned out to be less a research on borderline patients than a *research on ourselves*. Countertransference was a good topic, standing in the middle between the patient and the analyst. In my opinion, I considered that the way the Research Group had evolved was as promising, if not more so, than its initial aim had been. And I was convinced, once again, that before conducting any research on their patients as objects, analysts should first start to know more about themselves in comparison with others. As we know, a homogeneous corpus is a very important point for successful research. In other words, it seems to me a priority first to have a clear view of what we really are before starting to investigate what our patients are, as we see them, understand them, and treat them in different ways.

This naturally leads us to consider the usefulness of *conceptual research*. Our President, Daniel Widlöcher, has decided to open a new field of investigation. I agree about the necessity for conceptual research, but, again, one has to ask where the starting point will be. I consider that it is impossible to have conceptual research that would not be rooted in the history of psychoanalysis. I will submit a hypothesis for discussion. It would be interesting to consider the whole of the psychoanalytic literature, not only as a mass of writings, books, papers, and so on, but as, if I may say, a human organism, body and mind, which was born with Freud but has constantly changed from its birth on and even more since Freud's death. In this way, we would understand how new movements have appeared not out of the blue but, most of the time, as a reaction of disagreement with the preceding mainstream. For example—and very schematically—the object-relations movement was born in order to fight Freud's drive theory as solipsistic and self-propelled evolution. But in another direction ego-psychology believed in the existence of an autonomous ego and in a free area of conflict, both escaping the influence of the drives and serving purposes of adaptation. Following these two movements came the rebirth of narcissism with Kohut's self-psychology, which paved the way for the intersubjective movement. Transferring the battlefield to Europe after the Controversies between Melanie Klein and Anna Freud in England, new tendencies developed, promoted by Bion, who corrected Melanie Klein in his own way and whose ideas were closer to Freud's, and by Winnicott, who introduced paradoxical thought and overcame the distinction between internal and external. To end this brief panorama, in France Jacques Lacan tried to put psychoanalysis on the track of French structuralism, led by linguistics. So we can see that, in this history, which I have schematically drawn for you, there is at the same time a sort of coherence, notwithstanding a great multiplicity of orientations. But if we cannot dictate to history its course, we can at least try to understand its moves retrospectively. It should also be the task of conceptual research to investigate how the basic notions of psychoanalysis may have such different meanings for different groups in various epochs. For instance, is transference understood in the same way everywhere? What is an object according to psychoanalytic theory? Is there a specific psychoanalytic conception of time? Is psychoanalysis a psychology? And, if not, what is it? These are urgent questions that await an integrative knowledge.

Conceptual research has to be really *conceptual*, not only descriptive. Perhaps here we can have an opportunity to create a true epistemology of psychoanalysis.

I now come to a third approach about what fields are worth investigating, having agreed that both clinical and conceptual research were important priorities. I see different possible options. One option—which has its source in Freud, as we have been reminded in quoting the *Outline*—is the traditional body–mind problem. Is it possible today to connect the findings about brain processes and psychic activities? Or between Freud's psychic apparatus and the brain in a neuro-psychoanalytic conception according to Mark Solms? Is such an attempt wishful thinking, a utopia, or a working hypothesis? Contrary to many of our colleagues, I consider it to be of the utmost importance to be knowledgeable about the findings of neurobiology and, moreover, to remain informed about the attempts to build a new epistemology, which encompasses the knowledge from different fields. I shall return to this later.

We come now to the most important and very debatable problem of empirical research and, more especially, infant research. It is on this point that Peter Fonagy and I have the most important disagreements. But before proceeding, I would like to offer a clarification. For me, there are at least three Peter Fonagys. The first is the institutional man. I will not say anything about that aspect, as it is not proper for scientific debate. The second Peter Fonagy is the researcher. I admire Fonagy's very wide information and knowledge, but I have some difficulties in dealing with his ideas. I often disagree with him on his statements, choices, and options, and I usually criticize many of his position statements—for instance, when he firmly assures us that today we "know" that many of the factors that we were used to thinking about as created by the environment have, in fact, their source in heredity. I will question that on many grounds: Peter Fonagy relies on a conception of heredity that does not mention the role of epigenesis, as today all the interesting thinkers in the field try to sort out. Fonagy relies on quantitative studies, such as studies on twins, quantitatively based, which happen to analyse very superficial character traits. The question seems much more complicated and needs a more thorough examination. Relying on "behaviour–genetic data", we should observe that behaviour is a concept not for psychoanalysts, but for behaviourists. It seems that Peter Fonagy II wants to be everywhere: in the genes, in the cells, in the brain, in the behaviour, and also, if possible, in the transference. Such a one-man show is not possible. Good science implies a limited number of controllable parameters. This too all-embracing perspective tries to accomplish an impossible synthesis. I see no relationship between these theoretical options and the material of the patient. Using Paul Whittle's expression, we have, here, two tectonic plates. For an analyst, the problem is not heredity vs. environment, but "how the mind of the patient works in that specific treatment situation provoking reactions (thoughts, feelings) in the mind of the analyst". The interesting problem is not the source of the influences, but the outcome in the individual's mental life and his relationship to his internal life.

Fonagy, like many others, believes in attachment theory. I would like to express, in a few words, my reservations about this. The baby is not attached to the mother, and neither is the mother attached to the baby. They are both in love. Would Peter Fonagy undifferentiatedly use being attached and being in love? Being in love is not being attached: it is to be irresistibly attracted—an entirely different issue.

Another example of relying too much on biology is the total rejection of the death instinct, proposed by Freud, as inconsistent with the present state of knowledge in biology. In fact, we now know, with the discovery of the phenomenon of *apoptosis,* that, in some instances cells can receive the order to die, which means to destroy themselves, committing what is called cellular suicide (Ameisen, 1996). So let us not be too impatient. What constituted, some time ago, evidence against a psychoanalytic concept proves false and becomes a support for it some years later. But Peter Fonagy's main concern is the study of development. Two facts, at least, must be remembered here. There is, in the present state of knowledge, no agreement on the theory of development. The infant observed by Spitz, Margaret Mahler, Daniel Stern, Esther Bick, Lebovici, Emde, or Winnicott is not the same child, and the findings are significantly different from one researcher to another. The ideas of Winnicott and his findings about the transitional object and the transitional phenomenon, making a fundamental step forward that was not limited to development, have described important features of psychic activity in the adult.

The second observation is that Freud's conception of time in psychoanalysis, as I have shown in my book bearing that title (Green, 2002), is a very complex and articulated one. The developmental point of view is just one out of ten others, which I can only mention here. Double orientation of psychic activity as progression and regression, timelessness of the unconscious, after-effect, which Laplanche translates as after-wardness, the action of primal phantasies categorizing the experiences, the sexual theories of children, repetition compulsion, the concept of historical truth, and so on. It seems that, after Freud, instead of thinking how to articulate and to build the psychoanalytic concept of time, which Freud neglected to do, some orientations of psychoanalysts have reduced and simplified it into a developmental conception, which has greatly impoverished Freud's theory. For all these reasons, I do not think that the research oriented in that field can be significantly helpful for psychoanalysts. I do not discuss the value of these findings for infantile psychology. Psychoanalysis is neither biology nor sociology, and even less psychology. As Charles Sanders Peirce was aware a long time ago, psychic doesn't mean psychological. And even if one remembers that Freud equated psychoanalysis with depth psychology, here we are rather in superficial psychology. Depth psychology, which means the study of the psychic activity related to the unconscious, has, in my view, practically no links with psychology. I know that this statement will create many disagreements, but as Freud says: there is no help for it. Observation is not very appropriate for psychoanalysis. Mother–baby observation or any observation can only observe the external manifestations of each partner. What is expressed outside and can be observed is *not* a translation of what happens inside, in the internal unconscious world. The only thing we can "observe" is psychic phenomena. To explore the internal world, we have no direct tools, only indirect devices such as speech expressing thoughts, dreams that are reported, fantasies that can be guessed, plays that can be understood or shared. In other words, because the material is symbolic, the tool must possess symbolic qualities.

And now we come to Peter Fonagy III. Peter Fonagy III is the clinical psychoanalyst, a colleague of mine. This colleague I respect and can have discussions with very fruitfully, being in agreement with most of his understanding and interpretation. To speak the truth as I see it, I still do not understand the connection between Peter Fonagy II and Peter Fonagy III. I hope that as time goes by, Peter Fonagy III will develop in such a way that Peter Fonagy II will grow closer and closer to Peter Fonagy III.

To some extent my position, which I expressed some time ago (Green, 1996), is not an isolated one. More specifically, it is in agreement with the reservations of many French psychoanalysts. In 2002, the *Bulletin* of the Paris Society (Perron, 2002) reported the opinions of twelve colleagues (and one Swiss) stating their disagreements with the standards and decisions of the committees of the IPA. One should note the strong reservations of Roger Perron, who is not only a senior colleague but a researcher in psychology also (see chapter 6).

I wish to end my lecture with some final remarks, which I have not seen quoted in our circles. We must be aware that for the last half-century scientific knowledge has been undergoing a revolution. I do not allude to computers, artificial intelligence, or cognitivism: I have in mind broader areas of epistemology. There is a group of biologists—among whom I will list G. Edelman, H. Atlan, H. Von Foerster, J. Didier-Vincent, F. Varela, A. Prochiantz—who have promoted or advocated *the theory of hypercomplexity*. The mathematician R. Thom can be added to the list, and E. Morin has extensively studied the topic in his five volumes, *The Method* (1997–2001). After reading his work, I thought Freud can be considered a precursor of this new trend.

Morin distinguishes between different levels: living—human individual—social—species. The tools of the hypercomplex thought are trifold:

1. *hologrammatic*: the part is in the totality, which is in the part.
2. *recursive*: causes produce effects, which retroact on the causes.
3. *dialogic*: uniting the terms of a relationship that is, at the same time, both complementary and antagonistic.

Such tools organize a plural thinking regulated by the laws of organization and disorganization. The highest levels of complexity include strategy rather than programme, the promotion of creativity. The result emphasizes pluralism, autonomy, multiple communications, a hierarchy of levels of organization.

The complex organization includes uncertainties, freedom, disorders, antagonisms, competition. Morin concludes by proposing the individual as the centre of conscience in and for society. "The individual mind–brain is more complex than society, more complex than earth, more complex than galaxy" (Morin, 2001, p. 107; translated for this edition).

In the end is my beginning. [T. S. Eliot]

3

Plurality of sciences and the unity of reason

Michael Hampe

Two contrasts

In all scientific as well as non-scientific investigations, two different strategies to gain knowledge—a unifying and a differentiating one—can be distinguished. There is the attitude of research—let us call it the Platonic one—which looks for one unifying principle, such as the Theory of Everything in physics, or for one universal paradigm of knowledge, like the axiomatic mathematical theory, or which believes in one fundamental form of experience—for example the simple registering of colours, shapes, and sounds—a form of experience that all other experience leads back to.

On the other hand, there is the differentiating attitude—let us call it the Aristotelian one—in which progress means detecting differences and where knowledge means finding one's way in complicated structures. It is no disappointing message for this mentality that knowledge does not have just the one and only source but many origins, that the forms of theorizing in mathematics, physics, biology, history, psychology, and sociology are different, and that the experience in a laboratory and historical, clinical, and social experience are all different forms. That these different forms of experience cannot be brought back to a common core—the collecting of sense-data, something nobody believes in any more, in any case—does not lead to an embarrassing confusion for this mentality; it is not a loss of unity but shows that one has learned to find one's way around in the complicated landscape of human knowledge—that it is no longer necessary to look for the one principle in everything.

A second important contrast between epistemology and the philosophy of science is the one between contemplation and action, between knowing that something is the case and knowing how to do something. It is typical of most of the traditions of Western science to reconstruct knowledge according to the model of contemplation, of detached observation, and to consider technical knowledge and skills as epistemically second-class, as a mere application of insights that were originally gained through detached observation.

Both contrasts—the one between unification and differentiation and the one between contemplation and technical skill—are very important for philosophy of science in general, and especially for the philosophy of psychoanalysis.

Unified science and pluralism

Unlike the biological sciences or the humanities, psychology and psychoanalysis are sciences that have interpreted themselves as part of a unified science, dominated by the paradigm of physics—a physics that formulates its theories in a mathematical language, deductively, and tests them by experiments. Applied to human knowledge as such, the model of unified science meant that all sciences would one day form one great system—a system that is free of contradictions and rests on a finite set of absolutely evident axioms. There is a concept of reason that is connected with this model, according to which coherence is the cardinal virtue of all scientific knowledge. A pluralism of sciences that does not make up a coherent system becomes something unreasonable in this understanding of unified knowledge. The theoretical paradigm for this coherentism is mathematical and logical theory: the deductive system. The paradigm of unified science and the implicit coherentist concept of reason also lead to fundamentalism, because deductive systems have an axiomatic fundament that consists of evident and coherent propositions that guarantee, together with the rules of inference, the validity of the system (see Toulmin, 1983, pp. 69 ff.). This model was developed by logical positivism, especially by Rudolf Carnap (1938). The humanities challenged it, because they could not recognize themselves in this idea of knowledge and reason and they would have been integrated into such a system of unified science only by giving up what knowledge and reason was for them. Instead of explaining the phenomena in general mathematical and experimentally tested theories, the humanities saw themselves as a knowledge that understands and interprets processes of life and culture. This was the difference between explaining and understanding, between deductive science and hermeneutics.

If you think of the works of Ricoeur, Grünbaum, Habermas, and others, the theory of psychoanalysis was haunted for almost the whole of the twentieth century by this alternative between explanatory natural sciences and the hermeneutical humanities. But it is very helpful to remember that this dichotomy, brought about by the reaction of some traditions of knowledge against the idea of a unified science, was a simplification in the philosophy of science. It was a simplification already by the end of the nineteenth century. The level of reflection that neo-Kantianism had reached in 1840 with Trendelenburg's *Logic* (1840) and the works of Rickert and Cassirer made it, in principle, impossible to believe that there can be a unifying principle of all human knowledge (Rickert, 1926, 1929). In Cassirer's *Philosophy of Symbolic Forms* (1977), the resulting pluralism of the neo-Kantian school had a profound articulation, and Nelson Goodman developed this pluralism in *Ways of Worldmaking* (1978) into an independent contemporary philosophical position.

To reject a philosophy that believes in one principle of all human knowledge, as neo-Kantianism did, does not mean dropping all principles of reason. The coherentist concept of reason is not the only one possible. Despite coherence and integration into one system or deductive connection with the one and only set of evident propositions, there are other criteria of reasonableness, like the explicability of rules for knowledge and action, the intersubjectivity of beliefs and experience without appeal to authority and charisma, and, last but not least, methods of continuing projects of inquiry that are independent of particular persons. These are criteria of reasonableness that are not bound to the concept of a unified science and to the paradigm of the deductive system. They are criteria of reasonable procedures that organize developments and transitions into a single science and between different sciences. The concept of reason in coherentism and fundamentalism is applicable not so much to procedures as to results and to states of sciences. It is a postmodern overreaction to believe that because the idea of unified science and the static concept of reason (see this characteristic in Toulmin, 1983, p. 106) connected with it failed, the concept of reason has become useless in general when we look at scientific enterprises. In fact, at the end of the nineteenth century and the beginning of the twentieth, neo-Kantianism had found a way between the artificial constraints of a unified science and the *laissez faire* of postmodernism.

Heinrich Rickert had already found a cross-classification in the philosophy of science that was much more useful for reconstructing what happens in active academic disciplines than was the dichotomy between explaining and understanding that left out enterprises like geology and mineralogy or jurisprudence and economics. Rickert distinguished between generalizing and individualizing sciences, on the one hand, and evaluating and non-evaluating, on the other. That there are sciences that investigate individuals without necessarily being hermeneutical, like geography and mineralogy, is taken seriously in this classification. And that there are sciences that operate at a very fundamental level with evaluative terms like "just and unjust", "wealth and poverty", "health and disease" is again an insight that is essential for any pluralistic understanding of human knowledge. For example, German and English jurisprudence are, according to this scheme, individualizing and evaluative sciences, because they aim at the understanding of particular legal systems—the German and the English, respectively—and they operate with a contrast in values between the just and the unjust.

Any science that deals with human beings—sociology, psychology, medicine, or psychoanalysis—is individualizing because mankind is a finite set of individuals, very different from the unlimited realm of applications dealt with by the physical laws in relativity theory or quantum physics. And when a science about human beings deals with evaluative terms like "health and disease" or "normal and abnormal", it is, like jurisprudence, an individualizing evaluative discipline. This classification says nothing about the methods by which the individualizing insights are gained and how the evaluative terms are justified.

Also, in experimental physics—in which, for example, a natural constant is fixed by more and more exact measurements—the message is individualizing. Mathematical concepts, especially when they are applied in the theories of measurements, allow the recognition of something individual with greater and greater exactitude. It is a mistake to believe that generalizing knowledge is always related to causal processes and aims at universal explanations, whereas individualizing research should always aim at simply understanding (the psychologist Lewin, a student of Cassirer, had already pointed out this mistake in his study of the theory of science—see Lewin, 1981, pp. 233–278). The exact determination of the brightness of a star or the speed with which a galaxy moves in space leads to an individualizing insight, an insight that might have general theoretical consequences, for example, for the determination of the age of the universe. But the involved empirical methods of measurement are strictly directed onto something individual without being hermeneutical.

Psychoanalysis may be in a very similar position: investigation of the early childhood problems of a neurotic through more and more exact analysis and procedures of recollection that lead deeper and deeper into the history of the person are certainly aiming at knowledge of something individual. However, this knowledge might have consequences for the general theory of neuroses. That psychoanalytic research is individualizing at one level—that of clinical investigation—does not necessarily mean that psychoanalysis is a hermeneutical investigation. Thus, I disagree with both Ricoeur and Habermas, who take psychoanalysis to be a hermeneutical science. In *Erkenntnis und Interesse*, Habermas took the associations in dreams of a patient as texts that are to be interpreted (see Habermas, 1968, pp. 262 ff.). But because the question "What is true?" is much more complicated in psychoanalysis than in literary criticism, and because the consequences for metapsychology of a particular psychoanalysis are very different from the consequences that the interpretation of an individual text might have for the general theory of texts, it is an oversimplification to consider the hermeneutical work of a literary critic and the interpretive work in psychoanalysis as instantiations of the same method.

Between individual and generalizing sciences and sciences that operate with and those that operate without evaluative terms, reductive relations are impossible. Take, for example, pathology, for which the difference between "health" and "illness" is essential: it cannot be reduced to anatomy. And the difference between "healthy" and "ill" cannot be reduced to the difference between "just" and "unjust". Certainly, there are relations of application between the disciplines: there can be no pathology without anatomy. But these relations of application do not lead to a unified science. There will never be a single theoretical language and a unified form of experience for disciplines like physics, clinical medicine, and jurisprudence. Precisely this absurdity should be a reality according to the model of unified science. It is obvious, however, that the idea that the legal theory of guilt should be formulated in the same language as the one used for elementary-particle physics is absurd. Different realms of knowledge and different themes of investigation need different languages of description and different forms of experience. Although physical, legal, and psychoanalytic research are aiming at relevant, articulated, and exact insights, relevance, clearness of articulation, and exactness nevertheless mean something different in each of these disciplines. These theoretical virtues can only be understood in the context of the particular languages of these theories, and the methods of disciplining experience are equally relative to their respective sciences. The realization of these values is possible only by acting in the particular disciplines (Hampe, 2000). The paradigm of rationality put forward by the model of unified science that is orientated at the deductive logical mathematical system concentrates on a rationality that is realized by the syntactical concatenations of substitutive signs (see Whitehead, 1898, pp. 3ff.). But the internal and external relations between the concepts of the empirical sciences are of a semantic nature. The interesting questions about the relations between the empirical sciences are always if and how the meanings of concepts are to be related to each other. To relate the meanings of fundamental terms from different sciences to each other, we need methods of translation that produce transitions between the sciences that are reasonable in the sense of being intersubjectively acceptable. The fundamental presupposition for such translations is that they are relevant and, in an ideal way, of a heuristic value for the involved disciplines. The meaning of juridical terms cannot be translated in a relevant way into the meaning of physical terms. Therefore, there is no systematic relation between these sciences. But that does not mean that there is a lack of formal coherence in human knowledge. It only means that different themes of knowledge exist; but these topical differences are usually put aside in formal considerations.

Contemplation and action

How important is the second contrast between contemplation and technical skills for the understanding of modern sciences, and especially for the understanding of psychoanalysis? In the first half of the twentieth century, John Dewey already showed that it is a myth to believe that there is such a thing as pure contemplation leading to a fundamental theory on the one hand and a purely practical secondary form of knowledge that is nothing but the application of theoretical insights on the other. In his sociology of knowledge, Dewey claimed that this idea originated from the interests of a priest class in privileging their own form of knowledge against that of craftsmen and technicians (Dewey, 1982, ch. 4). At least since the so-called pragmatic turn in the philosophy of science—that is, at least since Ian Hacking's *Representing and Intervening* (1983, Part B)—it is clear that all knowledge is founded in forms of action. Experience, if it is the experience of a scientific investigation, is always the result of disciplined action. Such disciplined action may consists in the correct use of a microscope or a telescope, in the disciplined attention of a philologist carefully reading a text, or in the differentiating view that a radiologist develops when he analyses an X-ray picture. Scientific experience is never the result of a passivity that is free from any conceptual constraints. To have an experience never means just to register what is given. In experience there is nothing that is simply given, free of conceptuality. "The Given" is a theoretical fiction of empiricism, as Quine (1951) and Sellars (1963) have shown. And Carl Friedrich von Weizsäcker wrote about the empiricism that produced this idea that it "was searching for experience. But what experience could be, empiricism thought to know a priori, e.g. inductive logical conclusions from sense-perception. A consequent empiricism would have to have learnt from experience what experience is" (Weizsäcker, 1988)

Nobody who has just sense-impressions has an experience. And the person who looks through a microscope has a type of experience that is different from that of the one who is listening to the associations of a neurotic client. In analogy to the insight that there is not merely one form of rational theorizing, the mathematical deduction from general laws without any value-terms, we have to accept that there is not just one form of scientific experience; instead, sciences develop simultaneously with their forms of theorizing experience, and both are methods to give discipline to our actions in order to gain knowledge.

As long as the philosophy of science believed in a strict borderline between theory and experience, any scientific experience was taken to be a testing of theory. This test was first interpreted as the attempt to verify a theory. The insight that general propositions about infinitely many individuals can never be verified by finite experiences leads to the idea that scientific experience could at least falsify or confirm theories (Peirce, 1877; Popper, 1934). In order to be able to do that, an experience has to be acknowledged as being relevant for a theory. But neither the concept of confirmation nor the concept of relevance could be clarified by a modern philosophy of science (Toulmin, 1983, p. 77; Whitehead, 1938). It is always an option for a scientist to declare that an experience that falsifies his theoretical assumption or does not confirm his theories is irrelevant for his hypotheses. To date, it has not been cleared up what kind of scale we could ever use to be able to measure the degree of confirmation a theory has gained from experiences. If we take as our criterion only the length of time a theory has survived without being falsified, then Ptolemaic astronomy would still be better confirmed than the Copernican. Since it has become common sense in the philosophy of science that all empirical terms are theory-laden, that scientific experience is gained by disciplined actions, experience is no longer considered a test of theoretical hypotheses but a form of theorizing—a theorizing via means that are different from pen and paper. A voltmeter or a microscope are as much conceptual tools as a formula or a text, since they instantiate the theory of electricity or optics. In the same sense the tools of free association or dream interpretation are instantiations of the psychoanalytic theory of the unconscious.

I am not denying that there is a difference between theorizing with pen and paper and performing experiments and observations. Theoretically, one can write down with pen on paper whatever one wants to, whereas a voltmeter or a telescope do not necessarily show what the theoretician wants to see, and the client does not necessarily dream and say what the analyst is expecting. Empirical action has its own manner of resistance, whether it proceeds experimentally, observationally, or clinically. It is this resistance that gives creative relevance to scientific experience. This resistance drives the theorizing mind into directions it would never move into without experience. This creative relevance of empirical research is the main function of scientific experience and not its supposedly verifying, falsifying, or confirming function (see Rheinberger, 2000). Because scientific experience is disciplined and guided by methods of investigation, it leads to a rational intersubjective form of creativity that is different from the more irrational and inspirational forms one might find in the arts and in religion (see Whitehead, 1929).

Undoubtedly, the creative procedures in the sciences involve selections of propositions, observations, and methods. Old beliefs become relativized or are dropped, new ones are integrated into the web of beliefs. Drawing consequences for the theory from certain empirical procedures is also a form of scientific activity that happens according to implicit rules—and these rules need to be learned as much as do the language and the methods of research in the specific disciplines. The physicist learns to experiment, just as he learns to draw consequences from experiments. The historian learns to decipher documents, just as he learns to draw consequences—say, for his view of an epoch—from these documents. The art of this activity is to avoid hasty consequences. I presume it is similar in psychoanalysis: apart from the language of psychoanalytic theory and the therapeutic praxis, the analyst learns to draw consequences from the praxis for the theory of the unconscious and other metapsychological constructs.

The ability to draw consequences from the more empirical activity for the more theoretical activity is thus a competence relative to the different disciplines, and it is a competence of judgement, because it has to do with evaluating and balancing old and new beliefs and experiences against each other (Leuzinger-Bohleber, 2000, pp. 153ff.). Because this balancing is a process of evaluating factors that compete for relevance, there cannot be an inductive logic as a system of rules for drawing conclusions from empirical data valid for all empirical sciences (Goodman, 1972, pp. 357 ff.). The way a competent and creative researcher produces experiences and draws conclusions from them cannot be fixed in a system of rules, because it is not independent from the content of the experiences and theories that are to be related in the considered process of investigation. But, again, this does not mean that inductive procedures are basically irrational. What cannot be described in general rules is not necessarily irrational, as long as there are specific rules and paradigms that can make it plausible why this procedure of drawing a theoretical conclusion from certain facts is right and why the other procedure was wrong.

As soon as you do not accept the categorical distinction between contemplation and skill, you also have to drop the sharp distinction between theoretical and practical reason. It was another mistake of the programme of unified science to take only theoretical reason in the form of logical structures to be important for science and to consider practical reason a topic of ethics. Science is scientific activity with very specific goals, and, as in all other activities, it is confronted with the question of whether its goals are reasonable and whether it pursues these goals in reasonable ways. Thus, questions of practical reasoning are as essential for reconstructing scientific procedures as questions about the logical coherence of the dogmatic systems a science may produce. Stephen Toulmin saw this very clearly when he wrote that "the rationality of a science . . . is not to be found so much in its *systems* as in the *procedures* of discovery and change over time" (Toulmin, 1983, p. 106; translated for this edition; italics added)

Rationality

There are some characteristics of relativism that can be interpreted as an entry of postmodernism into the philosophy of science: on the one hand, some reservations about the possibility of an inductive logic, reservations about a general system of rules for scientific research, and, on the other hand, the insight that values of knowledge like accuracy, and relevance, and clearness of articulation must be explicated and learned relative to the respective scientific disciplines. But there are important differences between Paul Feyerabend's "Anything goes!" and the acceptance of scientific pluralism, differences that depend primarily on the theory of rationality and truth.

The distinction between pluralism and relativism is not an extremely explosive subject as long as one analyses only sciences that do not employ evaluative judgements but follow merely theoretical aims. But as soon as one turns to questions of health and disease, of justice and injustice, and as soon as a therapy makes people ill and a legal system is unjust, one can hardly bring oneself to say "Anything goes!" Since therapies are supposed to make people healthy and legal systems are supposed to bring about justice, before the background of instrumental rationality, it would be unreasonable to accept even the mere possibility of harmful therapies and unjust legal systems. It is a precondition of instrumental rationality that there is an absolute consensus on the ends—that is, that there must be an agreement on what is meant by "health" and "justice" among those who decide whether or not a certain therapeutic technique or a legal system is to be continued. If the terms of "health" and "justice" are plausible only relative to a certain form of therapy and a certain legal system, then the criteria of instrumental rationality vanish, as instrumental rationality requires that the ends can be made explicit independently of the various means through which they could be achieved. The generation of ends is not the task of instrumental rationality. Rather, it presupposes an agency that sets ends. Hence, instrumental rationality itself depends on another form of rationality: a higher-order rationality that creates ends and determines what is meant by "health" and "justice". In order to avoid relativism when comparing different kinds of therapies with each other, there must be a neutral and external point of view. From this neutral and unbiased perspective, one can compare different therapies that are supposed to serve the same end. (Neutrality in the sense of an unbiased point of view is a characteristics of Toulmin's theory of rationality—see Toulmin, 1983, pp. 56 ff.)

The situation becomes even more difficult not only if there are conflicts of instrumental rationality, but if there arise internal conflicts within the higher-order rationality that poses ends. Is it possible to develop an unbiased and external point of view that allows the comparison of the different ends of human action and knowledge? This question is important for two reasons: because psychoanalysis operates with terms of "health" and "disease" and because it pursues two special aims of knowledge—first, it analyses the knowledge of human unconscious, and, second, it examines the self-understanding of persons by means of their knowledge of their own unconscious. One could perhaps even say that psychoanalysis connects those two aims with each other: either it regards self-transparency as a means to the achievement of lasting mental health, or it considers that striving for self-transparency can have mental health as its side-effect. The latter could be possible even if self-knowledge were to be regarded as an end in itself pursued by the psychoanalytic process, and even if self-transparency is seen as a good even higher than health—according to the Socratic conviction that only a life reflected on is a life worth living.

In this combination, a conflict of ends might arise. For its solution, one needs an unbiased mind to decide. The pursuit of health in the sense of unhampered managing of professional and private commitments can turn out to be problematic. This might be the case if health is pursued via the overlooking of conflicts in the life of the individual or in society and if individual and collective self-knowledge is intentionally neglected, since its recognition would lead to even greater suffering. If there is no possibility at all of changing the conditions that bring about suffering, then there are only two options left: either to deny the conflicts—that is, to perform self-deceptive strategies—or to enhance the capacities to cope with the situation. If I am right, psychoanalysis claims that all individual and social strategies of self-deception carry the risk of reproducing pathological processes. Therefore, it must regard the enhancement of self-transparency as reasonable. Believing this, psychoanalysis commits itself to an ideal of rationality that stems from the Enlightenment. According to it, an increase in reflexive abilities and self-knowledge leads to greater human autonomy and freedom and potentially enhances mental health; whereas a lack of reflexivity is considered to bring about suffering and dependence. Nevertheless—and this is a legitimate criticism of the Enlightenment ideal of rationality—psychoanalysis regards reflexivity and self-transparency not as human capacities given in advance, but as gradually developed competences that can be suppressed or supported. Above all, those competences, with respect to the unconscious processes that are the objects of their research, have to be supported at any rate. At this point, we have reached a new level of the theory of rationality: now we are no longer discussing the rationality of a particular science, nor the reasonable organization of the whole of human knowledge: rather, the question has to be raised whether the beliefs and actions of an individual human being are reasonable, whether or not that person is able to lead a reasonable life. It is obvious that for psychoanalysis as well as for psychiatry this personalistic conception of rationality is of the utmost importance. Presumably, there are various correspondences between the value terms "healthy" and "unhealthy" and "reasonable" and "unreasonable".

Reason can be regarded as a reflexive ability, as the individual competence of persons to distance themselves from their own interests and habits and at least sometimes to take on/adopt an unbiased and neutral point of view on the conflicts of their own lives. But this temporary detachment does not mean that individuals have command of a language or a logical system that is not relative to—and entirely detached from—a personal point of view and that would provide absolutely objective measuring rods/standards. Rather, here at the level of human individuals, there is a conception of rationality that is entirely different from the coherentist and fundamentalist unified science, the conception of unbiased detachment that is supposed to protect people against self-deception, illusions, and superstition. Though Sigmund Freud signed a declaration of his scientific *Weltanschauung*, that does not necessarily mean that he felt committed to the ideal of a unified science, although he was looking for a possible connection between psychoanalysis, biology, and neurology. At the end of the nineteenth century, a "scientific *Weltanschauung*" also meant the refusal of religious and philosophical obscurantisms. Whoever followed a scientific *Weltanschauung* intended to participate in the project of the Enlightenment to support the collective and individual disillusionment of the human race. There is no doubt that Freud, in this sense, regarded himself as a supporter of the Enlightenment rather than as a biologist or physicist, although he used thermodynamic and drive-theoretical models.

Thus, the enlightened ideal of rationality is not primarily a coherent systematization that judges intellectual projects by the way they fit into a general system of sciences. Rather, it is an emancipatory project that makes it possible for human individuals and societies to autonomously reflect on their beliefs and wishes and to decide about their own circumstances. The question of whether something is or is not able to be systematized is secondary. The primary question is whether a certain nexus of beliefs, of needs and life, can be reflected on and judged by the person who lives it, or whether it remains opaque and the person remains more or less captive to unconscious mechanisms of thought and feeling.

Insofar as psychoanalysis is committed to an enlightened ideal of rationality and takes this to be universally applicable to all human beings, it can hardly understand itself as a mere clinical technique, a technique that tries to realize a dictated end of mental health with appropriate means. For this reason, psychoanalysis is not comparable with other procedures that interpret themselves simply in terms of instrumental rationality and that are easily integrated into a certain system of scientific medicine. Insofar as psychoanalysis is committed to the enlightened ideal of rationality, it also inherits the burdens of Enlightenment. Thus, it becomes the one to decide what it means to lead a reasonable life, free from subordination, superstition, and illusion. This essentially refers psychoanalysis to practical philosophy.

This becomes even clearer if, apart from the concept of rationality, one considers the relevance for psychoanalysis of another conception—a conception that has also been discredited in relativist postmodernism. I am thinking of the notion of truth—in particular, of the conceptions of truth and truthfulness.

Truth and truthfulness

If I understand rightly the methods of free association and dream-reporting as technical procedures used as means to explore the unconscious, then these methods presuppose that when a patient refers to the dream-scenario, he is recording absolutely truthfully what spontaneously pops up in his mind. A physicist can perform an experiment correctly or incorrectly, and a radiologist can interpret an X-ray picture in the right or the wrong way. But an experiment or an X-ray picture does not lie. The data of psychoanalysis manifest themselves in a certain attitude towards events that could be characterized as either truthful or deceptive. The aim of psychoanalysis seems to be to enhance patients' ability to be truthful and to weaken their tendency to deceive themselves and the psychoanalyst about their true convictions and wishes. When every person has his or her own truth and truth per se is nothing but a plausible construct, to set such an aim of the therapy would be entirely mistaken.

Thus, psychoanalysis seems to be committed not only to the universalized ideal of rationality that the Enlightenment has supported, but also to a strong conception of truthfulness. Furthermore, psychoanalysis seems to presuppose that individuals differ in their capacities to recognize their own underlying beliefs, motives, and wishes. It seems to me central to the theory of the unconscious that there are real facts of the structure of beliefs, motives, and wishes of a person about which that individual has no idea, which he or she cannot understand and comprehend without the help of psychoanalytic techniques. If a person believes that he/she believes P and therefore wants X, but in reality, he/she believes non-P and therefore wants non-X, this situation creates an internal inconsistency, being a contradiction between a false self-understanding and the true state of the self. A woman may think that she is convinced that her father is a lovely person and wishes to care for him and attend him, but in reality and in the sense of unconsciously and as a willingness to act she does not believe that her father is a lovely person and she thus does not want to look after him but is desperate to avoid it, she presumably is lost in such a sickening conflict between the belief that is real and the belief that is wished to be real. Contradictoriness, following a coherent ideal of rationality, is not rational, and, following the insights of psychoanalysis, in some cases it can cause psychic and bodily disease. This disease makes it impossible for people to reach their aims, thus becoming an objective fact in their lives.

If this reconstruction is right, then, in the form of the symptoms that psychoanalysis diagnoses, it is shown as an objective fact that there is a difference between truth and falsehood, and that it is not only a question of the perspective taken and the point of view from which it is regarded, but that contradictoriness is more than a mere matter of formal logic or of semantics. Rather, there is real suffering that arises from falsehood and contradiction. By means of truthful reports of their own associations, suffering persons are supposed to learn to accept the truth about their action guiding beliefs, motives, and wishes. This ability to recognize sets them free from the necessity of generating illusions about themselves and thus coming into conflict between psychic state and self-image. This is why the coherentist conception of rationality on the level of individual personality gains an enormous importance for psychoanalysis. The idea that the requirement of non-contradictoriness is a necessity for the systems of motives and beliefs of a person must be thought in relative terms, regarding the background of psychoanalytic experience. As persons, we may play different social roles, and there may be contradictions between the beliefs and motives the one role or the other requires. But the variety of systems of motives and beliefs a person can live in does not necessarily mean a release. Obviously, there are fundamental contradictions that bring about diseases, a kind of irrationality that is not re-interpretable as tolerance but as an unsuccessful life.

Such a conception is, without doubt, in accordance with the philosophical conception of realism with respect to truth and deception, rationality and contradiction: it presupposes that there are real facts, not only fictions and constructions of the psychic state of a person, and that contradictions and coherences are facts of the very state of that person's psychological situation. I am well aware of the fact that I have to neglect the scope and differentiation of psychoanalytic schools, theories, and methods. But it seems evident to me that classical psychoanalysis starts out, at least, from a strong realist conception of truth and a coherentist theory of rationality, as far as Freud's own writings are considered. The fact that a coherence theory of truth is not applicable to the whole range of sciences does not imply that we have to abandon a coherentist theory of rationality in every respect. In a context that excludes incoherences, it does not make sense to strive for coherences. What does it mean that a proposition drawn from elementary-particle physics contradicts a legal one? We cannot imagine such a contradiction, because even though the two sciences have some formal basics in common, using formal operators like "and", "or", "not", "if . . . then", and so forth, they do not share a common terminology. From this, in turn, one can infer that one can look for coherences only where there is a common topical ground that concerns the subject matter. Only if brain science and neuronal-network theories on the one hand and psychic research and psychoanalytic therapy of neuroses on the other hand share their terminology and their topics to a certain degree is there a chance of finding either coherences or conflicts between the two sides. Hence, at the level of science, the coherentist unity of rationality is a relative term: this unity has to do with the fact that different sciences overlap in their topics and semantics, whereas these overlaps can be found or produced. It seems reasonable to suppose that there are thematic overlaps in the belief system a person produces. It is self-evident that there is a striving for coherence and that whenever it is unsuccessful, this produces pain and suffering.

Bernard Williams (2002, pp. 11ff.) has recently pointed out that it is a characteristic of contemporary reasoning that a conception of absolute truth has become degraded, has become meaningless. Simultaneously, in many areas there is a striving for truthfulness, and there are various projects of unmasking at work. Social scientists, historians, and political scientists cultivate an atmosphere of suspicion. As Williams writes, they try "to look behind the façade—above all, behind the respectable scenery—to recognize the real structures and motives behind them" (Williams, 2002). Although perhaps we no longer believe in an absolute truth in the form of an ultimate universal system of all sciences, we keep on believing in particular falsehoods and truths—for example, that Stalin has falsified documents, or that an American human geneticist has deceived the scientific community with his false twin experiments. Since the Enlightenment, there have been efforts at unmasking going on in all aspects of human life, and it is a universal project of enlightened rationality to enable people to lead a life as free of illusions, deception, and self-deception as ever possible.

Since Freud, psychoanalysis has been committed to this aim, and thus to the unity of a universalized enlightened rationality. This rationality is indivisible, since we usually tend to reject any relativism—for example, with respect to Stalin's falsification of history. We do not believe that before he forged the documents, it was true that Stalin met certain Jewish intellectuals, and that it was false afterwards. There is just as little ground for believing in the truth of a person's statement during repression—that he or she has never had a certain traumatic experience—and after the dissolving of repression to consider this statement still to be true. The rejection of a universal truth in the sense of ultimate laws of nature, valid for an unlimited range of experiences, does not mean that we have to give up a strong conception of truth with respect to particular statements and affairs. Above all, we should not give up the notion of truth with respect to systems of beliefs of individual persons, regarding truths simply as pleasant "constructions". Perhaps those insights that psychosomatic therapy practice gains from the diseases of its patients, who suffer from the untruthfulness and inconsistencies in their own lives or of the society they live in, may help in overcoming the postmodern conviction, stated in relative terms, that we no longer need rationality and truth. It is possible that with regard to certain historical or biographical events, we cannot decide any more whether or not they have taken place. Here, we have to be content with narrative plausibility. But this does not mean that it would not seem more reasonable to us—and in the context of clinical experience even healthier—to know the truth about a fact instead of being fooled. It would be a great help to sober philosophical reasoning if the experiences gained by psychoanalytic therapy through the suffering of humans who cannot cope either with the untruthfulness and contradictoriness in their lives or with social circumstances were to help to relativize the postmodern conviction that reason and truth are no longer needed.

4

Between hermeneutics and natural science: some focal points in the development of psychoanalytic clinical theory in Germany after 1945

Werner Bohleber

To begin with, let us briefly look at some of the motives that prompted me to consider the development of psychoanalytic clinical theory in Germany from a particular viewpoint. What drew my attention to the psychoanalytic theory debate of the last 50 years were the intersubjective, narrative, and constructivist conceptions of contemporary psychoanalysis, most of which were formulated in the United States. I could not help asking myself two questions. First, what were the reasons why the international psychoanalytic community paid virtually no attention to the conceptualizations of the psychoanalytic process and psychoanalytic understanding that had been developed here in Germany; and, second, why have these contributions only been adopted rudimentally, if at all, and reflected upon by ourselves? In a strange way these approaches sank into oblivion, which made it impossible to expound on them, to build upon them, and to develop them further.

To illustrate my point by two examples:

1. In Germany, Gadamer's philosophical hermeneutics, Horkheimer's and Adorno's critical theory, and Jürgen Habermas's

Translated by Elisabeth Vorspohl.

philosophy of communicative action gave rise to productive debates about the status of psychoanalysis, both as an intersubjective theory and an emancipatory hermeneutic science that is critical towards ideologies. These discussions anticipated in no small part ideas that we readily adopt today as issues of the international psychoanalytic debate. Common to intersubjective theories is the assumption that the analytic process does not take place between a knowing analyst and a patient as the object of knowing; instead, it constitutes a subject–subject relationship. Psychoanalysis is viewed as "the dialogic attempt of two people together to understand one person's organization of emotional experience by making sense together of their intersubjectively configured experience" (Orange, Atwood, & Stolorow, 1997, p. 5). This view presupposes modern philosophical developments—that is, the shift from subject philosophy to intersubjective conceptualizations, along with a linguistic turn. What intersubjectivism describes in terms of a subject–subject relationship has been thought of in the European philosophically informed tradition as the I–Thou relation and the I–Other question, respectively. The intersubjective relationship is seen here as the counterpart of the instrumental I–It relation.

2. The term "encounter" is at present resurfacing in discussions about the therapeutic relationship. The term was used, for example, by Isidor Berenstein in his plenary address at the IPA Congress in Nice, 2001. He distinguishes between an object relationship that emerges in the analytic relationship as a transferential manifestation on the one hand, and a relationship between subjects, in which the Other appears as an Other and not as an object, on the other. For both partners this encounter contains something novel, a presence of the being-other of the Other that has not been represented before in the internal world of the interacting partner

In a different context, the concept of "moments of meeting" (L. Sander), originating in infant research, is also identified as a phenomenon of the analytic relationship (Stern et al., 1998). The concept of "moments of meeting" emerged from the study of adaptational developmental processes. In contrast to the interpretation of transference–countertransference processes, a moment of meeting creates a non-determined open space that makes accessible other aspects of the relationship that are relatively free from transference–countertransference aspects. It establishes a new intersubjective contact between both partners by which their shared implicit relationship is changed.

The term "encounter" derives from the socio-ontological philosophy of dialogue. In the 1950s—hardly remembered now—it already played an important part in anthropological–psychoanalytic thinking.

In Germany, philosophical and sociological debates proved to have a specifically stimulating effect on theoretical concept formation in psychoanalysis. The ensuing dialogue was indeed one of the characteristics of the development of psychoanalytic theory. The peculiar breaks and faults that marked this development in Germany were another special feature. They resulted from often hidden dynamics, produced by attempts to deal with the National Socialist past and the Nazi involvement of German psychoanalysts. History of tradition and generational history merged in this process of dealing with German guilt.

I wish to emphasize that my remarks here do not cover the whole of the development of psychoanalytic thinking in Germany; instead, I focus on certain crucial aspects.

Anthropological–psychoanalytic thinking in the 1950s and the triumph of ego-psychology

With the National Socialist seizure of power a creative period of psychoanalysis, which had been flourishing especially at the Berlin Psychoanalytic Institute, came to an end. In the course of the process of *Gleichschaltung*, non-Jewish German psychoanalysts separated from their Jewish colleagues. At the same time, the expulsion of Jewish psychoanalysts resulted in the shifting of the centres of psychoanalysis and their development from Vienna and Berlin to London and New York. Though the majority of German analysts wished to preserve Freud's psychoanalysis, they found themselves more or less compelled to cooperate both in the association of psychotherapeutic schools and in the project of a "German" psychotherapy. Most of them turned a blind eye to the fact that their manifold compromises fundamentally betrayed the psychoanalytic cause. Psychoanalysis became incorporated into a national project that was to be developed on racial biological bases. After the collapse of the Nazi regime, German psychoanalysts were in the main convinced—as Werner Kemper put it—that all the depth-psychological schools had "by historic necessity . . . rallied their forces behind the façade of the German Institute" (Kemper, 1947, p. 7). This way of synoptic thinking characterized the scientific and theoretical outlook of all psychoanalysts who had stayed behind in Germany. Two groups in particular gradually distanced themselves from this way of thinking and tried to rejoin the international psychoanalytic community: on the one hand, Carl Müller-Braunschweig and his Berlin group, who founded the German Psychoanalytic Association in 1950; and, on the other, Alexander Mitscherlich, who established his Department for Psychosomatic Medicine at the University of Heidelberg. It is not possible here to detail the institutional history that formed the bedrock of the scientific development. Instead, I am going to focus on the history of ideas and theory.

Because German psychoanalysis was cut off from international developments in the years after 1933, ego-psychology, which had gradually moved centre-stage, was no longer adopted here. Instead, traditions of psychoanalysis that originated in German Romanticism emerged, while at the same time psychoanalytic theorizing was drawn into contemporary philosophical currents. This connection between philosophy and psychoanalysis became increasingly apparent in the late 1940s and the first half of the 1950s, especially in terms of a philosophically based critique of psychoanalysis as a drive psychology and natural science.

Carl Müller-Braunschweig had, originally, been a philosopher rooted in the neo-Kantian tradition. In his project for a depth-psychological anthropology, published in 1947, Müller-Braunschweig considered man to be both a part of natural reality and at the same time a being whose reality is yet to be determined. In accordance with neo-Kantian philosophy, he also considered man a medium of an ideational realm, a world of ought (of moral precepts) awaiting its realization, from which something new may emerge in the life of the individual, something that cannot simply be deduced or predicted from the past. Once this new element has entered the world of events, it can be subjected to the unitary examination guided by natural law. Müller-Braunschweig followed Nicolai Hartmann's theory of layers and linked it to the topographical model of psychoanalysis. Each higher layer depends on the layer below. Urges and forces, drives and passions, feelings and ideas can be subjected to higher mental purposes and their inhibiting, fostering, controlling, and educating influences. The neurotic personality, however, has very little freedom to influence his internal states consciously. His psychic life "has assumed the character of a relatively dissociated mechanized system, a state in the state, a relatively independently proliferating psychic part-organisation" (Müller-Braunschweig, 1947, p. 203). This metapsychological–philosophical foundation also shaped Müller-Braunschweig's theory of psychoanalytic technique, published in 1953. The analyst's task is to help the patient to master his neurotic–mechanistic system and to subject it to a maximum degree of independence and control—that is, he must be helped to move towards autonomy and to be fulfilled anew as a moral being. In this view, transference is not simply characterized by the tendency to repeat the past, but also by a tendency to break the very fetters of that past. To this end, it is not enough to render the unconscious conscious; what is further needed is a "thorough mental revision" (p. 681) through which the analysand gains control over what was before in control of him. This step is facilitated and mediated by the therapeutic relationship, which does not constitute a mere "repetition of past tendencies" but provides the patient with the previously unknown experience of a "significant new human encounter" (p. 683).

* * *

"Encounter" was a central concept of German philosophical anthropology in the 1950s. Initially formulated in the philosophy of dialogue as developed by Martin Buber, Franz Rosenzweig, Ferdinand Ebner, and others in the 1920s, it was introduced into psychotherapeutic theory formation by Ludwig Binswanger, Viktor von Weizsäcker, and others. (The following remarks draw on Michael Theunissen's excellent 1977 study.) For one thing, this philosophical school opposed the assumption of a universal subject, a core concept of German *Idealismus.* Like Martin Heidegger's fundamental ontology, it focused on the factual *Menschen–Ich.* The second front line was drawn up against transcendental philosophy and its assumption that the world is constituted through the subjectivity of the individual. Martin Buber replaced an original, philosophically isolated "I" with an origin in the "Between", in the mutuality of a direct relationship—that is, in the I–Thou relationship that overcomes all means–end relations and instrumental relational structures (as represented by the I–It relation). Buber described this Between as a phenomenology of the encounter. The encounter is not achieved by the I and Thou as fully developed beings; instead, both emerge from the pure event of encounter. It is not the Thou that makes it possible for the I to become a person; instead, both acquire their personhood in the encounter. In this way the encounter as the "Thou–I" is elevated to the true subject. In Ludwig Binswanger's (1942) thinking, the Between assumed an even more fundamental significance. Binswanger described the constitutive primacy of duality and regarded love as the most supreme and genuine mode of this duality. The We-hood as an ontological entity also challenged Heidegger's views, who conceptualized the Being-with of the Other [*Mitsein des Anderen*] only in terms of a Being-there-with [*Mit-Dasein*]. In agreement with Buber, who had already determined the encounter as a fact beyond all that is physically existent, Binswanger understood the encounter of the I–Thou as a pure transcending of the Being-in-the-world. The intimacy of I and Thou in love "traverses" space and time.

* * *

This concept of the encounter was also of central importance for Felix Schottlaender (1952). The personalistic approach introduced by Ludwig Binswanger enabled Schottlaender to bridge the gulf between the various psychotherapeutic schools. In his view, it is impossible for the analyst to function as an objective mirror, for as such he would merely embody a "cold science" and fail his patient, whose neurosis must be acknowledged as his existential problem. The analyst is required to establish a communicative contact with the patient's world if he is to understand his world view and way of existence, and this can only be achieved in a true encounter that transcends the transference–countertransference dynamics. For this reason the relationship between analyst and patient becomes an autonomous and previously unknown communicative experience. Transference and encounter are both of essential importance if the therapy is to be successful. Through the analysis of the transference the analyst must help his patient to abandon his infantile demands and advance to an unconditional acknowledgement of reality and a genuine relationship. The aim of therapy is to open up a true Thou-horizon and enable the patient to devote himself to the world.

Common to all these approaches is the emphasis on the fundamental importance of intersubjectivity, both in interpersonal and in therapeutic relationships. In spite of their empirical–anthropological outlook, however, they undermine the actual Thou and the factuality of the relationship. Here, the intersubjective meaning of the relational immediacy, which the concept of transference cannot fully encompass as an intersubjective experience of encounter in the here-and-now of the therapeutic relationship, is methodically inadequately conceptualized. It becomes a metaphysical and transcendent fact; and in the final analysis, it proves to be religiously substantiated.

On the other hand, the metaphysical essence of the philosophical–psychotherapeutic concept of encounter was matched by the critique that psychoanalysis represented a reductionist approach in looking at human existence exclusively from a scientific and mechanistic drive-energetic viewpoint. In 1936 this reproach was paradigmatically articulated by Binswanger (1947) in his lecture on the occasion of Freud's 80th birthday. As Binswanger put it, the scientific conception of Freud's psychoanalysis created the idea of a *Homo natura* and thereby a scientific construction that depended on the destruction of the anthropological unity of human experience. The totality of human existence, the interpersonal We-relation, the communication of existence and the self constituted by the We, were dissolved. "If this self is objectified, isolated and theorized into an ego or into an id, an ego and a superego, then it is cast out from the realm of its true *Dasein,* from existence, and throttled ontologically and anthropologically" (Binswanger, 1947, p. 181). In Binswanger's perspective man is always placed in a structure of meaning. The explication of this structure makes it possible, then, to determine the locus of psychoanalytic inquiry and psychological realization of man. What is comprehended in this process is but the context of meaning, not the real connection between psychically real experiences. The context of meaning creates a unity that can then be subjected to hermeneutic explication. In this way Binswanger conceptualizes the psychoanalytic method of interpretation as a special case of the hermeneutics of the humanities developed by Wilhelm Dilthey. Freud himself did not really know what to do with

Binswanger's ideas—in a letter to Binswanger (10 October 1936) he wrote:

> Of course I don't really believe you. I always used to stay on the ground floor and in the basement of the building—you have it that by changing one's viewpoint one catches sight of an upper storey, the dwelling of distinguished guests like religion, arts and others. You are not the only one to take this view, most specimens of the *Homo natura* do so. In this respect you are conservative, while I am revolutionary . . . but probably we are talking at cross-purposes. [Freud & Binswanger, 1992, pp. 236–237]

The subject matters that Binswanger, relying on Husserl, Heidegger, and Buber, described as categories of a structurally informed analysis of the cognition of existence [*Daseinserkenntnis*] were to return later and in different philosophical contexts: in Gadamer's analysis of hermeneutic experience and in Habermas' discussion of the scientistic self-misunderstanding of psychoanalysis.

In the middle of the 1950s ego-psychology, in its American form as the natural science of the psyche, began its triumphant advance in Germany, thus putting an end to the isolation from international psychoanalytic developments. The ensuing scientific debate also challenged trends in psychoanalytic theory formation that were markedly influenced by anthropology. Natural scientific methodology was now defended as being perfectly appropriate to the cause of psychoanalysis. Gerhard Scheunert (1956), one of the protagonists of German ego-psychology, established the exploration of the *Homo natura* as an inalienable strength of psychoanalysis, because the interplay between man and his social environment is invariably taken into account by psychoanalytic exploration. Scheunert saw human corporeality as socially determined by ontogenesis from the beginning. Critique also focused on the intersubjective conceptualizations of the encounter. If the anthropologically influenced view of analytic processes had brought the psychoanalytic attitude of abstinence and neutrality into discredit, Scheunert (1959) now attacked the concept of encounter on the grounds that its unfathomable depth resisted any thorough exploration. Scheunert stated categorically that the subject of the analyst's epistemological attitude and of his use of countertransference must be the patient as an object of study, if both are not to founder in an "illusionary emotional exuberance".

The introduction of ego-psychology radically changed the German theoretical landscape of psychoanalysis. Defining itself as an objective natural science, ego-psychology helped psychoanalysts to get rid of the conceptual vagueness typical of the eclecticism of the German psychotherapeutic tradition. Apparently any possible progress of German psychoanalysis within the international context depended on a clear caesura, a definite break with that tradition. At the same time, however, several fruitful and potentially promising aspects of this thinking were also dropped. They made their reappearance later, in the debate about the scientific position of psychoanalysis and in the intersubjective concepts of treatment.

This ego-psychological influx into Germany was, of course, not a homogeneous one. Moreover, the object-relations theories of the English Middle Group and especially of Michael Balint also began to flourish during those years.

Philosophical hermeneutics and the scientific status of psychoanalysis

In the middle of the 1960s new scientific methodological approaches came to the fore. They were made possible by a new foundation of scientific hermeneutics as conceptualized by Hans Georg Gadamer in his epochal work *Truth and Method*, first published in 1960, which sparked off the discussion on hermeneutics and ideology critique in the social sciences led by Jürgen Habermas. In order to get a better grasp of this development, we must first briefly look at some central ideas of Gadamer's philosophical hermeneutics. A dialogically achieved intersubjective understanding is the basic concept of Gadamer's view of the hermeneutic phenomenon. He emphasizes the dialogic nature of understanding, which he explicates phenomenologically in terms of a hermeneutic experience. Its object of study is the tradition of texts and hence their interpretation. These texts are, however, no antiquated, dead objects; instead, we establish a relationship with them that is comparable to what happens in conversation. They are language, and tradition speaks to us as to a Thou. Gadamer then elaborated the intersubjective relation between I/Me and the Other on the basis of the structure of question and answer inherently embedded in the text. The encounter with the text or with the Other as a Thou in a dialogue starts off by something addressing us. However, the Other is only able to address us when we are prepared to suspend our prejudices—that is, to allow them to be challenged. It is only under the premise that this preconception—in the sense of a prejudice that is called into question—comes into play that the Other's claim to truth can be experienced at all. The dialogic nature of the I–Thou relationship fulfils itself in the understanding of the Thou, or, to be more precise, in the immediacy of the claim with which the Thou is confronting the I. The Thou can only be experienced as a Thou if the I does not ignore his claim but is ready to listen. According to Gadamer, the hermeneutic priority of the question rests in the fact that we never begin to question something *ab ovo*; we exist, instead, from the very beginning within the flow of tradition and contexts of meaning. For this reason our ideas do not simply come to mind, but they presuppose questions—though questions are not so much actively posed by ourselves but force themselves upon us—"Hence to ask questions is less in the nature of acting than in the nature of endurance" (Gadamer, 1960, p. 372). This priority of the question is indispensable to an adequate understanding. In order to understand a text or, likewise, a certain way of behaving, we must first regain the question to which what is to be understood is an answer.

Wolfgang Loch's conceptualization of the psychoanalytic process and his hermeneutic concept of the countertransference

Gadamer's view of hermeneutics inspired Wolfgang Loch to a deeper theoretical exploration of transference and countertransference in the psychoanalytic process. As a theorist, Loch attempted to synthesize the different theoretical psychoanalytic approaches: ego-psychology and object-relations theories, explaining and understanding, and psychoanalysis both as a natural science and as hermeneutics. Loch considered the psychoanalytic method to be a method of research, informed by the search for truth and owing its therapeutic effect to that very pursuit. In his view, the use of the object relationship is of no less significance than is interpretation as an analytic method. In his postdoctoral thesis of 1965, he examined the background of the analytic process on the basis of general hermeneutic principles formulated by Heidegger, Gadamer, and others. According to Loch, the patient's psychopathological manifestations are encoded messages, constituting a text that is to be interpreted. Any understanding of this text requires the analyst to be aware of two preconditions: (1) each single word the patient articulates and each piece of behaviour is an answer to a question that we do not know but have to understand in order to be able to interpret word and action; (2) prior to any understanding, there is a preconception with which the interpreter approaches the text, and only by contributing this preconception to the process and holding himself ready to be changed by the text can the analyst hope to understand it at all. On this hermeneutic view of the understanding of the other's psyche, which Loch owed to Gadamer, he established his psychoanalytic theory of countertransference. Because every word and action of the analysand is in the nature of an answer, they involve a transference and point to an object relation that the patient is repeating. He has developed his reactions in response to his primary caregivers, whose behaviour, in turn, is seen by Loch as the countertransference onto the patient. In order to understand the analysand, the analyst must aim at a trial identification with this countertransference of the patient's significant others by empathically immersing himself in and interpreting it. Within this perspective, countertransference reveals itself to be a prerequisite of all interpretative processes; this also means that it precedes transference. The analyst's first task is to ensure that the question, to which the patient's behaviour and emotions are the answer, can fully evolve in himself, the analyst. In agreement with Freud, Balint, and Bion, Loch developed a conception of the analytic process that congenially integrated hermeneutics and object-relations theory. Later he elaborated this conceptualization in numerous contributions (see especially his collected essays: Loch, 1972, 1975, 1986).

Loch understood interpretation as the third element of the psychoanalytic situation. It remained questionable for him, however, whether the explanations and reasons that are implied in the interpretation and sound plausible to the patient were true before—that is, whether they actually existed all along or whether it is only at the moment of conviction that they become what they are: determining motives. Seen in this way, interpretation creates a new reality shared by analyst and analysand. This interpersonal agreement rests on a consensus conception of truth. A consensus presupposes a common framework. This is constructed by the tacit assumption of both analyst and patient that there is a reality independent of themselves, which also implies the idea of the true life (Loch, 1974). Here Loch takes a middle position between those who regard transference as the rediscovery of something past and the modern view that it is co-created by analyst and patient in the analytic relationship.

Hermann Argelander's concept of "scenic understanding" as a method of psychoanalytic understanding and its function in the psychoanalytic process

Initiated by Horkheimer's and Adorno's critical social theory and the search for an adequate scientific methodology in the social sciences, for scientific objectivity and hermeneutic interpretative understanding, an immensely stimulating and fertile culture of discussion developed in Frankfurt during the 1960s. These discussions drew upon psychoanalysis as a theory, while the ensuing dialogue between local social scientists and psychoanalysts, especially at the Sigmund-Freud-Institut, gave rise to seminal developments within psychoanalysis itself.

In the exploration of the specific perceptual and cognitive processes needed by the analyst to comprehend the strange unconscious of his patient, Hermann Argelander did unparalleled research. In several contributions published between 1968 and 1974, Argelander developed a psychoanalytic hermeneutic approach. He did not try to identify the psychic causes and motives of actions in order to use them for a construction of causal explanations. Instead, he was concerned with the meaning of actions. He asked how it was possible to know the unique individual whose peculiarity is determined by unconscious conflict and ego aspects. To do so, the analyst must, in the analytic situation, distance himself from the everyday meaning of what is being said—in other words, he must challenge the meaning of everyday speech in order to grasp the unconscious meaning. According to Argelander, an empathic attitude is not enough: what is needed is a specific, hermeneutically informed way of perception, characterized by evenly suspended attention and other basic hermeneutic rules such as the *Gestalt* principle, the contextual principle, and the interference principle. The most important perceptual instrument, however, is "scenic understanding". Argelander assumes that the unconscious meaning is represented not only in verbal exchanges but also in the situation as a whole. This "situational information" enables the analyst to decipher the unconscious fantasy that the patient enacts in their shared interaction. Argelander draws attention to a misunderstanding frequently encountered in discussions on transference: the equation of the current situation and the infantile scene. In opposition to this equation, Argelander emphasizes the *Gestalt* change that an unconscious conflictive constellation undergoes when it is fitted into a new situation. In this process unique unconscious phenomena of expressions are produced, the meaning of which is influenced both by the latent conflict and by the patient's present situation with the analyst. What becomes manifest in the scene is never a single infantile experience, but an infantile configuration that evolved from many scenes on the basis of screen memories. The infantile constellation is not simply a repetition of the infantile reality—it is a creation of the psychic apparatus. Fitting it into the present situation represents a specific ability, which Argelander calls the "scenic function of the ego": a preconscious process informed by general *Gestalt* principles. On the analyst's part it is matched by "scenic understanding".

There is something fictional about the scene as a hermeneutic concept revealing the unconscious conflict and thereby conveying its meaning (Raguse, 1998), for its meaning is always bound up with the two partners involved in this particular scene—that is, it cannot be isolated from them. Transference reactions derive their significance as a vehicle of meaning entirely from this configuration.

Here I cannot dwell on Argelander's contributions in detail. However, it is evident that he maintained the position of the analyst as an objective observer, while linking it to a novel hermeneutic conception, according to which transference does not constitute an entity inside the patient awaiting its activation. The scene is a dynamic construction co-created by both analyst and patient, not simply something in the past that faces them. Basically, scenic understanding represents a kind of modern constructivist understanding of transference, ahead of its time.

Alfred Lorenzer's way from scenic understanding to a hermeneutics of corporeality [Hermeneutik des Leibes]

The concept of "scenic understanding" was, in fact, introduced by Alfred Lorenzer, who worked at the Sigmund-Freud-Institut at the same time as Argelander. Lorenzer (1970, 1981) considered scenic understanding to be part of a psychoanalytic conception of language and symbol. Unlike Argelander, Lorenzer rejected ego-psychology on the grounds that it distorted the critical potential of psychoanalysis. He intended to conceptualize a new psychoanalytic metatheory. An adequate understanding of the genesis of this conception requires a brief review of a debate that established the significance of psychoanalysis as a socio-critical and ideology-critical method of self-reflection. (For documents of this debate that are important for psychoanalysis, see Habermas, 1968, 1970, and his critical review of his own position of those years in Habermas, 2000; see also Gadamer, 1967, 1971.)

Jürgen Habermas challenged Gadamer's proposition of the hermeneutic claim to universality. According to Gadamer, we are always placed within the history of the impact of the tradition that determines our awareness. Habermas qualified this claim to the authority of tradition. In his view, the power of self-reflection is able to overcome the dogmatic force of tradition. Language is also a medium of authority and social power, and hence hermeneutic experience is invariably confronted with the dependency of the symbolic context on the factual relations and the material social practice. For this reason, a dialogically agreed-upon understanding may derive from an ideologically masked structure of power. [I cannot consider Gadamer's reply to Habermas' critique in detail here, but, briefly, Gadamer disputed that self-reflection transcended hermeneutic experience and its linguistic realization. He also criticized Habermas's critique of authority, which he regarded as prejudiced. According to Gadamer, authority cannot simply be opposed to enlightenment and be equated with coercion. He postulated a natural authority that is acknowledged by love and by the choice of an example. Gadamer also disputed that understanding culminated in the clarification of unconscious motives. Instead, understanding must extend the lines of meaning beyond the restricted horizon of the individual to enable tradition to speak. In a psychoanalytic perspective, this subject matter is yet to be thoroughly explicated. The inevitable incompleteness of psychoanalytic processes, for example, also has something to do with a surplus of meanings in the cultural contexts of (democratic) societies (Lear).] According to Habermas, any consensus is suspected of having been obtained by force in a pseudo-communication. What is needed, therefore, is depth hermeneutics. Hermeneutics is expanded into an ideology critique, and self-reflection enters the centre of a critical social theory. In those years psychoanalysis provided Habermas with the only tangible example of a scientific discipline by which self-reflection was methodologically employed. The power of therapeutic reflection can break up the dimension of both the subjectively presumed meaning and the cultural tradition. Habermas applied the psychoanalytic model of neurosis to the formation and development of social institutions. Later he abandoned this approach, while maintaining his communication-theoretical interpretation of psychoanalysis. It was Lorenzer's distinction between public communication and privatized symbols rendered unconscious that facilitated his search for an understanding of communication pathologies.

* * *

Lorenzer started from Freud's differentiation between word presentations and thing presentations. Unlike language, the scenic structure mentioned above is largely stored in sensorimotor interactive memory traces. The unconscious is generated by those scenic relations. In neurotic conflicts, individual symbol formation is mutilated by defensive processes. Repression means that the conflict is dissociated from language. Excommunicated from ordinary language, it manifests itself mainly in action and in interactive scenes. Transference makes the analyst a participant in the patient's life practice, which enables him to gain access to those life projects of the patient that are not integrated into the social consensus, and to his nonverbal forms of interaction. From this it is evident that countertransference plays a fundamental part in Lorenzer's theory. Participating in the scene, the analyst invariably becomes included in the patient's dramatic conception as a concordant or complementary co-actor. By engaging in the patient's play, he comes into touch with and fathoms the layer of unconscious forces. Meaning that has been rendered unconscious then reveals itself by the interactive patterns represented in the scene. In other words, access to the unconscious cannot initially be gained through language, but only through the analyst's participation. By an act of symbol formation, this participation can then be elevated to an understanding participation and be given verbal expression.

In Lorenzer's view, the analytic project is the reconstruction of deconstructed language, and psychoanalysis is a hermeneutic reflection science. In his later contributions, published in the 1970s and 1980s, he discarded this conceptualization as a mutilation of psychoanalysis. Returning to Freud, he developed psychoanalysis as a genuine science of the "hermeneutics of corporeality", which he defined both as scientific discipline and a discipline of the humanities. Seen in this perspective, the *Homo cultura* must not be played off against the *Homo natura,* as it was by Binswanger. Neither is the unconscious nothing more than the excommunicated consciousness containing the repressed. What matters is no longer the "destruction of language" alone. The unconscious constitutes an autonomous realm of meaning, a system of concrete life projects that are nonverbally organized and make up a system that opposes the prevailing consciousness of the speech community and the prevailing circumstances. These life projects are the precipitations of a direct sensual exchange in the early mother–child unit—that is, of the instinctually determined forms of interaction, a scenically structured "system of bodily life projects" that cannot adequately be conveyed by language (Lorenzer, 2002, p. 150).

Idealization and forgetting: dealing with the Nazi past

In the wake of the international pluralization of psychoanalysis, the multiplicity of psychoanalytic schools became known in Germany, with object-relations theory playing a central part. Along with interpretation and insight, framed in ego-psychological technical terms, especially in Eissler's standard model of technique, the therapeutic relationship gradually obtained primacy over the technical rules of treatment. In this context, I would like to remind the reader of Wolfgang Loch, who has already been mentioned, and of Johannes Cremerius and Helmut Thomä. Each of them was rooted in the tradition of Michael Balint and object-relations theory, and each distinctly enriched and shaped clinical theory in Germany. Cremerius (1984) and Thomä (1981, 1983; Thomä & Kächele, 1985) extended psychoanalytic relational concepts into a dialectical and procedural view of the analytic technique. Both of them aimed at a liberation from an idealized superego identification with the so-called classical technique. No longer did the rules of treatment constitute an ideal instrument; instead, they were seen as an integral part of the creation of the analytic relationship, relativized and informed by the aims of the analytic process. Within this perspective, each rule is placed in an operational context. Time and again the analytic attitude is to be asserted in the flux of transference–countertransference developments. In this way, the analyst's behaviour and his contribution to the creation and maintenance of the therapeutic situation is given central importance.

In the 1970s the study of severe personality disorders and their treatment began to predominate in psychoanalytic discussions. Within the German Psychoanalytic Association a technical debate ensued, which at first focused on the pathology of structural ego-disorders (see, for example, Argelander, 1977; Fürstenau, 1977a, 1977b; Loch, 1977). However, contrary to the developments mentioned above, this debate did not stimulate original contributions to the treatment of these severe pathologies. Instead, discourses evolving around this subject matter reveal a strange, defensive attitude, which in those years also characterized the discussions on psychoanalysis versus psychoanalytic psychotherapy. Focused on the essentials of psychoanalysis, those debates were nourished by the concern that these very essentials would be thrown overboard by those psychotherapeutic methods that derived from psychoanalysis proper. It seems as if many analysts felt threatened in their psychoanalytic identity by those discussions on modified treatment concepts for severe personality disorders. They were concerned that the "essential analytic tasks"—interpretation and free association—would lose their significance and that the contact with the unconscious world and its meaning, which is to be explored, would be lost (Argelander, 1977). The expanded scope of indications for psychoanalysis threatened to break up the homogeneous technique, which was to be preserved as an "undivided integral technique" (Loch, 1977). This apprehensiveness created a vacuum that was then filled by the adoption of international research. At first, discussions focused on Kohut's self-psychology and Kernberg's method for the treatment of borderline cases and narcissistic personality disorders, until in the early 1980s Kleinian psychoanalysis gained an increasingly stronger foothold in Germany. Kleinian concepts provided and confirmed a homogeneous technique for the treatment of neuroses and severe personality disorders.

* * *

What are the reasons for the stagnation described here? I will consider one single aspect: the attempt to deal with the Nazi past. In the years following 1980, the whole problem of the National Socialist involvement of German psychoanalysts, which had not been worked on, or at least not adequately so, gave rise to fervent discussions. Questions were asked now, especially by younger psychoanalysts. The whole complex of unanswered questions and guilt feelings had formed the underground on which an idealization of psychoanalysis had developed in the 1950s and 1960s—an idealization that has been taught to the next generation. The generation of younger analysts, in turn, experienced self-doubt and feelings of devaluation. They did not feel confident about their ability to live up to their ideal, and they had to struggle with inflexible, rigid attitudes without being able to understand the underlying connection with their teachers' feelings of guilt. The confrontation with the Nazi involvement of their teachers' generation aroused disappointment in and a suspicious attitude towards their analytic fathers. From this suspiciousness and distrust grew a contempt for their predecessors' scientific achievements and a neglectful attitude towards their own psychoanalytic traditions. During the following years this disappointed estrangement led to a renewed idealization of different psychoanalytic schools from abroad, especially of Kleinian psychoanalysis. Deficient skills and inadequate knowledge was compensated for in this way, but dynamically these idealizations also served as a counteridentification.

CONCLUDING REMARKS

Reflection about these connections and the clarification of generational boundaries facilitated a creative mastering of the specific blockades that had been characteristic of the German psychoanalytic community. By focusing on currently presenting problems, I have tried to highlight contributions to the discussion of psychoanalytic theory and scientific theoretical issues of psychoanalytic research that originated in German psychoanalysis—contributions that are ready to become integrated into and elaborated by international discussion.

5

Freud and psychoanalytic research: a brief historical overview

Alain de Mijolla

I want to begin by citing the words written by Freud to his fiancée on Monday, 21 April 1884, when he announced to her that he had just learnt of the existence of a substance, cocaine, the effects of which he was planning to study: "As you know, an explorer's temperament requires two basic qualities: sanguine in the attempt but critical in the work" [*Du weisst, das Temperament des Forschers braucht zwei Grundeigenschaften: sanguinisch beim Versuch, kritisch bei der Arbeit*] (Freud, 1960a, p, 108). We will find, in fact, that these characteristics are mixed in variable proportions throughout his life, which I will divide arbitrarily into three main stages: laboratory research, psychological clinical research, and psychoanalytic research. Though the latter was initially centred on clinical work, in the final decades it became increasingly oriented towards anthropology.

That Freud had already shown in his childhood that he had a curious mind and was a compulsive reader, eager for knowledge, is a familiar fact on which I do not need to dwell. He himself gave us the keys with which to analyse the motives of this *Forschertrieb,* stimu-

Abridged from "Freud et la recherche psychanalytique", in A. de Mijolla, *Freud. Fragments d'une histoire* (Paris: PUF, 2003).

lated by infantile sexual curiosity, and he supplied numerous illustrations, of which his study on Leonardo da Vinci has been considered by many as being the equivalent of a self-analysis.

Neither will I enlarge further on his adolescence, on which I have already commented elsewhere (Mijolla, 1996), nor on his correspondence with Eduard Silberstein or Emil Fluss, where on each page one can follow the accumulation of a cultural baggage that he was to enrich throughout the course of his life. Nor shall I dwell on his first years at university, where the philosophical discussions stimulated by the lessons of Franz Brentano bear witness to his enthusiasms and the ardour that fired him at that time in the intellectual duels that were often aroused by quite disparate centres of interest.

This brief overview of "Freud the investigator" begins, in fact, with the announcement made to his friend Wilhelm Knöpfmacher on 8 August 1878: "During these holidays, I have moved into another laboratory where I am preparing myself for my real profession—flaying animals or torturing of human beings—and I find myself more and more in favour of the former" (Freud, 1960a).

In fact, this activity was to form the essential part of Freud's life for nearly 20 years, and Frank Sulloway's book (1979) has shown its importance for the formation of his thought, as well as the conceptual terrain on which his first psychological hypotheses were elaborated. Certain excesses notwithstanding, it provides us with some explanations for the curious silence that Freud insisted on maintaining with respect to this crucial period of his existence and his research. Among these, we may note the fact that "in most of his psychological theories, Freud reacted against the hereditary and somatic tradition of the medicine which had immediately preceded him" (Sulloway, 1979). He probably thought that the official history of psychoanalysis should not appear to be marked by his years of training as a laboratory researcher or as an organic neurologist but, rather, to spring solely from the understanding of dreams and bungled actions and from the interpretation of neurotic symptoms in the light of unconscious processes.

Nonetheless, the early research work in zoology carried out by the young Freud soon earned him the respect of his teachers and recognition in scientific circles. In the laboratory set up by Karl Claus in Trieste, where he was one of the first students to receive a grant, he was scarcely 21 when the painstaking dissection of hundreds of animals enabled him to confirm the existence of testes in the male eel, previously thought to be hermaphrodite, and, in spite of his young age, to present this discovery to the Science Academy in March 1877. His paper was published a month later (Freud, 1877b) and marked the end of this period of apprenticeship in research under the tutelage of Professor Karl Claus, with whom his relations later cooled despite these rather auspicious beginnings.

Freud's departure from this zoological section and his admission to the laboratory of Professor Ernst Wilhelm von Brücke—the director of the famous Institute of Physiology [*Physiologische Institute*] in Vienna—whom he considered to be his first teacher and one of the most important for his training, marked a turning-point in his career. In October 1896 (he was 20), Freud was still only a "*famulus*" [a sort of research scholar]; but the work with which he was entrusted led him to make an important discovery concerning the rear nervous fibres of the Petromyzon (lamprey larva)—a discovery that showed a continuity between the cells of the nervous systems of higher animals and those of so-called lower species, which the defenders of Darwin's then highly controversial evolutionary theories were keen to demonstrate. For some authors, like Ernest Jones, he was on the verge of discovering the theory of neurones. Jones insists on this point: during all these years of research, Freud constantly restrained his creative imagination and seemed not to dare to go beyond the bounds of scientific rigour; this meant that he just missed making the discoveries that were to bring others the fame and fortune for which he so ardently longed. He remained attached to the anatomical method, histology, and work with the microscope (moreover, he later invented a technique for staining nervous tissue with gold chloride), but he did not venture into an experimental field that might have offered him a more dynamic or physiological approach. Jones reads into this a manifestation of Freud's tendency to passivity and of his preference for the eye over the hand (Jones, 1953).

In 1878, however, Freud carried out this other type of research at the level of experimental physiology, in Professor Salomon Stricker's laboratory. But nothing productive came of it; nonetheless, while he was there, he learnt a technique for carrying out microscopic examinations *in vivo,* which he would later use for studying crayfish under Brücke, to whom he returned in 1879.

After carrying out a few unsuccessful experiments on gases in Prof. Karl Ludwig's Chemical Institute in 1881–82, his life, as we know, changed. In April 1882 he met Martha Bernays. In June, Brücke advised him, on account of his poor financial background, against pursuing a career in research in his laboratory. As a result Freud determined to prepare himself for clinical practice by living and studying in a hospital for the next three years. In May 1883 he served in the psychiatric clinic run by Prof. Theodor Meynert, who became another important figure in his existence. It was at this point that he began specializing in neurology and conducted his anatomo–pathological researches, which would make him known and bring him recognition in the medical world during the next 15 years. I shall not cite the numerous publications that he devoted to the exposition of his observations in this field, though it is worth mentioning his work on aphasia, published in 1891. This was not linked to a particular piece of research; instead, it synthesized the ideas about its functioning that had been inspired by his histological observations on the genetic development of the nervous system.

Before coming to his important contribution to infantile neuropathology, it is important to remember the forages Freud made, with mixed fortunes, into the domain of psychopharmacology, of which he may be considered to be one of the forerunners, owing to his studies from 1884 to 1887 on cocaine. Much stress is laid on the fact that his wish to be united with his fiancée deprived him of the fame of having discovered the anaesthetic properties of this substance. I would point out, however, that his work at that time had the nature of genuine "scientific research" with therapeutic aims, even if Freud was taken in by what he read of the results published on the other side of the Atlantic, where the use of cocaine was widespread, which constituted the basic literature available on a substance that was recognized as being both magic and anodine.

He began by trying cocaine on himself—we know, moreover, that he continued to use it orally at least until 1898—and on his hospital colleagues, such as Carl Koller, or on his fiancée, and he deduced that the substance presented no serious addictive danger. He described its stimulating and euphoric effects and thought that he had finally found a drug capable of treating depressive states or states of asthenia that could not be treated by the psychiatric and neurological approaches of the day.

The "critical" side of the investigator that he was led him to measure experimentally, with the help of a dynamometer, the effects of cocaine on muscular efficiency and the time delay prior to the onset of a psychic reaction after swallowing the product, publishing a very precise table of results in 1885 "in order to show the effects of cocaine according to a scale of measurable values". With his "optimistic" side getting the better of him elsewhere, he, too, quickly prescribed its administration by injection—a new method at that time—and its employment as a substitute substance, without secondary effects, in the treatment of morphinism. The results of this palliative on his friend Ernst Fleischl-Marxow were to prove catastrophic; and soon more and more evidence emerged, which resulted in cocaine being designated as "the third scourge of humanity".

Ernest Jones saw this adventure as a sign of Freud's tendency to attempt to generalize from a singular fact he had observed—a double-edged sword that was nonetheless at the origin of his most brilliant future discoveries, such as the "Oedipus complex", perceived during his self-analysis. Other investigators share this opinion—Michaël Schröter, for instance, who underlines Freud's early conviction "according to which a singular but characteristic example, 'a wonderfully pure case' (letter, 27 November 1893, [Freud & Fliess, 1985, p. 61]) which manifests what is typical, had a paradigmatic value" (Schröter, 1989).

The anatomo–pathological investigations were less exalting, less likely to bring fame and riches, but over the years they enabled Freud to establish a reputation for himself in infantile neurology, in sharp contrast with the reception that his psychological theories were subsequently to receive. They also helped him to develop a rigorous mental approach to observed phenomena. The influence of Brücke—a partisan of Helmholtz's school—led him, above all, to confine himself to scientific observations and to distrust metaphysical explanations—a credo that he would reiterate in 1932 in his lecture on the *Weltanschauung* (Freud, 1933a [1932]).

It was in part thanks to Ernst Brücke that he obtained the grant that made it possible for him to go to Paris to dissect infantile brains in Charcot's clinic. We know what the outcome was of this research project, which soon became secondary among his preoccupations. Yet it was still in pursuit of his investigations into infantile neuropathology that, on leaving Paris, he was to spend a short period in Berlin, gaining experience in Professor Baginsky's clinic, and that then, from 1886 on for the next ten years, he held a consultation in paediatric neurology three times a week at the Max Kassowitz Institute in Vienna (Bonomi, 1994). In conjunction with Oscar Rie, who was assisting him at the time, he published some papers on infantile paralyses that made his name as a neurologist; these ranged from the "Clinical Study on the Hemilateral Cerebral Paralysis of Children" in 1891 (Freud & Rie, 1891a) to "Infantile Cerebral Paralysis" (Freud, 1897a), which summarizes his earlier publications on the same theme.

But Freud was already elsewhere. He had, in effect, now entered the second period of his activity of research, which has been designated as "psychological research", combining clinical observation with the most daring theoretical speculations. He had started this when he was beginning his practice, because he was not satisfied with understanding nothing of his patients' symptoms and, above all, with being able to do nothing to heal them. The model offered by Josef Breuer's experience with Anna O would serve Freud as a terrain for clinical experimentation; and we are all familiar with the history of these years from his correspondence with Wilhelm Fliess.

What is sometimes overlooked is the research that Freud wanted to undertake on Jewish *Witz* and the collection that he was making of stories he had been told. There is also a tendency to forget the major research project that he wanted to carry out with Wilhelm Fliess, in 1893, on neurasthenia, the elaboration and failure of which has been described at length by Michaël Schröter (1989). In this article, which is particularly important for understanding Freud's activity as an investigator in psychology, Michaël Schröter shows that the initial aim of this research, for ordinary private practitioners, was to match the findings published by university clinics, because it was supposed to be based on "one hundred cases of anxiety neurosis" and "a corresponding number of male and female neurasthenia and the much rarer periodic mild depressions", plus "a second series of one hundred cases of non neurotics" (Draft B, in Freud & Fliess, 1985, p. 44). Nothing profitable came of this "neurosis collection" (letter to Fliess, 21 May 1894, ibid., p. 73), but this crucial moment in Freud's research activity clearly illustrates the theoretical and empirical mode of investigation that was to characterize it from then on, as described by Norbert Elias (1983).

Freud was interested, in fact, in the other forms of neuroses that his patients presented, which could not be treated so easily by uncovering "primitive scenes". They were included globally under the term "neurasthenia", and it was in order to see more clearly in this nosographic chaos that he decided to explore them. Was there a relation between them and sexual problems, as seemed to him to be the case in hysterical states? Were they psychological, organic, or linked to current behaviour such as masturbation or *coitus interruptus*? Isolating a "specific aetiology" thus became the primary aim of Freud's research, and to this end he began questioning his patients systematically, at the risk of losing a stunned clientele. It was sexuality in general, past and present, that was now incriminated; only later on, in the psychoanalytic era, was infantile sexuality to be designated in particular. "No one has ever asked me about that before!" his patients would exclaim (letter to Fliess, 6 October 1893, Freud & Fliess, 1985, p. 57). His discussions with Fliess continued, giving rise to the articles that the latter then devoted to nasal reflex neuroses. They constitute the only evidence of their aborted attempt to collaborate, along with the correspondence, which I can only invite you to read again. Drawing on his clinical observations and his aetiological hypotheses, Freud, for his part, continued over the next few years to examine in greater depth the notions of actual neurosis and psychoneurosis of defence, and he isolated the "anxiety neurosis" from neurasthenia.

But, as we shall continue to see, he was a solitary investigator, and the researches he undertook with others or that he asked others to undertake did not produce convincing results. In the context of a university study, which included the statistical demonstrations resulting from the previous study, a young physician from Berlin, Felix Gattel, set himself the task of verifying Freud's theories on the sexual aetiology of actual neuroses, neurasthenia, and anxiety neurosis on the basis of a sample of 100 cases in Krafft-Ebing's psychiatric clinic in Vienna during the summer and autumn of 1897; but here again the collaboration came to a sudden end, and Freud came to the conclusion in September 1901: "My pupil Dr Gattel was a disappointment." Felix Gattel published the results of this research under his own name in a book entitled *Über die sexuellen Ursachen der Neurasthenie und Angstneurose*, and Fliess suggested that Freud was offended by this.

In 1901, however, Freud rediscovered his nostalgia for these studies, in the form of statistical evidence, as can be seen from what he wrote to Fliess on 15 February—an announcement that contains an amusing metaphorical association with the "scientific" instrument of the early experiments on cocaine:

> I am collecting my notes on neurotics that I have seen during consulting hours to show what even such necessarily superficial observation reveals about the connections between *vita sexualis* and neurosis, and to comment on them. In other words, I am doing roughly the same thing Gattel did at the time he made himself so unpopular in Vienna. Since I need new cases and my practice is very sparse indeed, I have only six examples in my collection so far and those are not the best. I have also introduced testing for left-handedness—with the dynamometer . . . and threading needles. [Freud & Fliess, 1985, letter of 15 February 1901, p. 436]

We could no doubt learn more about this episode from Ludger Hermanns, who, along with Michael Schröter, has carried out a fine research study on Felix Gattel (Hermanns & Schröter, 1992a, 1992b; Sulloway, 1979).

We know at least that these notes, the large part of which probably disappeared in the *auto da fé* of 1907, were put to good use in the case history of Dora. For now we have entered the third period of research, which, from then on, Freud designated definitively in his writings as "psychoanalytic examination"—that "irreplaceable method of research" (Freud, 1906a).

Here, again, I shall not dwell on what the various biographies of Freud have already described and commented on at length. Instead, I shall just recall a few points of detail with which we are less familiar, but which show how Freud attempted to arouse in his pupils this taste for "psychoanalytic research" to which he devoted all his energy, at the risk of being reproached for preferring it to his therapeutic activity, as was true in Ferenczi's case. In the *Minutes of the Viennese Psychoanalytic Society*, one can find echoes of these research projects, which were also rarely followed by results on which their initiator could count.

On 22 April 1908, Eduard Hitschmann

> submitted a provisional questionnaire with a brief explanation: it is a statistical study of the sexual life of healthy and ill people. . . . Professor Freud is of the opinion that, in the general questionnaire, homosexuality should only be mentioned incidentally; a second questionnaire could be sent to those who reveal themselves to be homosexual. Freud will elaborate the questionnaire

> himself with the help of the suggestions he has received. [Nunberg & Federn, 1962–75]

The list of the 89 questions is in the *Minutes*; but there is no record of the manner in which they were followed up, or of the results of this survey that foreshadowed the future research of Masters and Johnson in the United States.

On the suggestion of Ernest Jones, Freud wrote to Ferenczi on 25 February 1910: "I want to ask Stekel to give a lecture on initiating research in collecting symbols and typical dreams. He should then become head of the committee elected to do that." The idea, which was adopted during the Nuremberg Congress in March, was only realized the following year owing to the publication of Wilhelm Stekel's book (1911); it then reappeared during a meeting of the Viennese Society on 10 May 1911 in which Freud

> proposes to continue the common research on symbols which was suggested at the Congress, and to gather together particularly convincing examples. . . . Professor Freud . . . expresses the hope that common collaboration will make it possible to verify Stekel's symbolism and to correct its weaknesses. [Nunberg & Federn, 1962–75]

In any case, he was to use this material in the additions to *The Interpretation of Dreams* (1900a—see the important papers by Ilse Grubrich-Simitis, 2000, 2002) and in his *Introductory Lectures on Psychoanalysis* (1916–17).

The discussions between Freud and Adler were going on at the same time, and it was only a few months after this meeting that the latter founded his "Society for Free Psychoanalytic Research" (*Gesellschaft für Freie Psychoanalytische Forschung*), pointing out that, in his opinion, the members who followed him

> would have the opportunity of seeing that the original Society wanted to tie its members scientifically to the whole range of Freud's hypotheses and theories. For these members, such a development seemed not only difficult to conciliate with the fundamental principles of scientific research, but particularly dangerous for such a young science as psychoanalysis. [Adler, 1912. quoted in Stepansky, 1983]

The same reproach is made by Carl Jung and, still later, by Wilhelm Reich; but Ludwig Binswanger, who had been at the meeting on 19 January 1910, had formed quite a different opinion:

> This meeting made a very good impression on me because I was able to witness the violent nature of the confrontations during which no one minced his words or held it against others for speaking freely. Even Freud, while he was revered, was often contradicted. [Binswanger, 1955]

The same day, Binswanger noted the movement of conquest that was to characterize the development of psychoanalytic research in the following years:

> It must be stressed, above all, that for Freud, the psychoanalysis of the neuroses is only a branch of his life's work; it is the aspect that has been studied most because the opportunity for doing so occurs frequently and because it has practical results. But Freud has always envisaged psychoanalysis as a total science, as the great and new method of research, which he would like to see applied to religion, history and art. [Binswanger, 1955]

The article of 1913, "The Claims of Psycho-Analysis to Scientific Interest" (Freud, 1913j), confirms this remark. It followed upon numerous examples of exploration of neighbouring fields that psychoanalytic research could and should "conquer", taken both from meetings of the SPV and from his correspondence with his pupils. Freud had employed the term in respect of mythology, but he goes further in this article by giving the specialists of the other disciplines that he enumerates—linguistic sciences, philosophical reflection, biology, history of development, aesthetics, sociology or pedagogy—the following opinion: "The psychoanalytic mode of thought acts here like a new instrument of research" (Freud, 1913j). Moreover, the extension of the psychoanalytic hypotheses to the study of literary works has always been considered, since his study on *Gradiva*, as a complement to clinical observation.

A new common research project was begun on 25 February 1914 on the Oedipus complex. It was necessary to answer the criticisms that rejected the existence in the child of this complex or considered it as a manifestation that is only found in the adult or in neurosis. In his presentation of the theme, Freud delimited his field: "We have various sources at our disposal: 1) direct observation; 2) previous observations, already known or published; and 3) biographies appropriate to the subject."

He himself suggested a few additional lines of research while asking "participants to take into account the degree to which the Oedipus complex reflects the parent's sexual behaviour . . . [or] the influence of the parents' presence or absence on the child's behaviour" (Nunberg & Federn, 1962–65). The First World War interrupted the planned publication of these various studies, of which there remains no trace, the minutes of the meetings having disappeared.

The questions raised by psychoanalytic research and the modalities of its functioning were to remain obscure during the war years but resurfaced in 1919, when Sándor Ferenczi's brief experience in Budapest posed the problem of the possibility of teaching psychoanalysis at university. Freud declared:

> To sum up, it may be asserted that a University only stands to gain by the inclusion in its curriculum of the teaching of psychoanalysis. . . . For the purposes of research, it should be sufficient for teachers of psycho-analysis to have access to an out-patient department for the supply of the necessary material in the form of "neurotic patients". For psychoanalytic psychiatry, a mental inpatient department would also have to be available. [Freud, 1919j, p. 173]

The union and reciprocal balance between research and practice was an increasingly important issue and was crystallized in the following decade with the growing opposition between the Berlin Institute and the disciples of Sándor Ferenczi or of Otto Rank. It was a vast "competition"—one might say a "research" project—that brought out into broad daylight the contradictions that had hitherto lain beneath the surface. I would refer you here to the work of Mady Jeannet-Hasler (2002), who has studied in detail the ins and outs of the announcement that Freud made in September 1922 at the Seventh International Psycho-Analytic Congress in Berlin: that he was inaugurating a "competition" for the prize of 20,000 marks on the subject of "The Relation between Analytic Technique and Analytic Theory". "The questions to be discussed are how far the technique has influenced the theory and how far they assist or hinder each other at the present time" (Freud, 1922d, p. 270).

As no text was forthcoming, the only contribution to this competition took the form of the explosive book written at the end of 1923 by Sándor Ferenczi and Otto Rank, entitled *The Development of Psychoanalysis: On the Mutual Relation between Theory and Practice* (Ferenczi & Rank, 1924). This is not the moment to go into the contents of this book, which were highly critical of psychoanalysts, who were described as *"Übertheoretiker"*, nor into the conflicts that persisted after the publication, following it, of Otto Rank's well-known *The Trauma of Birth.*

There is reason to think that Freud may have felt that he was regarded as one of those who privileged psychoanalytic research to the detriment of its therapeutic aspects, for he was increasingly attracted by theoretical questions that—although based on clinical experience and although he constantly referred to the hypotheses originating from them—pointed him towards the paths of philosophical or sociological speculation he had frequented in his prelaboratory days. His lectures and writings show this mixing of precise and original research, for instance, in *Moses and Monotheism* (1939a [1937–39]), with more general reflections on major human themes such as *Kultur,* religion, and war, synthesizing the acquisitions of his experiments and research.

I have already pointed out that from a very young age, Freud had been a researcher, an investigator, and the notes that have been preserved show that he remained so until the last days of his life. But although the form it took changed over the course of the years, the initial programme seems to have remained the same, "sanguine in the attempt but critical in the work". In the lecture on the *Weltanschauung,* his description in 1932 of scientific work takes up again, and summarizes, several other earlier reflections and sets out clearly his conception of the methodology of psychoanalytic research as he had applied it:

> The path of science is indeed slow, hesitating, laborious. . . . Progress in scientific work is just as it is in an analysis. We bring expectations with us into the work, but they must be forcibly held back. By observation, now at one point and now at another, we come upon something new; but to begin with the pieces do not fit together. We put forward conjectures, we construct hypotheses, which we withdraw if they are not confirmed, we need much patience and readiness for any eventuality, we renounce early convictions so as not to be led by them into overlooking unexpected factors, and in the end our whole expenditure of effort is rewarded, the scattered findings fit themselves together, we get an insight into a whole section of mental events, we have completed our task and now we are free for the next one. In analysis, however, we have to do without the assistance afforded to research by experiment. [Freud, 1933a (1932), p. 174]

It is certainly not just a coincidence that this text appears in the same volume as the lecture on "Dreams and Occultism" (Freud, 1933a, Lecture XXX), for Freud's relations with parapsychology cannot go unmentioned in this overview of his research activity. Traces of Freud's superstitious tendencies can be found in his correspondence with Wilhelm Fliess; but it was the arrival of disciples like Carl G. Jung, Herbert Silberer, and Sándor Ferenczi that, in addition to the frequent assimilation by the public of psychoanalysis and his own interest in dreams and the world of mysticism, led Freud to consider that researches should be carried out before any position was adopted on this dangerous ground. The correspondence with Jung, as the one with Ferenczi, provides numerous examples, and the latter's "clinical" observations with fortune tellers in November 1909 are related as objective experiments the relevance of which Freud questions in each instance while showing that he is shaken by what he has been told. The attempt to bring Jung and Ferenczi together in these explorations came to an abrupt end in the year 1911, especially as the publication of *Wandlungen und Symbole der Libido* [*Symbols of Transformation*] (Jung, 1912) was evidence, for Freud, that Jung's interest in these problems was distancing him from psychoanalysis.

A letter Freud received in 1921 from Hereward H. L. Carrington aroused his interest, and he replied on July 24 as follows:

> I am not one of those who dismiss *a priori* the study of so-called occult psychic phenomena as unscientific, discreditable, or even as dangerous. If I were at the beginning rather than at the end of a scientific career, as I am today, I might possibly choose just this field of research in spite of all difficulties. I must ask you nevertheless to refrain from mentioning my name in connection with your venture, and this for several reasons. First, because in the sphere of the occult I am a complete layman and newcomer and have no right to claim so much as a hint of authority in this connection. Second, because I have good reason to be interested in sharply demarcating psychoanalysis (which has nothing occult about it) from this as yet unexplored sphere of knowledge, and in not offering any occasion for misunderstanding in this respect. Finally, because I cannot rid myself of certain sceptical materialistic prejudices which I would bring with me into the study of the occult. [Freud, 1960a, p. 334]

He nonetheless consulted books on the subject and divulged the result of his reflections in a written communication dated 2–6

August 1921, which he read to the members of the Secret Committee during their last meeting in the Harz Massif in September. Having remained unpublished for a considerable time, it finally appeared under the title, "Psycho-Analysis and Telepathy" (Freud, 1941d [1921]), but only after Freud's death. On the basis of the two cases he presents in it, Freud only expresses the conviction that there must exist a "thought-transference" [*Gedankenübertragung*], an affirmation he was to withdraw before accepting it again in February 1925 (Note 2, Letter 1001F, Freud & Ferenczi, 1992–2000, Vol. 3), when he was ready to circulate the article that had hitherto remained secret, much to the displeasure of Ernest Jones, who was absolutely opposed to it. On 7 March 1926, Freud wrote to Jones:

> Now, the revision of *Traumdeutung* for the collected edition gave me the impetus to reconsider the problem of telepathy. In the meantime, however, my personal experience through tests, which I undertook with Ferenczi and my daughter, have attained such convincing power over me that diplomatic considerations had to be relinquished. . . . Despite telepathy, I hope you will not wholly lose confidence in me. [Freud, 1993]

The 1933 text remained reserved concerning occultism in general, but favourable to the hypothesis of thought-transference, which, Freud suggested, should be studied from a psychoanalytic point of view, adding that he no longer feared, as he had done for so long, that this realm of research might tip psychoanalysts over into spiritualism or mysticism.

* * *

It is time to conclude, or, rather, bring to an end this incomplete overview of Freud's activity as a researcher, which was a constant element of his life. So many commentaries and more or less wild analyses have been expressed on this theme that there is no risk of my adding anything new to them. I shall just recall certain points mentioned in passing. That Freud was a *solitary* investigator seems to me to be the essential characteristic. He never set up an organized team or "laboratory" that he could call his own, and all his attempts at collaboration either were broken off or failed. The research projects that he was able to propose to his various pupils were not, in general, very productive, and one can note the absolute sterility of all the attempts of an "experimental" type, whether sociological or statistical. In 1934, in answer to the American psychologist Saul Rosenzweig, who wanted to test experimentally the validity of some psychoanalytic theories, Freud said that if he found such investigation interesting, he saw little value in it, "because the wealth of dependable observations" on which psychoanalytic investigations rest "makes them independent of experimental verification". But, he added, "Still it can do no harm" (Gay, 1988, p. 523).

This is hardly surprising. The phase of "psychological research" that I have artificially isolated came to an end, in my view, in a very precise context: that is, at the beginning of Freud's self-analysis.

It was this that characterized the originality of "psychoanalytic research" and, in my view, it is this alone that characterizes it today. I think that:

> All research, whether it is "on" or "in" psychoanalysis, to use the fruitful distinction suggested by Daniel Widlöcher, is part of the permanent process of self-analysis which is characteristic of the psychical activity of any psychoanalyst. It draws its dynamism from this process and infiltrates, from its unconscious processes, the preconscious and conscious messages which are addressed to those who are aware of them and will then, in their turn, become subject to the self-analytic impulsion. [Congress of French-speaking psychoanalysts, "La recherche en psychanalyse. De l'auto-analyse à l'histoire de la psychanalyse", Brussels, May 2002]

The example of Freud, like that of other great pioneers, shows that it is from the encounter between what they find in themselves and what their patients bring them that an authentic psychoanalytic creation originates. It is for this reason that it can only be solitary in its origin, even if the exploitation of what has thereby been brought to light requires the participation and confirmation of others. Other types of research exist "on" psychoanalysis, inspired by sociology, epidemiology, or other scientific disciplines, but, in my view, the term "psychoanalytic research", inaugurated by Freud, should be reserved for the product of this very specific self-analytic process.

It is worth recalling that Freud never abandoned this mistrust of "certitudes" that, in *The Interpretation of Dreams* (1900a), had already suggested the existence of an unanalysable part, "the navel of the dream", and led him to repeat the words cited by Hanns Sachs: "*Man muss ein Stück Unsicherheit ertragen können*" (Sachs, 1944, p. 128). It was to Marie Bonaparte that he was to express most clearly his position concerning the limits of research, which eludes description:

> Mediocre spirits demand of science a kind of certainty which it cannot give, a sort of religious satisfaction. Only the real, rare. true scientific minds can endure doubts which are attached to all our knowledge. I always envy the physicists and mathematicians who can stand on firm grounds. I hover, so to speak, in thin air. Mental events seem to be immeasurable and probably always will be so. [in Jones, 1955]

His declaration to Wilhelm Fliess has been cited many times, but here it is appropriate:

> For I am actually not at all a man of science, not an observer, not an experimenter, not a thinker. I am by temperament nothing other than a conquistador—an adventurer, if you want it translated—with all the curiosity, daring and tenacity characteristic of a man of this sort. [letter, 1 February 1900, in Freud & Fliess, 1985, p. 398]

It is the "sanguine" side that is stressed by those who see Freud as a romantic and revolutionary, but one must not take completely literally this confidence made on 1 February 1900 in the slightly depressive mood of the "post partum" of *The Interpretation of Dreams* (1900a). The other Freud, the "critical" side, is always present, quick to tell Ferenczi:

> Allow me to confess that I have found in myself only one quality of the first rank, a kind of courage, which is unshaken by convention. Incidentally, you yourself belong among those who are productive and must also have observed in yourself the mechanism of production, the succession of daringly playful fantasy and relentlessly realistic criticism. [letter, 8 April 1915, in Freud & Ferenczi, 1996, vol. 2]

It was once again to Ferenczi that he wrote:

> . . . we are not suited for any kind of official existence, we need our independence on all sides. . . . We are and remain nonpartisan except for one thing: to investigate and to help. [letter, 20 April 1919, in Freud & Ferenczi, 1996, p. 348).

May this watchword serve as a conclusion.

6

What are we looking for? How?

Roger Perron

Having worked for many years as a researcher and teaching research, I have come to believe that we cannot do any good research unless we first answer these two questions: *What* do we want to know? *How* shall we do that? In other words: to begin with, we must define, as precisely as we can, the *object* of the research, and then the *methods* we intend to use.

So, if we psychoanalysts want to do a piece of research, then on what objects, by what methods? In this chapter I give a brief outline of the possible answers.

I discuss five types of answers as regards research *in* psychoanalysis or *on* psychoanalysis, following a distinction suggested by Daniel Widlöcher. We can agree to call "research *in* psychoanalysis" any work that aims to know better what happens during the treatment—that is, to understand better the analytic process itself—and "research *on* psychoanalysis" any approach towards psychoanalysis from the outside or from its borders—work on treatment indications, on the outcome, on therapeutic techniques, on the functioning of institutions, and so on—but also, within a broader scope, critical analyses of our concepts and hypotheses, hermeneutics of Freud's writings, studies on the history of psychoanalysis, and so forth. I think that research *in* psychoanalysis can be performed *only* by a practising psychoanalyst who has been well trained for this specific task; research *on* psychoanalysis can be done by somebody who is not a psychoanalyst, the condition being that he works in close association with psychoanalysts.

There are five types of possible answers, as outlined below, to my two questions: what are we looking for, and how?

Research on treatment efficacy

First, let us consider the research movement that has been developing for some years: work aiming to show the efficacy of our therapeutic actions.

I do not insist on the importance of such work: I think we all agree that it is necessary in the present context of health systems and their financial problems. Instead, I want to discuss the very meaning of a question that might, at first sight, appear rather simple: at the end of a psychoanalytic treatment, has the condition of Mr X, of Mrs Y, or of a group of patients improved? This is not so simple: what do we mean by "improved"? What criteria can we use to assess improvement? A number of studies base the verdict on the disappearance or alleviation of the symptoms that were exhibited by the patient at the beginning of the treatment—in other words, on the fact that the patient no longer belongs to the nosographic class to which he was at first assigned. In the interest of objectivity, one often uses checklists, scales, and so on, applied "before" and "after". This seems sound—but some objections may be raised:

- symptoms can grow again and grow elsewhere, so to speak—that is, they can be displaced: one symptom may disappear, but another takes its place;
- the disappearance of a symptom that originally had a mainly defensive value can lead to a worse condition;
- nosographic categories borrowed from psychiatry are of dubious value in psychoanalysis;
- there are some cases that may not have improved in terms of symptoms, but whom a psychoanalytic treatment allows to escape a far worse psychiatric career;
- and so on.

But there is a more important point: we must question from a psychoanalytic point of view the basic assumptions of such works. Psychoanalysis does indeed differ from psychiatry, precisely on this ground. From a psychoanalytic point of view, the meaning of a disorder, its economy, its dynamic functions are not in the symptom itself: the subject's personal drama does not become known through mere classification. What we consider essential are the *processes* producing the symptom, not the resulting symptom itself, which the psychoanalyst views as a by-product. Hence, can we assess the outcome of a psychoanalytic treatment using such cues as mere symptoms?

Some work seems to escape this objection by assessing the improvement on the basis of opinions given by the patient, or by his/her analyst, or by a third party (another analyst, relatives, etc.). Objectivity may then be hoped for through the use of questionnaires, scales, and so on. This fits better with the psychoanalytic approach, which focuses on the subject; but this should be a subject considered in all his/her dimensions, including the unconscious. Hence, what do such opinions mean? Patients may say that they feel better just in order to please the analyst, or not to discredit such a difficult, time-consuming, expensive endeavour, and so forth. Or they may, for reasons that are no better, complain that the analysis is fruitless and the analyst a bad one. . . . Are analysts themselves more reliable? This is not so evident: what is at stake is their reputation—and their income! Perhaps an agreement between patient and analyst would be better . . . but is it not a good place for a mutual illusion? And if the opinion of an "external objective judge" were to be sought—is there such a judge? What does "objectivity" means here, and what would be the basis for the judge's competence?

Nevertheless, I think that such researches on efficacy must be done. But we should seriously consider these objections and deal with them as research problems in their own right, the questions being: how are such opinions produced, and what are the underlying dynamics? In any case, one may understand the scepticism of all those whom we try to convince of the efficacy of our actions by merely producing opinions: there are plenty of so-called therapeutic techniques that can offer such "proof" based on the opinions of enthusiastic patients.

A third approach assesses improvement on the basis of indirect cues: a reduction in health expenses, in days off work, and so on.

This may seem minor, but perhaps it says more to the managers and finance people we want to convince.

However, the main problem is perhaps elsewhere. A treatment is successful when its aims are attained. What aims? Of course, sometimes these may be to eradicate a symptom or a distressing pathology, and so forth. But many patients want an analysis for less precise reasons: because of a feeling of repetitive misfortunes, the desire to be freed of a painful past, or some sad condition the patient cannot name nor clearly describe, often with the wish to know more about oneself. The aims of the treatment are then evident: from the patient's point of view, to be happier, or less unhappy, to have a freer, responsible, conscious life; the analyst, of course, agrees but should add to these to gain more intrapsychic mobility, with less rigidity and invalidating defences. Freud said that it is a good result if "psychic misery turns to ordinary misfortune". This is, of course, the case, and we are happy when it occurs. But how can we assess it? Let us take this seriously; let us analyse the way this is thought and felt by the two treatment partners. A whole methodology is here to be created, and I think this can be done only by psychoanalysts trained for research.

Work bearing on particular populations

A second type of research focuses on particular populations. We can study groups defined by age, such as babies, children during the latency period, adolescents, and so on, and work on problems specific to these age groups—such as mother–baby relationships, transference and countertransference in psychotherapies during the latency period, the revival of oedipal conflicts during adolescence, and so forth—or we may approach more technical questions, such as interpretation in child psychotherapies, problems of relations with parents, and so forth. Defining such age groups may at first sight seem simple; however, we always have to question the postulated homogeneity of a sample—for example, declaring that all children between the ages of 8 and 9 are "in the latency period" is obviously too simple.

The situation is much more delicate when the intended research work bears on an adult sample defined by a pathology or a particular mode of mental functioning. Here all the traps of classification open.

The most obvious of these traps could be avoided via a more careful presentation of the research. I am often amazed, when reading works so defined, about the surprising lack of detail about the way the population was really sampled. For example, we are told that the study was of a group of depressive patients. It seems that the sampling was based on the diagnosis of the first consulting psychiatrists, but nothing is said about their conception of depression, nor the criteria they actually used: we cannot take it for granted that all think and decide in the same way!

One often tries to overcome this difficulty by sampling on the basis of a scale. But we have then to avoid the trap of a naive realism that would induce us to believe that the group is really composed of depressive patients, and only of depressive patients, because they are so categorized on a scale that "measures" depression. Does it really "measure" something—and what does it measure? Of course, if it has been carefully constructed, one has assessed its metrological qualities, first of all its validity, which is to answer the question: to what extent does it accurately detect depression? But the only way to assess this validity has been to use an external criterion, such as the clinical judgement of qualified experts. We thus come back to the preceding stage, the difficulty then being merely concealed by the instrument—and concealed in two ways: because its use is easy and rather automatic, escaping the problems of a clinical approach, and because quantification gives the instrument a respectable look of scientificity.

These difficulties are of a technical kind. There is a more basic one, arising from the very fact of working on samples. By definition, this approach aims to show what is and what is not different: what the subjects of this sample have in common, differing in this respect from the subjects of another sample, be it a control group, a sample composed of patients with another pathology or another mode of mental functioning, and so on. For example, one concludes that depressive patients more often exhibit a particular personality trait, personal history, defensive reaction, and so forth, than do patients in other samples. This is certainly useful. But we then have to face the difficulty of every classifying approach. A class is composed of objects considered identical in terms of certain characteristics that are absent in objects not belonging to this class. This has worked remarkably well for zoology and botany, but far less well as far human beings and their mental apparatus are concerned. We know the difficulties psychiatry had to face when it attempted, on the basis of the somatic medicine model, to distinguish between patients under the headings of a nosology defined as a set of exclusive classes. Psychoanalysis focuses on the global character of mental functions taken as a functional whole; we are, then, very far from such a classificatory approach, many psychoanalysts refusing on this basis to accept the very idea of a psychoanalytic nosography.

Work about techniques

A third type of research work bears on technical modalities of our therapeutic actions. Here the field is broad, and the themes often deserve our attention because they are akin to our daily practice. I will consider, for instance, the possible research work on the handling of interpretations in psychoanalytic treatment. It is obviously interesting to perform such research in order to know better under what conditions we think it possible and useful to give the patient an interpretation, and what the effects are in the short, medium, and long term, this being done by distinguishing between different types and levels of intervention (from the plain "hmmm . . ." or supporting "yes", up to a construction, but also the suggestion of a link, the offer of a personal association in the analyst's mind, a transference interpretation, etc.). Of course, many publications are available on this topic: I refer here to new methodologies—for instance, collecting a number of interpretations as given by the analyst (with the conditions of their production) and looking for their effects as observed by the analyst himself or by other analysts discussing this material. Here a new methodology should be developed, specifying the ways to collect such a corpus and to process the data; I think this effort would be worth while.

This work is about the psychoanalytic treatment proper, in the couch/armchair setting, but a number of research actions are also possible and desirable about other therapeutic settings and techniques: about play and pictorial activities with children, mother–child therapies, family therapies, psychodrama, and so on. In all these cases, in the frame of a particular activity, one can collect and process a corpus of observations on the model here suggested.

Work on the analytic process

Let us now consider major studies that bear on the development and the functioning of the analytic process, all through the treatment. Obviously here we are facing complex phenomena, including: the development of transference, and its necessary counterpart, countertransference; the development of transference neurosis; the dynamics of drives and defences; the discovery, by many patients, of an inner life that is much richer than previously thought; access to a new capacity to unbind and rebind and hence to a greater mental mobility; the succession of phases such as honeymoon, desert wandering, negative therapeutic reaction, and so forth. These phenomena are so complex that they cannot be treated in only one research study, and I would be suspicious if somebody were to tell me: "I have in view a research on the psychoanalytic process" without delimiting *what*, in this large field, is to be considered. It is necessary to distinguish specific targets in this vast enterprise. Here, again, I think it would be a sound method to collect a corpus of treatment materials on a given theme, to be noted according to a well-defined procedure. Let us take as an example research designed to study unbinding and rebinding processes, where a binding operation is noted when something now said explicitly evokes something said earlier. This may be made by the analyst, aiming thereby to promote the development by the patient of this major aspect of the psychoanalytic process, or it may be made by the patient himself. The working hypothesis would be that, all through the treatment, this would progressively be made less and less by the analyst, more and more by the patient—we know that when a good analytic process is attained, we speak rather seldom. Of course, in such a scheme, it would be necessary to operationalize the procedures to collect the data, to rate them, and to analyse the results.

Work on concepts and hypotheses

I will now turn to work at the very core of psychoanalysis: that aiming to reassess the bulk of the concepts and hypotheses constituent of our theoretical apparatus. Of course, this work has gone on unceasingly from the beginnings of psychoanalysis, which owes all its progress to this effort. However, it is obvious that in this field controversies proliferate, opinions clash, and the success or failure of a theoretical proposal depends to a large extent on the prestige and sociological weight of its proponent. For all these reasons, one can now and then observe psychoanalytic "fashions": for example, a theoretical advance much favoured in one psychoanalytic group, the members of which often refer to this with the use of some "signal" terms, disappears some years later. Only time can validate a real theoretical advance. This being said, can we develop the theory by means other than those used by Freud and by us all after him?

Personally, I doubt it. A theoretical elaboration is a work of thought, and its worth is exactly the worth of the thinker: it cannot be replaced by any automatic procedure, be it as sophisticated as you wish—and certainly no more so if adorned with the prestige of computers. But we can try to attain more rigour when reassessing our theories. I will limit myself here to four points.

1. Any reassessing of a psychoanalytic concept or hypothesis begins in the first instance as a historian's work: we have to trace its origins, birth, life, and sometimes death, as exactly as possible.
2. Such work clearly springs from our clinical practice: the only function of theory is to organize observations as a coherent, intelligible whole. Our situation is the one familiar to all the "nature sciences", insofar as this term applies to all disciplines that can be defined in this way, in contrast to mathematics, logic, and so on that do not bear on observable facts. We face two opposing constraints: adjustment to facts and system coherence. The history of science highlights the fact that for any given discipline there comes a moment when new facts break up the coherence of the accepted system, which then has to be enlarged, remoulded, restructured—an operation Piaget called "increasing equilibration". In many disciplines one can see moments and people that emphasize coherence, neglecting any annoying facts that cannot be fitted in—something that Lacan may perhaps be reproached for towards the end—and other moments and people that try to gather a wide variety of facts and integrate them more or less into a theory loose enough to accept them—for which the so-called eclectics may be reproached.
3. Another difficulty is specific to psychoanalysis: it arises from the highly polysemic character of our language. It may happen that we find it difficult to communicate in our discussions, that misunderstandings occur, perhaps that we politely agree to get out of

them—all this because the same word has very different meanings for the discussants. Can we avoid such a situation? We can, of course, work towards specifying the terms, distinguishing and organizing their various meanings: a well-developed discussion should always be careful to be expressed in a good vocabulary. This polysemic character of our language is often criticized by people working in the so-called hard sciences, who accept only terms with one meaning, bound in relationships that are themselves univocal. However, I am of the opinion that in our field the use of some terms with multiple meanings is necessary. Multiple meanings are the very fabric of mental life, and working on this multiplicity is essential to the analytic process; I even happen to maintain that some misunderstanding fuels this work. Could we keep this richness with only univocal terms, with very narrow meanings and at risk of extreme fragmentation? I doubt it—but this is, I think, a major epistemological question.

4. Final point: we must be more explicit regarding concepts and hypotheses.

Concepts

In psychoanalysis, as in other fields, concepts are organized in tiers: the base is made up of well-delimited concepts that are open to observation and rather strictly defined; but as we climb the successive steps of this architecture, we find concepts that integrate the lower ones and are farther from immediate observation; at the top, there are one or two keystone concepts the function of which is, precisely, to guarantee the strength of the whole system. For instance, we may consider the concept "negation" [*Verneinung*] as basal: it refers to declarations that are easily spotted. Negation takes a structure that is readily identified (what is denied is, by this very act, accepted); interpretation is rather certain (if the patient says, "this person in the dream is not my mother", then by this very fact this person is the mother). The concept of the "death drive" or the Eros/Thanatos couple, on the other hand, are keystone concepts: they were created by Freud with the aim of ensuring the coherence of the whole system.

Very interesting work could be done to formalize this conceptual, probably tree-like architecture. In the first instance, this is work on psychoanalytic language, and collaboration with linguists would be valuable. Let me refer here to work we developed some years ago with our Paris colleagues about the thematic entries classifying the publications in our Sigmund Freud library. We were led to such a tree-like architecture laid out in tiers over eight or ten steps, detailed in up to about 200 narrower themes. We have in prospect such a study—probably with the use of a convenient computer program—about the entries in the *Dictionnaire International de la Psychoanalyse,* recently published under the direction of Alain de Mijolla (2002). The aim in such a semantic analysis of our language is to achieve a clarification of the concepts connoted by these words; of course, in the final analysis it is up to the psychoanalyst to judge whether the results are acceptable.

Hypotheses

Do we set hypotheses? Yes, if we consider the term within a broad definition, according to which a hypothesis is a waiting state, based on an interpretation. In this sense, we often set hypotheses in the practice of our treatments: according to our understanding of the material, we expect that the patient will say, evoke, experience . . . something. Of course, this expectation is often unfulfilled: what was expected does not appear, or something else appears instead. This need not to upset us, as we are then led to reassess our expectations and to question the theoretical reasons on which they seemed to have been grounded. The good clinician who is able to keep open this questioning of his own expectations is probably the one who is most able to propose useful theoretical advances. Let us note that in this he is not very far from the scientist, who knows perfectly well that progress will be made by questioning false or weak hypotheses.

However, one cannot remain with only this broad definition of hypothesis. In the current scientific meaning of the term, a hypothesis is a proposition about the conditions of production of certain kinds of phenomena, a proposition that is supposed to be experimentally verifiable by realizing these conditions: the reality answers with "right" or "wrong". Perhaps we are not very far from that when in the practice of the treatment we propose an interpretation in order to facilitate in the patient a representation, an emotion, a link, on the basis of which we can then verify whether—as Freud said—"the matter reacts" or not. Here, again, disappointment may be useful if examined. But the scientist will probably not be satisfied if we say only this: he will object that an experiment, to be conclusive, must be repeatable by any qualified experimenter and, if possible, be "crucial"—that is, with no possible doubt remaining. Obviously, we are very far from this: our "experiments" cannot be repeated exactly, and they cannot be, in any meaning of this term, "crucial". Psychoanalysis is not, and will never be, an experimental science in this version of "science"—and I willingly add: "Happily so!"

Now, do we have to conclude that we cannot set hypotheses beyond the daily practice with a particular patient—that is, that we cannot build propositions about the conditions that produce certain phenomena, these propositions being themselves built as a theory? I think we can. But we should take into account the following:

1. We have to define the level at which the hypothesis works. As a matter of fact, one has to distinguish the broad hypothesis and its operational translation. I call "broad hypothesis" a directive idea that is not directly testable. For instance, let us consider the hypothesis: "Transference interpretations facilitate the development of the analytic process." Most of us would, of course, agree. However, let us suppose that somebody were to want to verify this through research: he or she would have to admit that, as such, the hypothesis is much too broad and loose to be tested against facts. It has to be turned into an operational form—that is, the conditions pertaining to the interpretation, its wording, the moment of the treatment, the kinds of patients considered, and so on need to be specified. The corpus of interpretations to be gathered and analysed must be collected under these specifications, otherwise it would be so ill-matched that it would probably not be of any use.
2. Do we want to *prove* that the hypothesis is right or only to *show* its usefulness? I do not think that we can demonstrate anything in psychoanalysis, by this kind of research or otherwise—let us be happy if we can show something in a convincing way to a sincere opponent. We would have to develop here a more detailed discussion about the distinction between "demonstrating" and "showing": this is a major point, as what is at stake is the status of proof, and of the ways to prove, in our work. This is a difficult question, and I shall limit myself here to underlining its epistemological interest.

3. About the difference between what is true and what is useful: I think we cannot plainly state that "this hypothesis is true or false", as it necessarily supposes that we refer to some external reality that would be independent of the observer. Here I am deliberately being pragmatic: I think that we can never demonstrate, or even show, that a concept or a hypothesis is "true" in this sense—only that it is useful to build the meaning of what we observe, and the more so the higher we go in the conceptual architecture to which I was referring above. We can show that the concept of "negation" is useful to the interpretation of certain kinds of observations, or that the death drive is useful as a keystone. Anyone is free not to use these concepts, but I can try to show that by discarding them one loses theoretical instruments that are useful to give meaning and to build observable facts.

CONCLUSION

Only a few words to end with, as a conclusion does not appear possible: I have only tried to raise questions.

I think we must free ourselves from the fascination of scientific models borrowed from the experimental sciences and, more particularly, from the so-called exact sciences. We have to develop epistemological and technical models fit for our field, which bear on human mental functioning. On my good days, I think that this is the best service we can offer to the human community. . . .

7

What does conceptual research have to offer?

Anna Ursula Dreher

Conceptual research is, no doubt, in fashion. Nevertheless, if I look at all that goes by that label, I think that there are some misunderstandings. There is, if you like, a need for conceptual clarification—namely, for the concept of "conceptual research".

One thing needs to be mentioned in advance: there is no conceptual research as a *standardized procedure.* I would like to suggest that it should, rather, be seen as a *research programme*—which no doubt contains some of the ideas and arguments that are currently being discussed. Whoever works in the field of conceptual research is always asked—at least in the case of friendly curiosity—two questions: "What is it about?" "What is it good for?" I would like to comment on both questions and shall therefore speak less about individual research projects and their findings, but, rather, about conceptual research itself—about my own view of conceptual research, of course.

The composite term implies that one must bring two things—psychoanalytic concepts *and* research in psychoanalysis—into relation. Conceptual research defines itself by its subject matter: namely, psychoanalytic concepts, those tools of language by which we attempt

---

Translation by Eva Ristl.

to grasp empirical phenomena—especially clinical phenomena—theoretically. As a working definition, I would put it this way: conceptual research is concerned with the *systematic* investigation of the meanings and uses of psychoanalytic concepts, including their changes, in relation to both clinical *and* extra-clinical contexts. Now, one might ask: what could possibly be so problematic about concepts that it is of interest to make them even the *subject* of research?

Let me make a few basic remarks on this point.

A number of our communication problems result, among other things, from the fact that our concepts and those phenomena to which they refer do not have a simple, stable relationship. I would just like to illustrate one such problem in this field of tension between language and the world with a rather plain example from everyday life. What or who exactly counts as a "pedestrian"? This may seem only a trivial question. This spring, Germany's Federal Supreme Court heard a case in point where the question was raised whether or not inline skaters are to be assigned to the category of pedestrians. The court's judgement: inline skaters are considered pedestrians, not cyclists—which the party of the inline skaters would have liked. A new empirical phenomenon—inline skaters—is to be integrated into a body of rules with established conceptual categories like pedestrian, cyclist, motorist. The Federal Court decided—to no one's surprise—conservatively, upheld the old categories, and assigned the new phenomenon of inline skaters to the "pedestrian" category—a decision little favoured by many pedestrians and most inline skaters alike. The advantage of this expansion of the concept of "pedestrian" is that the old conceptual field does not need to be newly organized. Had the Court assigned inline skaters to the cyclists' group, that would have caused delineation problems towards the powerful group of motorists. And had the Court newly defined an independent category, this would have had far-reaching consequences for all road users—and would finally have given bureaucrats the chance to invent new traffic signs.

Of course, you may ask what this has to do with psychoanalytic concepts. As to its subject matter—certainly nothing; and, luckily, we do not have such a court either. But the example points to structurally similar problems we have in all those areas where "something new" meets a canon of established concepts. In psychoanalysis, we encounter new things daily and on a variety of levels—in clinical and diagnostic work, and also when we are studying research results.

1. How we deal with the "new" that a patient brings up in every session is a determining moment in our clinical activity and can, for example, lead to the question: how do I integrate new perceptions and experiences into my existing ideas about mode and pattern of transference? And this, of course, essentially depends on the question of what I consider relevant at all in terms of transference.
2. A second example: What happens to our diagnostic categories when specific forms of auto-aggressive behaviour, self-mutilation, or eating disorders come increasingly into the focus of our interest. Do we use our old categories—like hysteria, for instance—or do we need new categories for these symptoms—and if so, what is their relationship to the old and established concepts?
3. And this is particularly relevant for research: one must, of course, mention the manifold problems that can arise for our concepts from new empirical knowledge generated by research. There always is, and always has been, such a pressure to change. We are experiencing it right now, for example, in infant research, where some of our developmental concepts are being questioned and confronted with ideas from attachment research. We also experience it where new findings from imaging procedures in the neurosciences might even change our ideas about how memory functions and how traumata are processed, for instance. The latter might not only change our theoretical ideas about conscious and unconscious processes, it could even have consequences for the clinical work with traumatized people.

What these examples illustrate is that concepts do change: they live just the way scientific language games in general live. When the world changes, when there are new clinical observations or extra-clinical empirical findings, this can influence the meaning of familiar concepts. It is certainly possible to integrate whatever is new into the familiar system of concepts, but it could also make sense to reconsider the established use of the latter or even to introduce new ones and give up the old ones. That is the way it is in everyday life, and that is the way it is in all the empirical sciences.

Science researchers like Thomas Kuhn (1962) have shown us that such substantial changes of theories and concepts do not occur continuously—they happen in leaps—and also that those changes are not only due to an accumulation of new knowledge: parameters like institutional power struggles or struggles for prestige and money, parameters that can be grasped by sociology of knowledge, often play a role that should not be underestimated. And, of course, stronger defences against every pressure to change are also imposed on our theories: again and again there are attempts to dogmatically delineate concepts up to sect formation, not infrequently oriented at authorities. Kuhn thinks that the validity of dogmatic language games, which claim eternal truth, is often limited to the reign of one generation—but exceptions confirm the rules, of course.

What Kuhn has described regarding scientific progress in general is also true for concept changes: rather than just following rational and factual considerations and being oriented towards empirical progress, they are also dependent upon the *Zeitgeist* and the ruling mentalities. For this, trends in science—for instance, the movement towards the cognitive sciences, or recently towards the neurosciences—are prominent examples. I am convinced that these developments actually provoke not only the necessity to rethink or even to adapt our analytic concepts—both in clinical practice *and* in research—but they also, above all, provoke the necessity to make sure that the meaning content of our concepts—the *analytic* meaning content so-to-speak, which is so essential for our clinical work—remains preserved; and especially to make sure that reductions and empiricistic simplifications are avoided—again: both in clinical practice *and* research. A gripping tightrope walk. . . .

For, what precisely distinguishes our analytic concepts is that their meanings are charged with our theoretical assumptions and the pre-assumptions of our world view [*Weltbild*]. From the beginning, a central place for our concepts to prove their worth has been the analytic situation. An essential criterion for the quality of a concept is its usefulness in clinical work. There, we gain a special kind of experience with other people and with ourselves—some even consider this kind of experience "unique" and not to be reached in any other way. And one decisive aspect of analytic work is the special emphasis on the inner world—with its conscious and *especially* its unconscious processes—and the emphasis on the tension between "internal world and external reality", as the beautiful title of Kernberg's 1980 book puts it. What it also includes is our characteristic weighting of drive, emotion, affect, and cognition in experience and behaviour—something that is certainly not shared by everyone. And what is also a part of this is the subjectivity of the analytic situation, our controlled emotional participation in the analytic process—our attention, for instance, to physical responses in ourselves—all of which we try to communicate via concepts.

When we reflect on this clinical work and speak to others about it, then our analytic concepts are our everyday and usually unquestioned tools. Probably, precisely this "matter-of-course-ness", or, if you like, "ego-closeness"—with which each person uses a concept in his or her own sense, and also as identity-creating in the sense of using the language of "his or her" analytic reference group—is a source of resistance against a rational communication with people who understand a concept differently, in "their" very own sense. And the difficulty of going beyond this egocentric perspective in the understanding of a concept unfortunately often has the familiar social consequence of questioning whether "they" still belong to "us"—a question that not infrequently ends in fundamental debates about who has the correct analytic understanding or, even, the "true analytic identity". Of course, often people hold the conviction that their own conceptual understanding acquired in their own analytic socialization represents, if not the only truth, then at least a superior one, and that the others' concepts are more or less wrong.

Most of the time being so centred on one's own understanding is one reason for underestimating problems that a "regional" meaning and use of concepts can have with respect to a broader communication with others. Also, the view that holds that there is no disadvantage but, rather, a creative potential in variety or even arbitrariness—which is not to be denied—is more often than not an expression of a defence in thinking critically about one's own understanding of concepts. Both attitudes, though they may serve one's feeling of safety, do not necessarily support communication that ensures that we refer, at least remotely, to the same phenomena when we are using the same concepts.

Let me specify some of these *general problems with our concepts* a little further with the example of the transference.

The problems begin already with the manifold contexts in which we meet this concept. Working as an analyst in private practice for many years now, I feel like many colleagues who, while dealing with transference all the time, are nevertheless dissatisfied with the semantic inexactitudes of the concept—and sometimes even the contraditions in its use. This shows up whenever we think about our cases, write case reports, or participate in intervision groups. For example,

- in my own work with patients, I experience the phenomena of transference;
- in colleagues' case vignettes, I read or hear how they illustrate and discuss transference;
- in the various analytic traditions, transference receives a different theoretical weighting;
- in empirical studies, transference is supposed to be grasped by measuring on the basis of transcripts . . .
- . . . or to be elucidated in its affective structure on the basis of video recordings;
- and, last but not least, international conferences do not allow us to overlook cultural differences in understanding the concept.

How is one to reconcile the various usages of the concept of "transference" in such a diversity of contexts? Does everything that carries the label "transference" actually contain "transference"?

This is not an easy question to answer, because transference has the problems that are typical of most of our concepts. First of all, there is the problem of reference: what exactly does transference refer to in the world? We analysts say: to a burnt-in cliché—that is, an unconscious, ontogenetically acquired relationship pattern that is being actualized in the here-and-now. And a behaviourist would ask critically: how can one observe this cliché?

Not directly, we would answer. Transference is simply not an objectively observable behaviour, like, for instance, a manifest narrative or a typical affective pattern. Rather, transference is a theoretical construct of psychoanalysis, deeply connected with all our ideas about the conscious as well as unconscious functioning of the psyche. There is, therefore, no behaviour that, as such, "is" transference: there are merely any number of very different phenomena that one can *see* and interpret *as* transference—and what this is essentially about is the understanding of unconscious pattern. If someone asks about the correctness of this interpretation, then we shall point to its dependence on the concrete individual case and, last but not least, also to the indicators to be found in what we experience as countertransference.

Each of us, in our own individual practice, has probably found a quite reasonable way to deal with these problems. The question remains, however, whether there might be—at the level of scientific discourse—a reasonable and systematic way to survey and to structure the different views and also the different practical implementations of central analytic concepts. Even though we may not succeed in every instance in unifying the usage, it is nevertheless important to engage in clarifying communications on commonalities as well as on differences—a prerequisite also for a dialogue with other disciplines.

I think that conceptual research enables us to take such a decentred perspective on concepts and additionally to systematically reconstruct and critically discuss the changes in a concept arising from theoretical and empirical progress, but always as a consequence of cultural and societal change.

In the 1980s I took part, at the Frankfurt Sigmund-Freud-Institut, in a research group initiated by Joseph Sandler for the study of the history of and diversity in the usage of the trauma concept (see Sandler et al., 1987). Apart from the subject matter of trauma, my interest at the time was focused above all on such a general *methodical* approach for the investigation of concepts, which, I hoped, could be useful in reducing the conceptual confusion that was already then cause for much complaint.

For a long time, encyclopaedias have been much used to orientate oneself better in the complexity of surveying the meanings of concepts. In my own work, first Laplanche and Pontalis (1973) and then also Moore and Fine (1990) have been reliable companions; the new volume by de Mijolla (2002) will certainly also be one in the future. But what becomes evident in such a chronological sequence is this: even excellent dictionaries of basic analytic terms need an update from time to time. Within the context of conceptual research, one naturally does go back to this aggregated knowledge. However, in the focus of an actual project we do not have the complete spectrum of analytic concepts—that could not be done with justifiable means—but always one concept only or one narrowly circumscribed conceptual field. It is like looking through a magnifying glass, so-to-speak, at those concepts of particular interest, in relation to which current as well as acute problems are manifest. Some concepts—like trauma at the time—are "right in the middle of those tensions, which are caused by the constant rebuilding of the theoretical edifice", as Sandler (1983) put it, and contradictory as well as inflationary use may well be taken as a sign that a concept no longer fits.

In our trauma project we started from an idea that Sandler had contributed, based on his experiences in the Hampstead Index Project: psychoanalytic concepts have no exact definitions and thus no unequivocal and fixed meanings, but it is useful to describe them in an elastic meaning-space—a meaning-space with a core, but with indefinite and changing borders. Furthermore, there are not only aspects of explicit meaning in their practical clinical usage, but also quite a number of interesting implicit facets—which we hoped to elicit from the interviews with analysts reporting on the treatment of trauma patients. To grasp both phenomena—meaning-space and implicit conceptualization—we worked out and used an inventory of procedures that consisted of a mixture of different qualitative methods, literature analysis, interview techniques, and techniques of group discussion.

When we presented our project in the late 1980s, the reaction to the *methodical* procedure—quite contrary to the reaction to our considerations on the subject matter of trauma—was rather "measured", along the lines of: interesting, but what for? If I disregard the fact that possibly we did not convey our suggestion well enough at the time, I think that this reaction surely had other reasons:

- One was certainly that at the time conceptual research was simply unknown to many people. Could there be a research method that has concepts as its research subject and not, as usually, empirical phenomena, like, for instance, affects or infant behaviour? And why is it done "autonomously" as a *project* per se, and not merely as—at best useful—preparatory work for the "actual": namely, empirical research?
- A further reason might have been that the methods we used came from the "wrong" tool-box—they were mainly those from qualitative social science research and not the quantitative methods of experimental research, which had, at the time, become en vogue.

In any case, our idea that such autonomous research could yield gains—and here meaning gains both in clinical work and also in scientific communication—had only a few supporters at the time. In the meantime, at least the *label* "conceptual research" has become established. The Hampstead Working Group and later the project group at the Frankfurt Sigmund-Freud-Institut had initially used the term "conceptual research" only as a loose "working title" to characterize their research activities. In the history of psychoanalysis, such discursive attempts at conceptual clarification were not new: one must only think of the concept-study groups of individual analytic institutes in the United States, or of the panel discussions, each on one concept. The latter often follow a typical pattern, with speech [*thesis*], reply [*antithesis*], and conclusion from all arguments—that is, especially the attempt at a synthesis: a pattern that can definitely be seen in the tradition of Socratic dialogues.

When I began in the 1990s to discuss such research activities from the history of psychoanalysis under the label "conceptual research", and in addition tried to give this research tradition a methodological foundation (Dreher, 2000), the term was by no means common in the analytic community. Even just a few years ago, a prominent analyst asked me, with an undertone of friendly irony, whether we were actually the only conceptual researchers in the world, or whether there were others apart from us. At the time I considered this a typically German question, for at least in the English-speaking world systematic forms of discussing concepts are quite common.

Today we even have two subcommittees for research in the IPA—one for empirical and one for conceptual research—and there is much talk about conceptual research—though with very diverse motives and with different goals. But when they say "conceptual research", does everyone mean the same thing? I doubt it. Who does conceptual research? Every clinician who uses a concept to describe some particular case? Every empirical researcher who, in the context of a study, operationalizes a concept as fittingly as possible, thereby attempting to grasp it by measuring it? Or everyone who is thinking about a concept anywhere in any way?

Of course, "psychoanalytic conceptual research" is not a protected term. However, I suggest making a distinction between conceptual *research* and various kinds of conceptual *reflection.* By conceptual *research,* I would only understand those activities that deal with concepts and their role in conceptual fields in a systematic and method-based way. Whoever *reflects* on concepts—and this should actually be a regular procedure for each clinician and each researcher—is certainly doing something important and useful, yet this is not automatically engaging in conceptual *research*: conceptual reflection is a necessary but on its own not a sufficient condition for conceptual research.

Thus, if the aim is systematically to grasp, clinically and extraclinically, the meaning and usage of concepts and their changes as well, then there is—beyond, of course, the ever-important reflection—a need for a certain system in the procedure and the attempt to integrate different convictions regarding a concept. The panels I mentioned and the concept-study groups are established and generally accepted models for such activities, which, so-to-speak, meet the minimum requirements for conceptual *research*. But sometimes one just wants to know more about a concept: how and why the current use of a concept developed over time, or whether a concept is used in a logically consistent manner, or what ideas neighbouring disciplines have about it. There can thus be more comprehensive research questions, which can only be answered by a whole range of different methods. Examples here would be various forms of literature analysis, computer-based consistency analyses, interviews, questionnaires, or perhaps also expert ratings.

In practice, conceptual research will typically be carried out as a project. A proper and respectable research project—meeting regulations—will, of course, have a specified aim, a structured working plan, and adequate consideration of the methods chosen and about the data evaluation. And a proper research project ends in a report, which makes the results communicable and criticizable. It goes without saying that such work can often only be carried out by a team. The work of such a team could, for instance, begin with a systematic literature analysis, which traces the usages of a concept in a historical longitudinal perspective as well as in a cross-sectional contemporary context. Further sources for evidence would be, above all, statements from clinical practitioners, because the classical place—where our concepts must prove their worth and also where changes may present themselves—is in the analytic situation. Of course, there are also the designated experts, if you will, for each concept, among whom I would also count, in addition to analysts, relevant researchers from neighbouring disciplines. Insofar as conceptual research intends to overcome the boundaries of the various schools, it will often be interdisciplinary—but always rooted in our *common ground*.

I hope to have countered, with this outline of a prototypical example of conceptual research, the prejudice that conceptual research consists merely of sitting in an arm-chair and free-associating about one's own understanding of a concept, or commenting on colleagues' usage of concepts, or just briefly consulting a dictionary. A concrete project may require a great many resources, depending on the questions asked, and, last but not least, the financial requirements, too, may be considerable—and as far as money is concerned, things are not a bit different with us than with anyone else: things become serious. . . .

* * *

I want to remark briefly on the selection of those methods that can be useful for conceptual research.

Occasionally, one hears that conceptual research uses qualitative methods, whereas empirical research employs quantitative methods. I consider this opinion to be based on a misunderstanding about how research works. Conceptual research and empirical research do indeed differ as to the subject matter of their research—their *"Erkenntnisinteresse"* [epistemological interest], if you like—but not necessarily in the methods used and not at all in their intention and aim, which is the widening of psychoanalytic knowledge. Meaningful empirical research, just like meaningful conceptual research, can be based on the use of both qualitative and quantitative methods. Naturally, because of its subject of interest, it is clear that conceptual research deals intensively with language and the analysis and interpretation of verbal data—a fact that only bothers those who consider words as primarily opaque and numbers as always exact.

That a research process also consists of structured as well as structuring reflection and discussion with the aim of achieving synthesis is evident to everyone—but not that this discursive moment is *systematically applied* and understood as *essential.* For not only the fact that concepts are themselves made the subject of research, but also the particular weighting of this discursive element may be unusual to some. Without this attempt to communicate systematically about the reasonable rules of usage and to look for social consensus, the goal of conceptual research—an improved concept usage—would be unattainable. Thereby, in the course of the research process, a concept is repeatedly put on the test-bench of reflection, discussion, and criticism. This spiral structure of the procedure is important not because conceptual researchers like to run around in circles, but because an attempt must be made to integrate new aspects gradually into the meaning-space so far elaborated: starting with one's own previous knowledge and a systematically acquired knowledge base, the task is, indeed, to consider clinical understanding as well as expert knowledge. Such working through with the aim of a slow movement towards a reasonable concept usage is—if you like—a hermeneutic process; at its best, it is that "progressive spiral" described in the context of the Hampstead Index (Sandler, 1987, p. 317).

Such continual work on a concept, of course, follows a pattern different from the heuristic step of a conceptual clarification typical at the beginning of an empirical project—in the important context of operationalization. This is necessary in empirical projects in order to move from theoretical concepts to observable variables. And with the selection of the measuring operations it is indeed exactly determined which aspects of a concept will be grasped—and which ones will not be.

One repeated criticism of many operationalizations refers to the fact that—through the selection of measuring procedures—the complexity of analytic concepts is not sufficiently taken into account. What makes analytic concepts so unwieldy? One of the central problems in dealing with our concepts has been identified in the work of a research group that ten years ago began to operationalize analytic concepts for diagnostic purposes in Germany (Arbeitskreis OPD, 1998). The evaluation of the situation by this OPD working group—which oriented itself more along the lines of quantitative empirical research—could not have been formulated any differently, had it been made from the point of view of conceptual research; the authors indeed complain about the ambiguity and lack of precision of many concepts (p. 18). They even talk about "conceptual neglect" (p. 19) and state their aim: namely, the reduction of psychoanalytic arbitrariness and the establishment of accepted and communicable standards (p. 8).

Of course, they, too, carried out this clarification not only for their own use, but for the benefit of other clinicians and researchers. They write:

> In order to be able to operationalize psychodynamically at all, it had to be assumed regarding the future user that he acknowledges the existence and justification of basic psychoanalytic

> concepts like the dynamic unconscious, transference and countertransference, inner conflict, or internalized self and object representations. [Arbeitskreis OPD, 1998, p. 8]

If one is to take this argument seriously, it would also mean that one will have to include our basic concepts, our "model of the mind", when examining the meaning and usage of concepts. There is no usage of analytic concepts without at least partial acceptance of the analytic world view [*Weltbild*]. The achievement of precision or formalization, as we know it from the natural sciences, seems hardly attainable for our concepts, at least for the time being—and beyond that, I doubt whether this is desirable. The authors of the OPD working group believe that it is "an unsolvable paradox to want to operationally define unconscious processes which play an important role for psychoanalytic understanding" (p. 8). I would not be so sure about this, for an operationalization appears only "unsolvable" to someone whose criteria for the grasping of conceptually relevant phenomena are closely oriented at the maxims of experimental sciences.

One possible consequence of those—from a methodological point of view, admittedly stubborn—aspects of our concepts would be to do without them and to adapt to the predominant trends in the behavioural sciences. But we could also more vigorously defend the analytic potential of our concepts—concepts, the usefulness of which has also been of profit to other therapy methods. Actually, the situation is paradoxical: when we analysts work clinically, we base our work in essence on precisely this profile of our concepts; but when we move into the field of research, some are quite willing to put such aspects last. Incidentally, we as analyst do not have to hide with regard to this dependence of the concepts on the world view, for this sort of problem—namely, the dependence of the meaning of psychological concepts upon pre-assumptions about human functioning—is not ours alone. The convictions of many cognitive scientists and some neuroscientists are based on the *pre-assumption,* again not shared by all, that the human mind functions like a computer—that it actually even is one. Of course, the computer metaphor is considered more "modern" than the system of our fundamental convictions derived from Freud's metapsychological considerations, but whether this image of man [*Menschenbild*] is generally better, or clinically more adequate, than ours may well be contested.

One additional thing I would like to mention here: such clarity and explicitness in concept usage—as is done in the context of every operationalization—is much easier to analyse and evaluate than some other idiosyncratic or even vague usage. However, such a precise formulation has a useful consequence: it is easier to criticize it. Researchers who are orientated to Popper's ideas could actually see this as an advantage—they, too, should be interested in increasing the validity of their investigations. And if well-founded criticism of whatever concept usage—also of an operationalization—is not seen as personal disparagement but as constructive criticism to improve our concept usage, this alone would be a success.

Such a critical function is, indeed, actually an essential aspect of a conceptual research programme, but it is basically descriptive, not prescriptive, and not at all a kind of Supreme Court for conceptual questions. It can stimulate discussions with its own suggestions at best it can act as a moderator in the discourse, but it cannot lead it on its own. A reasonable usage may only gain prevalence through good argumentation, not through authorities—at least, I would hope so.

Certainly, conceptual research can also take a perspective of cultural theory [*Kulturtheorie*], for the changing trends in the field of research—concerning subjects, methods, aims, and the associated concept understanding—do not withdraw from reflection. What exactly were the reasons in Germany two decades ago for the shift of research interests to observable or even measurable behaviour? How and why do treatment aims change as a function of socioeconomic changes in the health sector? What are the reasons for the trend towards concepts that can currently be noticed?

A fundamental fact becomes evident when dealing with such questions: namely, that the relationships between theory and reality, between a concept and the empirical phenomena, cannot only be seen as a two-digit relation: one should reasonably see them, according to the old semiotic tradition, within the framework of a triangle. What is added here is the person of the user of the concept, and thus the dependence of the meaning on historically grown, socially shared language games embedded in various human life forms. If one adequately considers this, one can become sensitized to the contingent usage of concepts—and, of course, also to one's own contingent usage. The importance of the influence of different cultural backgrounds is demonstrated primarily in the two research traditions discussed here—the Anglo-Saxon and the continental one—which also differ perhaps in the role and function they ascribe to concepts in a research process.

If one disregards for a moment the fact that dichotomies imply the danger of splitting—and thus easily of an inappropriate division into "good" and "bad"—and if one equally disregards that dichotomies may well lead to a little constructive *divide et impera,* then dichotomies definitely do have a pragmatic ordering function. This should not, however, lead to the misunderstanding, in view of the apparent dichotomy between conceptual and empirical research, that the two are best kept strictly separate. Just as the empirical and the conceptual are in a dialectic relationship with each other, so research activities, which have either empirical phenomena or a concept as their subject, are dependent on each other: without recourse to the findings from empirical research, conceptual research can be a "glass-bead game" [*Glasperlenspiel*]; empirical research without conceptual reflection can be poor or without clinical relevance.

Cooperation based on an *acknowledgement* of the different methodologies—not on claims of exclusiveness—is conceivable, as all kinds of researchers, and certainly clinicians too, strive for a common goal: the best possible theory, formulated in the best possible concepts. Last but not least, analysts, especially those working in a clinical setting, could be convinced of the practical use of analytic research in general—via the improvement of their important tool, namely, the analytic concepts—and perhaps gain greater access also to other research activities.

If "good concepts"—and good refers here to both domains, practice and research—are a goal that it is worth striving for on a long-term basis, then conceptual research must be seen as an ongoing research programme, as a task that has to be constantly redefined on the basis of the investigation of important conceptual fields that have come into the focus of interest and critique.

And if conceptual research were to succeed in strengthening the awareness of practitioners as well as researchers of the wealth that psychoanalysis possesses with its clinical experience and the concepts based on this knowledge, then quite something would have been achieved, though not a panacea for all problems—it cannot work miracles, no more than anybody else can.

Ideas for a research programme should be able to end with a vision: conceptual research and empirical research could together ensure that psychoanalysis stays psychoanalytic and at the same time does not miss the connection to the world. If the one could be the guarantee of quality assurance of the other, then both together would surely be invincible. I think we will see what of this vision becomes science, and what remains fiction.

8

What kind of evidence makes the analyst change his or her theoretical and technical ideas?

Ricardo Bernardi

Psychoanalysis, like any other discipline, changes throughout time, influenced by certain criteria of evidence that lead analysts to prefer some hypotheses to others. The aim of this presentation is to inquire, by combining a descriptive approach with a normative one, into the rational and emotional processes that guide the analysts' choices and changes in their theoretical and technical ideas. It intends to examine the phenomena of real change in psychoanalytic ideas and to inquire, at the same time, into ways that could bring greater conceptual depth and empirical validity to the new ideas.

This chapter presents the preliminary results of an ongoing qualitative investigation based on the analysis of published texts and on interviews with senior analysts who played an important role in a period of significant change in the history of psychoanalytic ideas in the Río de la Plata region (Buenos Aires and Montevideo).

Epistemological framework

The justification for changes in a discipline is not the same for the so-called "hard" sciences, the social sciences, and the humanistic disciplines. Undoubtedly, they are all influenced by cultural, historical, and socioeconomic factors, power and prestige struggles, and so on, but they differ in the epistemological criteria and the methodological procedures used to justify changes. These are the criteria that are supposed to serve as a guide to the argumentation in scientific controversies, and in internal personal reflection. The questions that then follow have to be what the reasons are that lead an analyst to prefer some psychoanalytic hypotheses over others, and whether the chosen criteria correspond to those of natural sciences or the humanities or whether they are *sui generis*.

Freud made it clear that his interest was in creating a discipline based on the observation of empirical facts. He argued that theoretical concepts of a science "can be replaced and discarded without damaging it", since the foundation of these concepts ". . . *is observation alone*" (Freud, 1914d, p. 77). Observation is based on the application of the psychoanalytic method, particularly in those cases in which "*we succeed in descending into the deepest and most primitive strata of mental development and in gaining from there solutions for the problems of the later formations*" (Freud, 1918b [1914], p. 10).

In its early days, the leading idea was of cumulative change in psychoanalysis, in which theoretical and technical advances supported each other. History, however, showed the difficulties inherent in this project. Freud tried to create a natural science based on interpretation—for example, a procedure related to the field of hermeneutics. In fact, these two orientations—the scientific and the hermeneutic—generate dilemmas that are still present in psychoanalysis. At present, there is a wide variety of psychoanalytic theories, and it is not always clear to what extent they coincide, contradict each other, or complement each other, or whether their relationship is incommensurable—that is, whether their concepts belong to fields that lack the mutual necessary semantic congruency and logical compatibility.

As I see it, the main problem to advance in debates lies in the difficulty with finding shared criteria of evidence. Nowadays it is not possible to reach a consensus regarding the criteria to which one has to resort: those of the natural sciences or those of the hermeneutic disciplines. Paraphrasing the title of a well-known book (Roth & Fonagy, 1996), the present situation could be called: "What kind of evidence works for whom?"

The existence of different criteria of evidence based on philosophical premises that are frequently incompatible makes it necessary to have at least a minimally neutral arena for their discussion, even if a completely neutral one may not exist. Theory of argumentation (Perelman & Olbrechts-Tyteca, 1958; Toulmin, 1958; van Eemeren, Grootendorst, Jackson, & Jacobs, 1993) offers a useful tool to establish a shared argumentative field within which the reasons in favour of or against different psychoanalytic positions can interact. This argumentative field is also the one that is supposed to be present in internal personal debates that guide each analyst's choice of his/her theoretical and technical positions.

Historical context

The development of psychoanalysis in the Río de la Plata region constitutes a suitable example for studying the changes of ideas. There are two different moments in the history of psychoanalytic ideas, separated by a period of crisis and political, social, and cultural changes during the 1970s that were very similar in Argentina and in Uruguay.

Between the 1940s and the 1960s, there was an increasing prevalence of Kleinian thought. During this period, great contributions were also made by local authors—Pichon Rivière, Racker, W. & M. Baranger, Liberman, Bleger, and others—who, though not questioning Kleinian theory, made contributions that went beyond Melanie Klein's concepts, particularly in the technical field. I am referring, for instance, to Racker's developments on countertransference, or to Pichon Rivière's and W. & M. Baranger's contribution on the psychoanalytic field concept, and so forth.

Since the 1970s, a period of increasing theoretical and technical pluralism has begun. Some groups of analysts continued to be faithful to Melanie Klein, while others enthusiastically took up authors such as Bion, Winnicott, Meltzer, or even Kohut, among others. But perhaps the most remarkable change was the interest of many analysts in the work of French authors, particularly that of Jacques Lacan. French thought influenced the way of reading Freud and constituted an unavoidable theoretical reference. At the same time as these changes took place, there was a loss of continuity in the tradition of Río de la Plata thought, as many of the original local contributions ceased their development.

Why was Melanie Klein widely adopted at the beginning and then, in many cases, abandoned in favour of other authors? It is possible to point out some incidental facts or historical tendencies that influenced this fact, but it is more difficult to try to make a conceptual reconstruction of the process of change that makes it possible to understand the processes of thought, the arguments, and the personal experiences that led to these changes. There was also a change of attitude towards the theory, as the idea of orthodoxy was gradually replaced by a positive assessment of theoretic pluralism.

Analysts who had been trained in the Kleinian tradition during the first period found themselves faced with an offer of new ideas, which led some of them to reaffirm their own previous theories and others to modify them or adopt a different psychoanalytic approach. Clinical practice and "private" theories (Sandler, 1983) might or might not more or less coincide with the changes in public discourse.

Questions addressed by the investigation

Two questions are considered:

1. What kinds of arguments operate in the discourse in public debates and personal internal debates? Does this debate make it possible to adequately explore the merits of each position and clarify agreements and disagreements?
2. How are changes in theoretical and technical ideas related to the analyst's personal and professional experiences?

Material and method

The public argumentative discourse was examined through the publications of the psychoanalytic societies during the 1970s. Although it is possible to discern the change of influences, works that systematically compare the new ideas to the old ones are rare. One of the most interesting controversies happened in 1972, on the occasion of the first visit of one of Jacques Lacan's disciples from the Freudian School of Paris to the psychoanalytic societies of Río de la Plata. The exact transcriptions of the theoretical and clinical debates held in Montevideo, in which the local Kleinian thought was confronted with S. Leclaire's thought, are available. This material was examined in another paper (Bernardi, 2002), and only some additional comments are included here.

In order to study the changes at a personal level, a qualitative study was designed, and 20 senior analysts from the region (10 from Buenos Aires and 10 from Montevideo) were interviewed, using the deep-interview technique. The sample was constituted by senior analysts who had played a relevant scientific or institutional role and with varying degrees of change in their ideas. The resulting material is still being analysed, and the influence of personal experiences in theoretical and technical changes is being examined, taking into account the criteria built in order to evaluate the reflective function (Fonagy, Target, Steele, & Steele, 1998). Some preliminary results are presented.

Results

A. *Public argumentative discourse*

From the analysis of the issues, it is possible to point out that:

1. The changes in the theoretical and technical positions do not go together with a systematic examination of the different ideas at stake and a specification of the reasons in favour of and against each one of them. As a general rule, in publications and during training, only the positive aspects of the preferred approach are stressed, and criticisms are generally omitted. Training does not include the systematic evaluation of alternatives, exploring the arguments in favour of and against each position.
2. As a consequence of the absence of argumentation, it is not easy to identify the epistemological model that guided the changes:
    a. There are no clear attempts to resort to refutations or even to the comparison between alternative hypotheses that eliminative inductivism requires; neither is there an accumulation of favourable observations like those found in the enumerative inductivism.
    b. We cannot speak of the exhaustion of one paradigm and its substitution with a new one, the way Kuhn describes it (Kuhn, 1962), since the previous Kleinian model remained

and was renewed. As a consequence, multiple paradigms coexisted.

c. In general, the arguments used in favour of the new ideas were those concerning their major conceptual richness and an advance that they presented in terms of sense, heuristic power, and plausibility. However, through a careful analysis, it is noticeable that generally this superiority does not derive from a detailed comparison of the usefulness of these ideas when applied to clinical problems; rather, it is considered as evident beforehand, in a kind of circular reasoning; it is also evident that this superiority is defended on the basis of the major prestige of these ideas at that cultural point in time. In most cases, these theories were used more as interpretative codes that permit a new way of decoding the clinical material than as groups of hypotheses that have to be confirmed by the material—though it is possible to find exceptions (e.g. Baranger, 1980; Etchegoyen, 1986), where there is a discussion of the arguments for and against the various positions (see Bernardi, 2002).

3. When controversies did take place, the less developed aspect was the one concerning the tangible consequences of each position for the outcome of treatments. As a general rule, the discussion turned towards the most abstract premises or philosophical assumptions.

These premises determine what each part considered to be the core of true psychoanalysis—a belief that prevented the discussion from questioning them, thus generating situations of apparent incommensurability between the positions. As a consequence, it was these premises that determined the kind of evidence considered valid and the ones that established which questions are legitimated and which should be excluded.

4. In order that the controversy should move forward, it would have been necessary that each part accept to explore the clinical consequences of their premises and then discuss the criteria of evidence at this clinical level.

As an example of what was said, I will examine the controversy between Leclaire and the members of the Uruguayan Psychoanalytic

Association, focusing on the discussion of the concept of body. During the discussion with the Uruguayan group, Leclaire questioned the Kleinian notion of an inside and an outside, and he suggested substituting Lacan's Moebius-strip model. The listeners objected that this model did not have an experiential character, and they defended the role of introjection and projection at the unconscious fantasy level. Leclaire pointed out that he preferred to conceive of introjection as an introduction of elements inside a structure, not as an image of the body that implies an inside or an outside. The discussion then turned to the implicit philosophical assumptions: the notion of structure (and the particular way Lacan uses it) and the notion of object, and the relation between this idea and Brentano's philosophy.

Up to that point, the discussion had succeeded in identifying the points of theoretical discrepancies. Now it was necessary to examine the clinical consequences of those theoretical differences. Five meetings were devoted to the discussion of clinical material, but it was not possible to create a shared argumentative field. The participants from Uruguay tried a moment-by-moment analysis of the session, looking for an understanding of the transferential–countertransferential movement in the Kleinian way. Leclaire, on the other hand, considered that in this way the patient's discourse was hindered, and he proposed a different, more silent way of listening. Again, the discussion allowed the identification of a series of points of disagreement (the notion of free association, interpretation, transference, the role of affects in the session, etc.).

At that point it was necessary to reopen the discussion in a different direction and to examine the consequences of one or the other position for the patient and for the concrete analytic work. It would have been necessary then to define different types of questions and establish the methodology to study them. It was also necessary to make explicit which reasons underlay each belief and ideal model on how a psychoanalysis has to be.

But this direction was almost unexplored during that discussion and has remained so since then. During the later decades there are few examples that show an advance in both the conceptual comparison and the examination of the clinical consequences. The arguments in favour of each position still rely today upon the persuasive qualities of the theoretical discourse, therefore offering an insufficient basis to choose or change a theory.

B. *Personal changes*

The study of the individual interviews makes it possible to analyse certain questions in depth:

1. *What changes?*

Changes in explicit theoretic or technical models are not the major transformation that analysts perceive in themselves but, rather, a freer attitude regarding their theoretical and technical models.

The introduction of new ideas does not replace the old ones, because the two often coexist. Sometimes the change only consists in the use of a new institutional or group language. At other times the new ideas are incorporated because they lead the analyst to new insights in the understanding of the patients and also of him/herself.

Two of the interviewees said:

> "With each change in the patient and even with each evolution of the analysis, the analyst changes his/her theories—I mean the operating theories. . . ."

> "I had no crises because I did not accept a scheme as definite and because my analysts themselves did not accept any scheme as definite."

The interviewee adds that even Aberastury, who introduced Melanie Klein in Buenos Aires, "worked with the [Kleinian theory of the] unconscious fantasy, but as she was analysed by Garma, she worked very often with other ideas. . . ."

2. *Why does it change?*

There is scarcely any reference or none at all by the interviewees as to the need of outcome studies, or to criteria similar to those of evidence-based medicine.

However, personal experiences in the work with patients, especially the negative ones, are mentioned as a source of significant changes in the patterns of understanding of oneself and of others. This suggests that the process of change occurs in a complex way and that analysts also test their own hypotheses, not only in their patients, but also in themselves. The relationship with analytic institutions is also a source of both submission and rebellion.

> "Changes occurred when people experienced certain levels of discomfort with the theories they were forced to work with . . . people change when they feel they are well interpreted by an author."
>
> "A homosexual young woman [a patient] said that I was an ideologist of heterosexuality. And I realized she was right, up to certain extent. My attempt to make a difference between science and ideology originated in that episode."
>
> [Talking about a treatment:] "It was an extremely uncomfortable experience for me. . . . There were things I should have handled in other ways. . . . Of course, I said to myself, I did not interpret enough the negative transference with him . . . as I saw him as a victim. . . . He made me change. . . ."

3. *How does it change?*

The reasons that lead to the change of ideas seem to be based on a particular combination of empirical and hermeneutic criteria and are related to moments or problems of great personal importance.

The change of ideas is often related to situations of personal crisis or difficulties with patients that had emotional consequences for the analyst, since his or her understanding according to the usual models was not satisfactory. The new ideas usually work as metaphors or analogies that offer new insights. Often these metaphors are of personal use, and they integrate the "implicit" theories described by Sandler (1983). In spite of their creative nature, they are usually not made public. This may contribute to their maintaining an open and changing nature, although sometimes it may be a factor that makes them arbitrary and not very coherent.

> "I then [when the seminars finished] began to use flexible schemes, I was never obedient as far as theory is concerned." [Examples are given.]
>
> [The analyst talks about conflicts in his matrimonial life. He adds:] "That is why I told you that it made me think that the

external object also plays a role. Many of the changes in my technique and afterwards in the theoretical part had to do with the flexibility to see what happens in each situation."

Discussion

In the sample studied, people renowned for their institutional and/or scientific importance were chosen. The results cannot be extended to the generality of analysts who may be more influenced by the leaders of the group.

It is possible that as they were interviewed orally, the answers emphasized the context of the discovery of new ideas, instead of their justification; this may have lead to more emphasis being given to the experiences than to the rational arguments.

CONCLUSIONS

1. *During a professional life, significant changes happen in the theoretical and technical models of analysts.*

These changes include the modification or the substitution of one theory by another, a more flexible attitude towards theories, and the development of implicit personal models.

2. *These changes are the result of a complex interaction between conceptual arguments and personal experiences.*

The motivation for change (or no change) arises not only from the presence of new dominant ideas in the psychoanalytic or cultural "milieu", but also, and in a significant way, from personal experiences. These personal experiences promote conceptual changes in a complex and indirect way. A high reflexive function is necessary in order for the analyst to be aware of his/her own process of change.

3. *An analyst's individual process of change is frequently not supported by an adequate training during analytic education.*

Analysts are not trained to make systematic comparisons that would clarify differences between various approaches. Psychoanalytic training usually does not offer the necessary methodological and epistemological training to adequately evaluate the arguments in favour and against different positions.

4. *Well-informed decisions in favour of or against the different positions require discussions in which the arguments of each part may interact. For that to be possible, the most necessary although problematic task is the construction of an argumentative field shared by the different positions.*

This task requires a minimum agreement on the criteria of evidence that will guide the discussion and procedure criteria when discussions collapse—that is, when the premises held by each party to the discussion make the argument of one party irrelevant to the other. In such a case the goal must be not to reach agreements, but only to clarify the positions and to explore the clinical consequences of each.

It also requires a clearer distinction among the different kinds of questions that come up during the discussion, and what sort of procedure or methodology allows the reaching of what kind of answer. Certain questions can be answered from the clinical evidence, at least with an acceptable consensus. Other questions, that are of a more abstract or speculative nature have no conclusive answers, and the discussion about them must be oriented towards exploring the heuristic qualities of the hypotheses. In a third place, we find questions of an empirical nature to which an approach by quantitative and qualitative methods may be useful. From this perspective the substantial question would be: What kind of evidence is necessary for what kind of question?

5. *Psychoanalytic training should pay more attention to the complex nature of the changes that happen during professional life, developing programmes of continuing education appropriate to this aim.*

These programmes of continuing education should place a special emphasis on facilitating the development of analysts' "implicit" models and help them to become explicit. But this is not enough. It is essential that the analysts be aware of the criteria of evidence that lead them to prefer some hypotheses to others.

Emotional and rational aspects have to be integrated. Given that some personal experiences play an important role in the change of hypotheses, it is necessary to have a greater discussion of this kind of experiences, focusing on the clinical problems that cannot properly be explained by the theories used by the analyst. The possibility of burn-out phenomena in analysts also has to be explored (Cooper, 1986).

In short, analysts have to be more aware of the theoretical and technical processes behind their change of ideas and to examine in a reflexive way the conceptual reasons and the personal experiences that lead to them.

9

The logic of psychoanalytic research

Jorge Canestri

In this brief chapter I should like to expand on some ideas that I developed in 1993 for a conference on the meaning of Jewishness in Freud's work, and to widen the field that I took into consideration at that time—the work of the creator of psychoanalysis—so as to cover the entire discipline. I must first say that the argument I develop here is very limited and certainly does not deal with all the epistemological problems that psychoanalysis itself raises. I will not therefore refer to the everlasting and never-resolved question, preceding all others, regarding the definition of the model of science to which psychoanalysis should refer, or the diatribes about the scientificity or otherwise of psychoanalysis as a discipline. My intention is guided by the statement that we must come closer—as close as possible—to the reality of our clinical experience *as it really is* if we want to have an appropriate epistemological reflection concerning the specific object of psychoanalysis and its remit. I will try to outline some ideas in this direction.

The title of this chapter refers to the classic, although much discussed, work of Karl Popper (1934). The author proposes again the well-known distinction made by Reichenbach between the "logic of discovery" and the "logic of justification": "If we make a distinction, as Reichenbach does, between a 'procedure for finding' and a 'procedure for justifying' [a hypothesis] then we have to say that it is not possible to reconstruct the former rationally" (Popper, 1934, Appendix I:2, p. 293). The impossibility of inserting the "procedure for finding" into the logical analysis of scientific knowledge is theorized by Popper as the "elimination of psychologism" from the context of epistemology.

Popper denies the possibility of deducing universal enunciations from particular ones, and he does not consider inductive inference to be valid: a "logic of scientific discovery" remains excluded from the epistemological field and becomes a subject of empirical psychology. This is the decision that I would like to discuss here.

Already during the years the work in question was first published in English, N. R. Hanson, in his *Patterns of Discovery* (1958), spoke of the inconsistency of this classical distinction, and in 1973 Herbert Simon, through his anti-realistic or conventionalistic definition of the discovery of the scientific laws, did the same thing. The first was based on Peirce's concept of abduction, the second on artificial-intelligence programs (such as the series by Bacon) presented as examples of "pure" inductive inferences—that is, as automatic and not socially contaminated. However, it is also true, as A. M. Petroni emphasized during an International Congress (1993) on the sociology of scientific knowledge at the Sorbonne, that in spite of the repeated declarations of the demise of the classical distinction between the context of discovery and the context of justification, "besides the ritual homage, no greater problem has been dealt with from a point of view that does not strictly refer to the context of justification". A useful distinction that the author introduces is that of considering that in scientific discovery there is a logical problem and a methodological problem: the logical problem consists of determining the logical relationship between data (from observation or experimentation) and scientific laws; the methodological problem is knowing how scientific laws are *de facto* discovered in scientific practice.

Petroni deals with the logical problem insofar as his thesis is that the elimination of the distinction between the context of discovery and the context of justification would allow for a different outlook on the problem of the realism/anti-realism of scientific theories (discovery/invention). He is sceptical concerning the methodological problem: no amount of knowledge about the interests of scientists, about their methods of collecting data, their internal or external conditioning in their research, and so on, will ever be able to tell us anything about the results of science. His scepticism—which may seem paradoxical if we consider the repudiation of the distinction introduced by Popper—leads his discussant (B. Matalon) to introduce in his turn a distinction between the different elements of a causal system producing scientific laws—that is, between the causal elements and those functioning as conditions for the action of the causal elements.

My own interest, on the contrary, is concentrated on the methodological problem—that is, that of knowing how theories are *de facto* constructed in scientific practice. I am aware that I have substituted laws for theories and discovery for construction. In the first case, I have simply widened the field; in the second, I have not intended to implicitly embrace constructivism or anti-realism against the realism of theories.

Perhaps, from my point of view, it was Imre Lakatos—albeit operating within the enlarged framework of the falsifying Popperian conception—who contested Popper's classical distinction most adequately.

In analysing the "logic" of mathematical discovery, Lakatos (1976) reveals a certain short-sightedness in Popper's approach. He says that when Popper (1934) separated the aspects of discovery into psychological and logical aspects in such a way as not to leave any room at all for heuristics as an independent field of enquiry, he obviously did not notice then that his "logic of discovery" was more than merely a *strictly* logical reconstruction of scientific progress. But Popper, who laid the foundations of this (fallible) logic of discovery, did not deal with the meta-question of what the nature of this enquiry was and did not notice that it is neither psychology nor logic, but an independent discipline: the logic of discovery, heuristics.

Lakatos's recognition of the existence of "an intrinsic unit of logic of discovery and logic of justification" is, in the words of the Italian epistemologist G. Giorello, "an attempt to understand *those problems, those procedures by trial and error, those tactics and strategies of research* that make scientific practice as fascinating an activity as any creative activity (1976, italics added)" (Canestri, 1993).

Considering Lakatos's concept as a useful framework for analysing the logic of psychoanalytic discovery, I proposed in my above-mentioned work (Canestri, 1993) a reflection on the strategy of Freudian research. For this purpose, I chose one of Freud's rather enigmatic works, but also one that held substantial evidence of the processes leading to its elaboration. I am referring to *Moses and Monotheism* (1939a [1937–39])—a text that reveals the pressing internal necessities that compelled Freud to write it. I only wish to summarize how I think research strategy functions in Freud, along with an example of the ethics that guide it. *Moses* is, among other things, a scientific work on the essence of Jewishness, on the "mystery of the Jewish essence", on the mystery of the essence of the author of *Moses*. This essence, he says (1941e [1926]), is indissolubly linked to the most intimate identity of Freud himself. What are the premises for this quest for essence? In a letter to the Editor of the *Judäische Presszentrale, Zurich* (Freud, 1925b), Freud explicitly declares that the Jewish religion arouses in him a purely scientific interest and is free from any emotional significance. The same thing does not apply to the Jewish people, with whom he admits to having a bond (in the psychoanalytic sense) that is impregnated with sentimental value. What is evidenced, and will justify an in-depth analysis, is the recognition of an element of his internal life that belongs to what we may call one of the very nuclei of the inner self and one, moreover, that has not been sufficiently worked out.

During the following year, Freud again takes the matter into consideration in his "Address to the Members of the *B'nai B'rith*" in these words:

> . . . what bound me to Jewry was . . . neither faith or national pride. . . . But plenty of other things remained over to make the attraction of Jewry and Jews irresistible—many obscure emotional forces, which were the more powerful the less they could be expressed in words, as well as a clear consciousness of inner identity, the safe privacy of a common mental construction. [1941e (1926), p. 273]

The relationship between the power of an emotional force and its expression in words is a concept known to psychoanalysts. "The resolution to go in search of this expression is implicit [in the Freudian text], and in his ability to recognize the powerful dark forces of emotion and to find a way of expressing them verbally with scientific dignity, we can identify one of the pivotal points of Freud's logic of research" (Canestri, 1993, p. 125). The response Freud proposes in 1930 in the Preface to the Hebrew edition of *Totem and Taboo* is in substance no different; on the contrary, the resolution is more explicit: "If someone were to ask him [to the author] what is there left that is Jewish, he would reply: 'A very great deal, and probably its very essence. He could not express that essence in words; but some day, no doubt, it will become accessible to the scientific mind'" (1934b [1930], p. xv). I do not believe that these quotations, and perhaps not even the entire *Moses*, reveal to us the essence of Jewishness. But I believe that they say much about the strategy that guided Freud in his research. *Moses* is in many ways the last step in Freud's self-analysis, his searching for *Ur-reste* on which depended essential forces to be analysed, forces that contributed to fostering the logic of research that had given meaning to his project. The core problem would have to be identified with this tension that furthers, by scientific means, the recognition and ceaseless transformation of what is most secret in a subject. From his exile in London he writes: "I am once more able to speak and write—I had almost said 'and think'—*as I wish and as I must*" [*wie ich will oder muss*] (italics added). Peter Gay shrewdly observes that Freud may be a free man "but is not free to stop writing about Moses". This observation could legitimately refer to the entire Freudian project.

In 1985, the careful research work by I. Grubrich-Simitis introduced us to the 1915 text, *Übersicht der Übertragungsneurosen*, and to some of the letters from the correspondence between Freud and Ferenczi, today complete. At the beginning of his letter to Ferenczi of 12 July 1915, we read: "Dear friend, in the preparation of *Übersicht der Übertragungsneurosen* I find myself dealing with fantasies that disturb me and it will be difficult for them to have any result for the public" (Grubrich-Simitis, 1986, p. 89, translated for this edition). I think it is important to emphasize the relationship between the fantasy that comes to light and its publication—a matter to which I will return later.

In a subsequent letter (which has been quoted frequently in a variety of contexts), Freud writes to Ferenczi: "I must state that one must not make theories; they must turn up like unexpected guests in the house, while one is busy enquiring into details" [*Ich halte darauf, dass man Theorien nicht machen soll—sie müssen einem als ungebetene Gäste ins Haus fallen, während man mit Detailuntersuchungen beschäftigt ist*].

I think these are some of the many indications that Freud offers towards a theory for a method of research that considers that theories, like fantasies, impose themselves on us like unexpected guests. In this case, the indication becomes the imperative, the *müssen* of the previous quote.

Two works published by Joseph and Anne-Marie Sandler (Sandler & Sandler, 1983a, 1983b) develop concepts that are very close to the ideas that I am trying to outline, since they implicitly contain an epistemological aspect regarding the construction of psychoanalytic theory and the production of new theories, models, and heuristic schemes. Their ideas are sufficiently well known, and I do not need to enlarge on them. It is sufficient to say that in the "three-box model", the second system includes "parts of the unconscious (structural ego) . . . as well as unconscious parts of the superego; and it embraces the Preconscious system of the topographical model" (Sandler & Sandler, 1983b, p. 420). This second system continually elaborates the derivatives of the unconscious. It is oriented towards the present in its search for adaptive solutions, and it is the creative centre of "current unconscious fantasies and thoughts" (p. 421). In the work I wrote in honour of Sandler, I said that: "A final characteristic of the second system (or second box) is that although it makes 'use of the most complicated secondary process . . . [it] has a high tolerance for contradictions' (Sandler & Sandler, 1983b, p. 421). This fact explains how essentially contradictory theories and thoughts can coexist without disturbing each other as long as they remain outside consciousness: 'This phenomenon has been described in relation to the creation of unconscious (preconscious) theories which may be contradictory but are tolerated outside consciousness. It was noted that the absence of contradiction was not that which is ascribed to the contents of the system Unconscious or to the id (p. 421)'" (Canestri, 1999). It is known that psychoanalytic concepts have multiple meanings: Sandler thought that it would be possible to carry out a productive research on these "dimensions of meaning" in the mind and in the clinical practice of every psychoanalyst. This operation would diminish the ambiguity of the concepts, clarify their meaning, and specify their use. But this is not the only possible aim—nor is it the main one—of research of this kind. These private schemata are, as Sandler pointed out, internally contradictory, not only because they are made up of parts of theories or of models that are incompatible or partly incompatible, but also because they include other "material" that is not necessarily linked to psychoanalytic theory *sensu stricto*. In 1967 the French philosopher

L. Althusser, in a work entitled *"Il existe une philosophie spontanée des savants"* (1974), hypothesized that scientists were "carriers" of a spontaneous philosophy that was to be distinguished from their *Weltanschauung*—the whole set of ideas that human beings have about the world and about themselves.

The spontaneous philosophy that Althusser studied in the works of some scientists included scientists' ideas—whether conscious or not—concerning their work and their science. He diagnosed the existence of two elements usually of a contradictory content, one of intra-scientific origin, the other of extra-scientific origin. The first regarded those convictions and beliefs that a scientists derives from daily scientific practice. The second comes from reflections on scientific practice that are linked to the philosophy of science. The first—intra-scientific—element may be a source of theories and models if it undergoes elaboration. This confirms its heuristic potential and brings it considerably closer to Sandler's formulations about the preconscious construction of a whole variety of "theoretic segments".

In her excellent book on conceptual research, Anna Ursula Dreher (2000) questions the denomination of preconscious—descriptively unconscious—theories given by Sandler to these "theoretic segments" that ought, logically, to be called "private" or "implicit" theories. I agree with her argumentation; however, I should like the role of the preconscious to be kept in mind in what I shall be dealing with now.

I wish to briefly remind you of a work on cognitive development that represented a milestone in its field—namely, the well-known book by L. Vygotsky published in 1934, *Thought and Language*. This Russian author has known alternating fortunes: initially repudiated in his own country, he was rehabilitated in 1956 with the publication of his complete works; he did not, however, escape censorship. In fact, in the Russian edition all references to Freud, Sapir, and so on, were eliminated, and in the U.S. edition all references to Marx, Engels, Lenin, and so forth were deleted, along with 150 pages of the original version. The translation of the title itself—*Thought and Language*, is imprecise, since the Russian *"Myšlenie i reč"* should be "Thinking and Language" (*Myšlenie* is the function of thinking and *mysl* is its product). [For these reasons, I refer here to the translation and notes from the Italian edition edited by Luciano Mecacci; the page numbers therefore correspond to this edition, which has been translated for this book.]

There are two ideas of Vygotsky that I am particularly interested in "making interact" with the present theme. The first is linked to the discussion with Piaget concerning the spontaneous and non-spontaneous—i.e. learned—concepts of children. Is it important to study the peculiarities of the thought (thinking) of the child and its spontaneous products (concepts, thoughts, "*mysl*") for the comprehension of the non-spontaneous, particularly the scientific, ones? Vygotsky, as opposed to Piaget, thinks so, and he carefully analyses Piaget's contradictions in the chapter, "Research on the development of scientific concepts during school age". He introduces the concept of a "zone of proximal development" to clarify the mechanism and the operation that allows for the learning of non-spontaneous concepts. I think that this concept may be of interest to us.

The second idea is about the distinction that Vygotsky makes between interior and external language: a distinction of great theoretical importance at various levels, but that also has a heuristic value in relation to our discussion.

Let us first consider the concept of "zone of proximal development": Vygotsky defines this as the area representing what the child manages to do (an area that can, therefore, be tested) through the collaboration of the adult. This happens in the learning process [*Obučenie*], defined "as a process of transmission and appropriation of knowledge, capacities, abilities and of the methods of man's cognitive activities. Learning is a bilateral process, carried out by the teacher and the student" (N. A. Menčiskaja, quoted by Mecacci). The child, therefore, succeeds in "elevating himself", by means of collaboration, to a superior intellectual level if this collaboration plays on an area of transition between what has already matured and what can mature.

Vygotsky starts from the thesis that concepts develop, and scientific concepts also develop, and they cannot be assimilated in a ready-made form (p. 205). But what is even more significant is that he hypothesizes—in contrast to Piaget—that between the child's spontaneous representations and those he has learned there is not only a limit, a division, but also a connection and a *reciprocal* influence (p. 211). The process of cognitive development begins with more elementary and primary forms of thought that reach more complex forms, but there is no supplanting of certain forms with others (p. 213). The process is conceived as a complex, continuous psychic process, never finishing with assimilation or with the formation of a concept. The fact that Vygotsky devotes his theoretical efforts to explaining infantile development does not mean that his observations are confined to development. All his statements relative to the relationship between spontaneous and non-spontaneous concepts and the area in which they connect with and reciprocally influence each other apply to the cognitive life of the adult.

Returning to the role of the preconscious, I should like to emphasize that at a cognitive level this area of mixture and transition, of conceptual "negotiation", has affinities with the role that Sandler, working on the two censorships and on the "three-box model", attributed to the preconscious. Psychoanalytic concepts, learned and official, must continually come to grips with the derivatives of the unconscious, with what is activated in the unconscious in clinical practice and forces the concepts to a constant work of evolution and re-elaboration. The unexpected guests mentioned by Freud continually turn up at the door. Psychoanalytic heuristics is based on the possibility of giving them hospitality. To avoid misunderstandings, it is important to clarify immediately—and Freud is very clear on this point—that the heuristic potential of these "scientific fantasies" may not have any real value at the level of justification. Nobody knows—*a priori*—whether one of these "fantasies" has real theoretical dignity until it has been verified (or disproved, according to the chosen epistemology) within the context of justification. My hypothesis is that a large part of the schemata that the analyst uses in his clinical practice is the result of a constant negotiation of "official" concepts, and that they are the result of different components of equally different origin. I cannot go into the specifics of this matter, as here I am only specifying certain epistemological reference points.

It might be interesting to note the difference between this design and the one that Popper proposes to distinguish between World 1, World 2, and World 3. Let us remember that World 2 corresponds to states of consciousness—or, more broadly speaking, to mental states—and that World 3 is that of objective thought contents, especially scientific thoughts. Popper (1972) thinks that there is a very important feedback effect from the world of thought objects onto mental states, but he says explicitly that an objectivistic epistemology studying the third world can throw an immense light on the second world, the world of subjective knowledge, especially on the thought processes of scientists; but that the reciprocal statement is not true. It is this difference between Popper's thinking and that of Freud and Vygotsky that leads him to deny the possibility of considering heuristics rationally. And it is this idea that I have tried to oppose, together with the idea of the separation of the context of discovery from the context of justification.

Let us now very briefly consider Vygotsky's second idea that I mentioned above: namely, the existence of an interior and an external language. As I said, I consider this distinction made by the Russian author to be not only pertinent but also rich in ideas from the point of view of philosophy of language and of linguistics and that, consequently, it has something to say also to psychoanalysis. This, however, is not the angle from which I present his idea today (see Carruthers & Boucher, 1998; see also the work of the Italian linguist R. Cardona, 1976, 1987). Vygotsky promotes a function of language—which is naturally not the only one—that is today described a "supra-communicative view of language" and is considered, at a cognitive level, as the function that ensures that language increases "human computation". We have already described how, from our author's point of view, public language, through non-spontaneous (learned) concepts, has profound effects on cognitive development. The interest that Vygotsky assigns to private language or interior language is that of guiding and shaping the solution to problems. In this case, the reciprocity of the influence of the spontaneous on what has been learned and vice-versa is also to be emphasized. This "self-directed speech" appears as an essential cognitive instrument.

In a paper entitled "The Mapping between the Mental and the Public Lexicon", Dan Sperber and Deirdre Wilson (1998) wonder what class of mapping can be configured between mental concepts and public words. They state: "We assume that there are mental concepts, and that they are not just internalizations of public words, so that the kind and degree of correspondence between concepts and words is a genuine and interesting empirical issue. . . . There are words which do not encode concepts and concepts which are not encoded by words" (p. 184).

In the wake of similar considerations, together with Werner Bohleber, Peter Fonagy (initially also Gilbert Diatkine), and other European colleagues, we are drafting a "Mapping Private Theories in Clinical Practice", within the research programme of the Working

Party on Theoretical Issues of the EPF. Our reflections lead us to define "theory" as the result of public-theory-based thinking plus private theoretical thinking plus the interaction of private and explicit thinking (the implicit use of explicit theory).

We cannot, however, escape the fact that having recognized the heuristic power of "private or implicit theories"—that is, the value of those that Freud called "scientific fantasies", to be welcomed like the unexpected guest and to put to the reality test—we find ourselves faced with an inevitable increase in theoretical pluralism and an increased babelization of psychoanalytic language.

W. R. Bion, in some undated notes that are probably from 1960, writes:

> Language has been invented; translation can be achieved; musical and mathematical notations exist; men compose and paint. And now psychoanalysis attempts to elucidate the barriers and links that hinder or promote the relationships that require a capacity for communication. Nevertheless, the success of psychoanalysis lies so far not so much in bringing communication nearer, as in showing unmistakably the feebleness of our methods of communication even in the communication of disagreement. But this does not touch a yet graver issue, namely the problem of communication with our successors, for it would appear on the surface that if we cannot communicate with our contemporaries, we are even less likely to be able to communicate with our successors. If this communication cannot be made, the future development of analysis is imperilled and the successful discoveries made so far could be lost to the world. [Bion, *Cogitations,* 1992, p. 173]

Various therapies for confronting this problem have been suggested by various authors (some psychoanalysts, others not), and we can probably say that none of these—neither the "logicization" of psychoanalysis attempted for a certain period by Bion and Lacan, nor the therapies proposed by verificationist neo-empiricism, nor the alternative ones of the falsificationist hypothetical–deductive method or of hermeneutics—has proved to be completely effective

What do we do about this? First, it is clear that we cannot deny reality simply because it would be nice to follow "logistical" routes that are more suggestive and epistemologically more correct. In physics we can investigate the universe in the matter *quantitate signata*; in psychoanalysis we do not have such matter, nor do we need such a scientific model. If, today—after the limitations that Popper attributed to logical neo-empiricism, those subsequently diagnosed by Kuhn in the projects of conjectures and confutations, or those that the post-analytic philosophy of Quine, Putnam, and Davidson formulated against "the three dogmas of logical neo-empiricism", and so on—we were to say what road to follow from an epistemological point of view, perhaps we should encourage epistemological realism: one that would consist of making a synthesis of those elements of the different epistemological currents that have proved useful for understanding the object with which we have to deal, choosing conceptual schema according to their greater efficiency in relation to the specificity of this object.

We must come closer to the reality of our clinical experience as it really is, with its inherent and irreplaceable subjectivity, with the use that we make in it of our own person and of our "private theories". What is private cannot be the object of scientific research until it has been made public. Bion says: "undergo transformation in the observer that enables them to be communicated to another . . . this process, which I call public-ation . . ." (1992, p. 119). Making public, and studying the methodology for doing so in a manner that is faithful to the reality of what we must communicate, is the task that awaits us.

10

Attachment theory and long-term psychoanalytic outcome: are insecure attachment narratives less accurate?

Mary Target & Peter Fonagy

In this chapter, while concentrating on qualitative, clinical research, we also touch on the whole spectrum of methods with which this volume, *Pluralism and Unity? Methods of Research in Psychoanalysis,* is concerned. In line with the spirit of the richness of different research strategies in psychoanalysis, we try here—through a small example that crosses the boundaries—to illustrate how these methods complement and reinforce each other in illuminating our subject of psychoanalysis, rather than dwelling on the relative advantages of different methodologies.

The example that we use is a study that at one point looked like a failure: an attempt to carry out a series of in-depth interviews, which had each been validated within other empirical research traditions, with a sufficiently large number of adults who had been in child analysis to be able to say something about the very-long-term effects of that treatment. We also included two untreated comparison groups—other children referred for similar problems but not treated, and brothers and sisters of the referred children, who had not themselves been referred for help. Thus, by comparing children with similar problems and with similar families (though, of course, no two children really have the same family), we hoped to get some idea of whether treatment affected long-term life-course. As in our first study of this group—a retrospective assessment of the changes over treatment shown by several hundred children in psychoanalysis and psychotherapy—we used the methods of the wider social science and mental-health research communities, hoping that we might make these communities more interested in and impressed by the impact of child analysis. If we learned something to surprise the child analyst along the way, then so much the better, but this was not our primary goal: child analysts do not generally doubt that their treatment works.

As it turned out, we did surprise child analysts to an extent, perhaps more than we surprised the wider child mental health world, in suggesting that the traditional "good analytic case"—the neurotic child with an adequate ego and reasonable environmental support—would do just as well, *in terms of symptoms and observable functioning*, in once- or twice-a-week therapy. In contrast, the child who *really needed* intensive psychoanalytic work, who did not get better without it, was the child with significant developmental problems, multiple symptoms, and/or pervasive social impairment: in other words, the child who had traditionally been thought unsuitable for analysis. We are not suggesting that the traditional view was wrong: they probably *were* unsuitable for traditional analysis, focused on the interpretation of the dynamic unconscious, oedipal conflict, and so on. They needed a different technique. However, that technique, and the skill to deliver it intensively, required a thorough awareness of ego functioning and primitive defences against mental processes, and how unconscious conflicts then, indeed, play out, but within a developmentally damaged psychic framework.

At this point in the programme of outcome studies at the Anna Freud Centre, we see a confluence between the empirical work we were doing and the tradition of conceptual and clinical research that had been carried out for many years beforehand. Any research, as Dreher has rightly explained in her recent book (Dreher, 2000), should be carried out within the context of conceptual clarification and an explicit theoretical framework. Anna Freud's work, together with the work of a number of systematic clinical and conceptual study groups—particularly, of course, the Hampstead Index Project led by Joseph Sandler (1962)—provided a solid basis for the understanding of our findings and for further theoretical elaboration consistent with them.

Anna Freud's model assumed that emotional disorders of childhood arose in association with the arrest or distortion of lines of normal development for which the child may find maladaptive solutions. The study we have mentioned, together with other research and clinical work, led us with colleagues to extend models of psychic change in child analysis—and adult analysis (e.g. Fonagy & Moran, 1991; Fonagy, Moran, Edgcumbe, Kennedy, & Target, 1993; Fonagy & Target, 1995, 2000). We delineated two models of treatment: the classical, or "representational", model involves the patient recovering threatening ideas and feelings, which had been repressed or distorted as a result of conflict and defence; the second, the "mental process" model, draws attention to the inhibition or stunting of basic mental processes. Our work has focused particularly on reflective capacities, or aspects of awareness of the mental states of others, as a major example of such a process, which may be distorted or underdeveloped in a number of ways, leading to various forms of psychopathology (Fonagy, Gergely, Jurist, & Target, 2002).

In deciding to follow up a proportion of the original retrospective study sample, along with their siblings and matched controls, we began with an empirical, quantitative design. The idea was to show, across a large-enough sample and with robust-enough measures to demonstrate statistical differences, that child analysis was capable of reducing the established lifetime consequences of childhood mental health problems. As Edward Glover pointed out as early as 1954, there is an urgent need for psychoanalytic treatments to include long-term follow-up assessments. For adult analysis, Glover believed, a minimum period of five years after analysis was necessary to assess the long-term outcome; but the success of a child analysis, he wrote, "cannot be satisfactorily checked until an after-history of 15 years has been secured" (Glover, 1954; see also Wallerstein, 1989). Since Glover put the case for long-term outcome studies in 1954, a number of substantial research projects into the nature and long-term outcome of intensive adult psychoanalysis—the Menninger Project (e.g. Kernberg, 1972; Wallerstein, 1986), the Boston Institute Project (e.g. Kantrowitz, Katz, Paolitto, Sashin, & Solomon, 1987) and the German DPV Follow-up Project (Leuzinger-Bohleber & Target, 2002)—have been carried out.

While these studies have been of great importance, their findings cannot be directly transferred to the outcome of child analysis. We therefore initiated a study, partly to see whether the pattern of post-treatment results that we had found across the large retrospective sample would hold up over decades of adolescent and internal and external experience. So, we predicted that subjects who had appeared to be suffering as children from pervasive and deep-seated psychopathology would show serious impairment of emotional and social adjustment as adults, *unless* they had received long-term and intensive psychoanalytic help, and also that differences between the outcomes of intensive and non-intensive treatment would be much narrower among the treated children with less severe pathology.

Incidentally, the follow-up study aimed to contrast different theoretical expectations about the long-term outcome of child psychoanalysis. Anna Freud's conservative view was that, when successful, analysis provided a bridge back to a normal developmental path. However, she did not believe that the child was then any less vulnerable than other children to the vicissitudes of later life events, losses, difficult relationships, and so on, which might cause a breakdown in adolescence or adulthood. In contrast to this view, we suggested that psychoanalytic therapy might enhance resilience in the face of later events, protecting the child from the full impact of these vicissitudes. We took courage from Freud's speculation after telling the story of "Little Hans":

> It may be that Hans now enjoys an advantage over other children, in that he no longer carries within him that seed in the shape of repressed complexes which must always be of some significance for a child's later life, and which undoubtedly brings with it a certain degree of deformity of character if not a disposition to a subsequent neurosis. I am inclined to think that this is so, but I do not know if many others will share my opinion; nor do I know whether experience will prove me right. [Freud, 1909b, pp. 143–144]

We hypothesized that this could happen not only through resolving repressed complexes, but also—especially in more deeply disturbed cases coming from backgrounds of emotional deprivation—through helping the child to understand and to predict his own and others' responses, particularly within relationships, through facilitating the capacity for mentalization, and through enhancing the security of internal working models of attachment relationships.

This plan turned to be only partly achievable, for two reasons. One prosaic problem was that it was very difficult to trace the subjects, and that not everyone agreed to take part. (Interestingly, there was a tendency for the untreated referred cases and for siblings of treated children to be more keen to participate in the very extensive interviews. Among the treated subjects, there was also a tendency for those with worse results in childhood to agree. Perhaps those who had had satisfactory treatment felt less need to talk or were less masochistically compliant. Nevertheless, there were some who agreed out of gratitude.) A further problem was that this study required a modest version of the kind of preparation that Marianne Leuzinger-Bohleber and her colleagues made when setting up the DPV follow-up study: gaining the cooperation of analysts in allowing their former patients to be interviewed for research purposes. Apart from fears that such interviews would reawaken disturbing memories and be experienced as very intrusive (fears that were justified in some cases), there is also the problem in relation to child analysis that the adult may have no memory whatever of having gone to a clinic to be assessed or treated. In a number of cases, neither sibling interviewed by us knew that one of them had been treated in the past: they were both told that the family had had some sort of contact at some point. The questions raised were sometimes problematic for the research subjects or their families. In the event, before we had to finish data collection, we assessed 75 subjects for an average of 15 hours each and coded all the interviews using the original coding systems and one or two of our own.

We did, of course, have a look at the data with the original questions in mind, and we discovered some interesting—and encouraging—patterns across the limited groups we had been able to study. So we did find, as we had hoped, that whereas in childhood the vast majority of treated subjects had suffered more adversity than had their siblings, in adulthood the siblings were more likely than the treated subjects to experience negative life events. In terms of personality functioning, the most important general observation was that successful childhood treatment was usually something of a protective factor—that is, if the childhood treatment outcome had been rated in the original, separate retrospective study as good, then the adult personality functioning was overall as good as or better than that of the untreated subjects. So, in work, love relationships, attachment security, reflective function, and coping with stress the treated cases were doing well, with the exception of those whose childhood outcome had been considered poor at the time. In the love relationship domain, for example, individuals with successfully treated disorders in childhood appeared to be doing somewhat better than were both their siblings and the untreated controls. None of those unsuccessfully treated in childhood had an adequate love relationship, and many had never had any sustained, intimate relationship. In terms of attachment security, those children whose outcome was relatively good appear to do as well as their siblings in terms of the likelihood of secure attachment. Those unsuccessfully treated appear to be predominantly preoccupied and entangled, whereas those untreated appear to be predominantly dismissing. In terms of the capacity to mentalize, to reflect on mental states, as predicted, the successfully treated group did somewhat better than all the others, whereas those whose outcome had been poor in childhood remained unable to conceive of mental states accurately. In brief, successful childhood treatment does appear to be something of a protective factor. However, there were some cautionary observations: even those who had been treated successfully appeared to be less good at making friends than were their siblings, and they were also more likely to have depressive or anxious personalities, although to an extent one would characterize them as cautious or mildly pessimistic rather than disturbed. We will return to this observation later.

We did not have enough material to answer all our original questions convincingly, or certainly to persuade the world of evidence-based mental health care that child psychoanalysis could put adult psychiatrists out of a job. However, this is where the story got more interesting for the world of psychoanalysis, in terms of methods and questions. Instead of having too little material to tell us how the groups differed in outcomes, we had a vast wealth of material—75 sets of recorded and transcribed interviews covering childhood, adolescence, adult life, families, friendships, work, love, physical and mental health, personality functioning, attachment, life events and resilience in the face of them, and so on. There was an interview about their memories of treatment, if they had had it and if they remembered it. In addition to this, we had contemporaneous records about the families, which were often detailed and extended over many years, together with the diagnostic and full treatment records of most of these cases. Many of them had been studied as part of the Hampstead Index Project.

Suddenly we had more data than we had the resources to deal with. And we needed different methods: we needed ways of coding the child treatment records, to collect more of the material from the histories, and to study the treatment process, its themes and techniques and changes—for example, in the child's capacity to symbolize, his range of affect, and the changing nature of the transference. We have been working on these since the time of the retrospective study, and we have made progress; but here we focus more on what we needed to study, and we report on the rich store of adult interview material: systematic, clinically based qualitative methods for the study of detailed autobiographical narratives. This work is still in progress, thanks to generous grants from the Research Advisory Board of the International Psychoanalytical Association and from the Anna Freud Foundation, and to the hard work of researcher psychologists, especially Abby Schachter, Doris Fillion, and Carolina Traverso, and of Nick Midgley, a child psychotherapist doing his doctoral research with us.

We will pick out a few lines of work that we are pursuing, to elaborate on some of the methods we felt were needed for the questions in which we were interested. We will offer a couple of examples to illustrate how we have changed our methods in the direction of the qualitative and the clinical. We are presenting this work as our attempt to explore what we believe to be a potentially very productive paradigm for psychoanalytic research that is, as yet, not widely used. This is the application of qualitative research methods as developed in the social sciences, and we can add to their development through the study of autobiographical data and discourse, such as we have in abundance in psychoanalysis.

An ideographic, case-study analysis of the sense of identity[1]

This study uses the method of interpretative phenomenological analysis (IPA), which we have adapted for this material. The method aims systematically to extract personal meanings from interview narratives about life experiences and to represent these first of all in the subject's terms and then try to discern underlying individual and/or relationship themes. The IPA method was not designed to look at unconscious meanings and motivations, but we are aiming to extend the method beyond the subject's conscious and preconscious beliefs to evolve an alternative to classical psychoanalytic research methodology. The study, which includes only three subjects, aims to offer what qualitative researchers call "thick"—rich and detailed—descriptions of the identity-related themes emerging from our in-depth interviews. The analysis focuses on the self-representations or "narratives of self" of these subjects and the way in which they have integrated the experience of childhood emotional disorder and a child analysis into their experience of themselves and the story they construct around their lives.

In this kind of research, data are processed in two stages: a stage of individual description and an aggregation phase. In the first phase, the analysis of each subject's interviews is written up as a detailed case study, using many extracts from the subject's speech as the "selected facts" from which a structure of meaning is created. Extracts that are experienced by the reader as recurrent (thematic), organizing (pivotal), or saturated (a single extract but one that is loaded with meaning by its unusual qualities of complexity) are selected. As in clinical psychoanalysis, the structure of description and explanation built in the listener's mind reflects not only the recurring, organizing themes in the subject's mental world, but also those that matter to the listener or that are salient in the analyst's theoretical and personal world. The intersubjectivity of the enterprise is admitted at the outset. In qualitative research the researcher's preconceptions and preoccupations are made explicit. We have recruited a number of researchers to work in parallel on the same data sets to see the extent to which common themes are perceived. This is part of the extension of IPA that our psychoanalytic considerations have brought—that IPA assumes that the declaration of the researcher's biases is sufficient, whereas we are aware that there will be unconscious as well as conscious preconceptions that will have influenced the selection of material. (In the DPV study, the same issue was addressed by introducing group discussion between clinicians and researchers.) As a second stage, there will be an analysis of themes *across* cases, in order to move towards some more general ideas about the narratives of personal identity in adults who have been in therapy as children.

We will briefly summarize one case, to give an idea of how the first stage works in practice. The case was chosen partly because of the very extensive documentation of it in childhood as well as through the adult interviewing. However, we wanted to look at a case where treatment had been considered successful in childhood, but where the subject did encounter further psychiatric and personality problems in adolescence and adulthood. This, as we have said, was statistically very unusual. As Marianne Leuzinger-Bohleber (2002) has stressed, we can often learn more from psychoanalytic failures than from our successes.

> "Michael E" was in treatment at the Centre three times: for some months when he was under 5 years old, and from the age of 6 for four years, on both occasions in analysis; finally, as a late adolescent he was seen by the same therapist approximately once a month for a year. The first referral was mainly for attacks of rage, which apparently responded well and then disappeared once his borderline and suicidal mother had abandoned the family following a series of traumatic scenes. At the age of 7, Michael was referred again for "completely unmanageable" trouble-making behaviour at school and being very difficult to handle at home because of the return of his frequent rages and "hysterical fits". His father saw him as very frightened rather than as aggressive.
>
> Detailed process reports of the analytic work from age 7 to 11 describe a background awareness of major problems in object relationships but an almost exclusive interpretative focus on sexual fantasies, fears, and wishes, which were attributed to his very alarming but exciting external situation. Despite serious problems in most areas of development—particularly affect regulation and learning—and multiple symptoms, Michael was seen as a prototypical neurotic child. He was used in a conceptual research group in the Centre for many years as a clear example of neurosis, with which to contrast borderline children. The technique was therefore classical psychoanalysis rather than developmental help, the latter being a form of treatment, aimed at developmental disorders, that was developed at the Centre. While the analyst acknowledged that Michael's anxieties might be linked to his mother's provocative and bizarre behaviour, her interpretative work was focused on Michael's incestuous wishes, primal-scene fantasies, his conflicts about his sexual desires for his analyst, his feelings of phallic inadequacy. For example, whenever she (the analyst) talked to him about his wish to have a mother, this was sexualized in the interpretation and presented as a wish for sex with his mother. After four years of analysis, the

analyst wrote that Michael had responded very well to analytic treatment. He appeared to be settled at home and at school, and all his symptoms and his school learning difficulties had gone. His much greater confidence and masculine assertiveness following the extensive analysis of his sexual wishes and anxieties were commented on, but his identification with an emasculated father was seen as still a potential problem, to be overcome in his adolescence. It was noted that the sexual transference towards the analyst continued, and Anna Freud decided it would be best to break off the analysis in order to allow him to get into latency before he tried to enter adolescence.

There were follow-ups and a further period of intermittent therapy sessions in late adolescence, because Michael was having another period of social difficulties, academic failure (despite a high IQ), and anxiety symptoms. He was striking in his prematurely conventional attitudes, he was unambitious, and he shunned the challenges and excitements of his age. Behind this wish to avoid life there seemed to be a complete lack of confidence.

We meet Mr E again at the age of 36, when he readily cooperated with the follow-up interviews, although he had experienced the approach to take part in the study as very stressful. The interviews are very interesting for being remarkably boring. Such interviews are rarely dull, but these are, despite a life that had—in both childhood and adulthood—been full of traumatic incidents, angry conflicts, and anxiety. Mr E leaves a lasting impression of being hesitant, repetitive, disappointed, puzzled—as though he is constantly asking himself, "what went wrong?" In listening to him, we end up asking the same question.

The content analysis of 12 hours of narratives identified four themes, each referred to by the word "thing", picking up a vagueness typical of the way Michael E describes himself: the "confidence thing", the "rejection thing", the "worry thing", and the "anger thing".

The first three are linked in his mind: the absence of confidence contributes to his feelings of being rejected, which, in turn, confronts him with persistent anxiety. None seems primary, but in combination they leave him feeling sad, empty, disappointed, with a sense of having missed out on life. His comments on suicide are telling.

> "I have thought about suicide [*small laugh*] a few times in my life, and I've always felt I couldn't do it. . . . I don't really feel I've got enough control over my own life to commit suicide [*small laugh*]."

A fourth theme concerns his fear of losing his temper. He is tormented by the possibility of causing damage by this, yet the suggestion is there that through anger he might break through to a now submerged identity:

> "If I get upset about something, because I keep it to myself, and then I lose my temper, but . . . I don't do it so much now [*small laugh*], I sort of keep calm, but still it's sort of—I feel I've got the choice either to shout my head off or something, I never know what to do, whether to bottle up my feelings or let them out, because they say 'you shouldn't bottle up your feelings', but if you don't bottle up your feelings you make the situation worse by showing your emotions."

Because of limitations to the length of this chapter, we will need to simplify a relatively complex and subtle picture of Mr E's self-representation that emerged from the fine-grained study of his narratives. Formulated within the classical frame of reference in which his analysis took place, Mr E has identified with the castrated father of his early childhood. Almost as if he had offered himself to his mother, in place of the father who had recovered through his analysis, somehow the idea that came to dominate his life is that access to the maternal object could only be found through this self-defeated, self-limiting identity. Often through the interviews he refers to how he has been saved by his marriage: his relationship to his wife feels crucial but is also maintained (in fantasy) by his endless neediness and hopelessness.

He now perceives his childhood as a progression from uncontrolled, angry exuberance to a frustrating, unfulfilled, inhibited identity. His experience of his analysis is hijacked to bolster this perceived shift. The analysis is thought about as something that drained him of infantile strength and vigour:

> "I think . . . um . . . I sometimes feel that I was more confident when I was much younger at school and . . . um . . . it might have been because I was disruptive or something [*feeble laugh*], and

> that's why I had a therapy, and when I came out of therapy I might have been more relaxed and less assertive and sometimes I feel . . . just that I'm not assertive as an adult—I sometimes think maybe I sort of had it taken out of me."

We can now see the analysis in his mind as another instance of having to subvert his masculine instinctual self to a dominant woman, that the formative experience was of submission to her demands. These fantasies are in stark contrast with the recorded history of the analysis and with the analyst's explicit aims for Michael. She gives a consistent impression, through her extensive process notes, in fact, of having appreciated Michael's livelier and more masculine side, and she wrote with regret, seeing him at 18: "This sober, somewhat strict, quiet young man with his approval of a safe job and a steady income, seems a long way from the lively, aggressive, highly imaginative small boy who was in analysis." It is striking how in his memory Michael has to force the analyst into the shape of yet another castrating female figure.

The discrepancy between the recorded history and the reconstructed history raises the question in the researcher's mind as to how a good and healing analytic experience comes to be subverted to the exigencies of internal economics. Here the researcher may speculate or interpret, and the criterion of truth is once again hermeneutic. It is possible that Mr E's current relationship experience imposes a template upon his memory of the analysis that makes his analyst into a figure who "takes away his strength". It is perhaps even more likely that the profound and well-documented traumatic experience of abandonment by his manipulative, impulsive, suicidal mother had created an organizing focus to which all subsequent experiences had to conform. There are many other possibilities along these lines, but all of them might be seen as exonerating Michael's therapeutic experience in itself. Was there any way in which the experience was unsatisfactory, which *might* explain the negative long-term outcome? There are a number of features of the treatment that, with hindsight, we might explore in order to learn something. One critical issue is the termination of Michael's treatment. The developmental understanding dominant at the Hampstead Clinic at the time of his treatment—now no longer sustained—considered a period of latency critical in the path from the oedipal period to adolescence. Yet Michael probably experienced the sudden ending as an indication of the analyst's incapacity to tolerate his boisterous sexuality. This might have retrospectively coloured the entire analytic experience as having been with someone who requires her partner not to express aggressive sexuality in an open way—in fact, requires a figure somewhat like the father. More pernicious, perhaps, was another aspect of the treatment, where reading the records one consistently feels that the analyst expresses a tantalizing partial understanding of Michael's struggles. While the objective trauma of his abuse and abandonment is generously acknowledged in clinical discussions parallel to his treatment, in the treatment Michael is continually confronted with the intense sexual fantasies that are considered to be the consequences of those early experiences. But the link is rarely made explicitly. What may actually have been happening is that in the transference he is re-experiencing the trauma of an exciting but misunderstanding, out-of-touch object, recreating the primary-object relationship. Related to this is the analyst's apparent unwillingness to see Michael as a profoundly damaged child. There is a consistent tendency for her to "normalize" Michael's sexual conflicts as neurotic and to ignore the underlying deficits in ego functioning that make it very hard for Michael actually to process these interpretations; he is constantly in danger of concretizing them and becoming more rather than less anxious. It is telling that his first response to being asked about his treatment, at 36, is that he really liked the receptionist, who was always kind to him and interested in him, in the waiting-room before his sessions. She gave him food and asked about his day and remembered him.

It is easy with hindsight to criticize clinical work, and the true test of the accuracy of such interpretations could only be accomplished in ethically very dubious research (involving deliberately wrong interpretations). As we can never envisage doing this, it becomes of great interest to study those whose analysis has not had the impact we might wish and to contrast these analyses with those—far more frequent—cases where the success of treatment is continued. Historically, Michael's treatment came at the cusp of a sea-change in the work at the Anna Freud Centre. Ironically, his case in its neurotic formulation was used by the Borderline Group of the 1960s and 1970s, which generated an entirely new therapeutic approach to cases such as Michael. We have evidence from our retrospective study of the tremendous successes that analysts at the Centre were able to achieve taking a more sophisticated developmental perspective that allowed for constitutional and early environmental faults in ego-structure and used the analytic context to help the child to engage in a rehabilitative enterprise regenerating parts of the mind. In Michael's case, this probably concerned the mental processes involved in the regulation of negative affect—the over-ready triggering of a sense of emergency that constantly undermined his sense of continuous existence. These basic developmental difficulties were not addressed; had they been, then the long-term outcome might have been much more favourable. In the therapy itself, he was able to use the analyst as an auxiliary ego; her evidently benign and encouraging stance helped him to organize his feelings, but only while she was present in his life and therefore in his mind. However, perhaps her belief—shared by her supervisor—that his unconscious conflicts needed to be brought to the surface actually served to make her into a figure whom he could not represent in a sustained way once the analysis had ended. Our understanding of Michael's current behaviour is that he is right to worry about what has happened to his earlier aggression and assertiveness: he constantly disarms and then deadens himself and his listener, and he can feel the loss all the time without knowing how it is happening. Whatever his analyst and his mother and other real, external objects did to him or failed to offer him in the past, the "taking something out of him" is now, of course, happening within his own mind. With hindsight, we can ask ourselves—as his analyst wondered at follow-up—whether Michael's progress could only have been maintained with continuing support from her as he faced adolescence (instead of her complete withdrawal for years, to allow him to withdraw from what she saw as his regressive, oedipal attachment to her) or whether the diagnosis of clear-cut neurotic pathology was mistaken, and an approach that was more focused on building and linking basic mental processes might have laid the basis for a better relationship to himself and his objects.

The possible role of trauma, recognized but not treated in analysis[2]

One could criticize us for making too much of Michael's early trauma and for suggesting that the absence of its exploration prejudiced the treatment outcome. In fact, our follow-up study showed that Michael was not one isolated case in the poor adult outcome group in having severe early trauma insufficiently explored in childhood treatment. An unanticipated observation in a small number of cases was that actual serious trauma—particularly physical abuse—remembered clearly in adulthood and causing continuing problems had sometimes not been addressed (or at times recognized) by the clinicians who were working decades ago. Some poor long-term outcomes seemed to be associated with analysts interpreting these children's reports as fantasy. Even though they knew that abuse of the kind their patients described was probably going on in the family, they felt that their role was to focus on psychic reality, and particularly on hidden meanings of the experiences, which could be leading to neurotic conflict. So, for example, actual frightening behaviour, such as the father chasing the child onto the roof or the mother locking him in a cupboard, dragging him by the hair, was worked with as an exciting masochistic fantasy. At the time of follow-up, these individuals could be seen to be reliving and being preoccupied with the traumata, for examples of intrusive memories or flashbacks that corresponded to actual experiences reported in the childhood file appeared in some Adult Attachment Interview (AAI: George, Kaplan, & Main, 1985) narratives. Perhaps it is not surprising that such individuals remained preoccupied, entangled in their childhood experiences, with their traumatic experiences unresolved, their psychiatric functioning impaired, and unable to adapt well to either work or social situations. Although we are not assessing this, one must wonder about the parenting capacities of these individuals and the likelihood of transgenerational repetitions.

An evaluation of the assumptions of attachment theory in relation to life narratives

The second example also involves studying the nature of reconstructions of the past, but it also entails comparing two conceptual frameworks: psychoanalysis itself, and its problem child—attachment theory. We will illustrate how we have tried to test some of the assumptions made in attachment theory and research, about the meaning of patterns of memory and speech, particularly as revealed in the AAI and its coding procedures. We will give two examples of questions we have been able to ask with this material, together with the detailed contemporaneous records:

1. Is the coherent and ready recollection of episodes from childhood that is characteristic of adults who are classified as "secure" an indication, as assumed by attachment theory, that their memories are much less defensively distorted?
2. Is the difficulty in producing memories to support positive descriptions of the relationships with each parent, as is characteristic of "dismissing" adults, an indication that their memories of rejection by their parents are suppressed in the service of idealization?

How accurately do "secure" adults remember their childhoods?

The most "secure" individuals who were functioning best in terms of their general personalities and relationships remember somewhat less accurately: their recollections are very coherent, but when set alongside the contemporary records, they emerge as tinged with idealization. They appear to smooth over or forget adverse experiences noted at the time of their assessment—even quite objective events: for example, the prolonged psychiatric-hospital admission of the mother when the subject was 12 years old, or major arguments leading to the divorce of the parents in adolescence. These mildly idealizing but persuasive subjects were much less likely to come from the treated group, even from those with successful outcomes. They came from the sibling group, who had grown up in the same families but had not been seen as problematic and had not been referred for help. The good-outcome treated cases were, as adults, also mostly coded secure, but they were somewhat less coherent. They seemed to have retained an accurate and mixed, inevitably more painful, and sometimes confusing memory in comparison to their siblings. These tended to be the most reflective subjects, still thinking about and struggling with their clearer, less comforting awareness of how things were. So, in AAI terms, the "earned secure" subjects were indeed honest and accurate, while the "unearned secure" carried around a nicer but too-rosy version of their childhood, packaged in a way that sounded true.

Are "dismissing" adults trying to idealize a rejecting childhood?[3]

This study has involved a sample of 8 individuals who were classified on the AAI as predominantly "dismissing". [There were 5 men and 3 women, who had been between the ages of 3 and 12 at referral (mean 7 years). The mean time between referral and follow-up was 30 years (range 17–45 years). In three cases the offer of treatment from the Anna Freud Centre had been refused; three treated cases had been in psychoanalysis and two in psychotherapy, for an average of 1.7 years.] We compared memory for childhood in dismissing-adult subjects to the historical information in the child-treatment files at the Anna Freud Centre, to see whether the AAI coder's inference of idealization and rejection could be substantiated. To do this, we independently coded actual experiences as described in the social history records, using the criteria for probable experience scales in the AAI manual.[4] We then did an in-depth qualitative study of the memories elicited by the AAI compared to the information found in clinical files. There is only time in this presentation to summarize the findings, which were that in half of the eight cases, the original AAI coding had made a false assumption of rejection by the parents, on the basis that the positive, unsubstantiated descriptions in the AAI reflected idealization. The reality in the history seemed to be quite consistent with the positive adjectives, and the dearth of memories reflected not a defensive forgetting of rejection, but something else. In two further cases there had been involving rather than rejecting behaviour by the parents, and again the broad descriptions were reasonably accurate.

CONCLUSIONS

The intention of our contribution to this volume was epistemological and methodological, rather than substantive. We are gradually trying to feel our way towards an application of qualitative methodology from sociology and social psychology to the detailed, fine-grained exploration of material collected in psychoanalyses and psychoanalytically orientated interviews. To conclude, we will highlight what we consider to be the defining feature of this (at least for us) innovative approach.

1. The material to be studied goes beyond the traditional case-study methodology in separating the role of the analyst and the investigator, the analyst implicitly becoming a subject of investigation. We are not saying that the narrative accounts of the analyst are not an adequate basis (i.e. that we need tape-recordings), but that we do not see the analyst's account as having the status of an objective, historical account. It is itself an object of study—as indeed Freud's clinical accounts have become.
2. We need clear procedures for the construction of "facts", and while these need not conform to traditional criteria of reliability and validity, the nature of psychoanalytic material dictates that procedures for controlling for the unconscious bias of the observer must be in place.
3. There needs to be a declared psychoanalytic conceptual framework within which the observation can be explored, given the very large number of possible frameworks for thinking about any material—for example, in the case of Michael E, the framework of neurotic vs. borderline pathology.
4. Qualitative, clinical exploration is a position in knowledge acquisition. We do not see a "developmental line" between conceptual (hypothesis-generating) and empirical (hypothesis-testing) research but, rather, a complementarity. There may also be thought to be a tension between the two positions, each sharpening the other, so that, for example, we could envision a randomized controlled trial combined with a qualitative study of the experience of being "randomized" by the participants, which would illuminate the quantitative findings.

We have worked for some time to address the crisis in the psychoanalytic knowledge-base. We think psychoanalysis would be helped by more rigorous data collection. We believe that harnessing the exciting new developments in qualitative research methodology will help in reorganizing our theoretical ideas, which, we think, cannot be achieved in the conceptual realm alone without the systematic study of clinical observations using a combination of qualitative and quantitative paradigms.

NOTES

1. The work using IPA on the adult interviews is being done by Nick Midgley with supervision from myself and Jonathan Smith, who developed the method. Nick has remained blind throughout to the childhood records.

2. This final piece of work was largely done by Susan Loden.

3. This study has been mainly carried out by Carolina Traverso.

4. The AAI coding was done by certified reliable coders. The ratings of case files were done by two coders separately: one certified reliable AAI coder (who had not coded the AAI), and a second rater scored using the AAI Manual without training. Inter-rater reliability for the 80 AAI experience scores assigned was .84 (Spearman's rho).

11

Psychotherapy with a victim of extreme violence: clinical case report and qualitative analysis

Sverre Varvin

In this chapter I present a qualitative process analysis of a psychotherapy with a patient, "Mohammed", who had suffered extreme traumatization. He was refugee from a country in Africa, and he had spent nine years as a political prisoner under the most inhuman conditions; he had been tortured, and he had seen others tortured, including his wife and daughter; furthermore, he had lost contact with his wife and six children.

I first discuss some significant perspectives on qualitative research, then present the methods used in this study, and, lastly, present some extracts from the analysis and results.

On qualitative research

Results in qualitative research are presented as *texts, narratives, dialogues,* and *descriptions* that cannot be reduced to quantitative measurements or fixed categories. The reduction of an often unmanageable quantity of "texts" is determined not by statistical principles but, among other things, by *the point of view* that is (consciously or unconsciously) chosen, on the material, and it occurs in several steps in the research process: selective observation, the attribution of meaning or significance to certain facts, and the selection of material to be analysed and of material for presentation. The criteria for selection are based on *phenomena* (significant from a certain point of view), not on the statistical mean. This implies that the process of research aims at the *new* and *specific* to the field or material that is being researched. In contrast, the aim of a group-based quantitative design is to determine whether or not a hypothetical property is present as a mean. In other words, in qualitative research the phenomena are analysed in their context, and generalizing is done, not at the level of data (*x* predicts *y*), but at the level of phenomena (an event understood in context).

The present study is part of an in-depth qualitative study on mental survival strategies after extreme traumatization (Varvin, 2002). The methods employed—with the exception of one earlier study (Varvin & Stiles, 1999)—have not been used on psychotherapy processes with patients who had suffered extreme trauma; moreover, to the author's knowledge there are no previous studies of a similar kind done on such patients. This study is thus situated in the context of discovery, and the aim is to find not general laws, but patterns and regularities across several cases.

In qualitative studies, the text creates a structure of meaning, which is then conveyed to the reader (Nielsen, 1995). The good case study is an example of this. A totality and coherence are created with an often convincing face-validity, implying a certain "seduction" in the dialogue between the researcher and the reader, which is necessary for the reader's appropriation of the research results. This "seductive moment" is then counteracted by the reader's critical apprehension of what has been read. This concerns the distinction made by Ricoeur (1991a, 1991b) between the *meaning* and the *significance* of the text. The first relates to its internal structure and the *way* it is constructed—that is, the internal coherence as a criterion for validity—and corresponds to the traditional meaning-constructing project of hermeneutics. The text must, however, also be understood as trying to say something about the world, as referring to something, and as having a message about a phenomenon. This is the *significance* of the text. If, for example, the object of study is psychotherapeutic dialogue, then there will be a journey from the reality of the speaking subjects, through field-notes, transcripts, analyses and working through, verbal reports, and, lastly, articles or written reports. Ricoeur's point of view is that the text must (again) be transmitted back to living communication and in this way be grounded in the experience of the reader(s). This process connects the text with another meaning and another experience (the reader tests the text's significance)—and new knowledge may possibly follow. These are the *external coherence criteria.* (In positivist science this part is usually termed "research dissemination". However, this has another significance: the point is not to ground the text or the results in the reader's experience as part of the validation process, but more to impart facts or knowledge to the uninformed reader or listener.) There is, following this, a strong emphasis on *pragmatic validation*—that is, the usefulness of the results, for example, in the clinic.

Appropriation is here seen as an active process of interpretation, which Ricoeur describes as a "struggle between the reader and the text". In this way the text may be actively appropriated by reading the meaning of the text, by its internal structure, and by establishing its significance through combination and comparison with other experiences, data, viewpoints, and theory. This perspective on psychotherapy research is relevant for the critique of the so-called drug-metaphor in psychotherapy research, which views psychotherapy as consisting of "active ingredients" the more of which should yield better results (Stiles & Shapiro, 1994).

Psychotherapy and psychoanalysis are, in contrast, seen as open-feedback systems, where both patient and therapist are constantly making more or less explicit adjustments to the other. This requires a research methodology adjusted to these characteristics of the research object.

The emphasis on the tentativeness of the conclusions in qualitative research accords, following this, with the open-endedness of "findings" during a psychoanalytic process. Laplanche and Pontalis say: "experienceеs, impressions and memory-traces may be revised at a later date to fit in with fresh experiences or with the attainment of a new stage of development. They may in that event be endowed not only with a new meaning, but also with physical effectiveness" (1973, p. 111). The new efficiency may be immediate in therapy and should be significant in the pragmatic validation of results in qualitative research.

Interpretations are made on the practice of language (e.g. texts and narratives) understood in context, and interpretation may never be final. What is at stake is "the broadening and deepening of knowledge about the human being", a "broadening of horizons", and pragmatic usefulness. The reader becomes thus the subject of the finished text (Nielsen, 1995). ["Neither in literary criticism, nor in the social sciences, is there . . . a last word. Or, if there is any, we call that violence" (Ricoeur, 1979, cited in Salner, 1989, p. 64). Or, phrased in more positive terms, this time by a poet: "Contrary to what is generally believed, meaning and sense were never the same thing; meaning shows itself at once, direct, literal, explicit, enclosed in itself, univocal if you like, *while sense cannot stay still, it seethes with second, third and fourth senses, radiating out in different directions that divide and subdivide into branches and branchlets, until they disappear from view; the sense of every word is like a star hurling spring tides out into space, cosmic winds, magnetic perturbations, afflictions*" (Samarango, 1997, p. 115; emphasis added).]

Methods: assimilation analysis and dialogical sequence analysis

I present here a summary of results using two qualitative methods—assimilation analysis (AA: Stiles, 2001; Stiles et al., 1990) and dialogical sequence analysis (DSA: Leiman, 1998)—in their revised version by the author (Varvin, 2002).

The assimilation model (Stiles et al., 1990) attempts to reconcile the scope and time-scale of the psychotherapy process (in-session events, usually observed on a scale of seconds or minutes) and psychotherapy outcome (changes in people's lives, usually observed on a scale of months or years) by considering smaller aspects of the identified themes (what is identified as the person's problematic experiences) and how they are negotiated and by studying each one separately and longitudinally. Problematic experiences are understood as derivatives of painful experiences, and they may be understood in an object-relational perspective as dialogical patterns as they appear in relational scenarios—complex mental schemata for being with others, expressed in explicit and implicit behaviour and conveying meaning and significance (see Gullestad & Killingmo, 2001; Varvin, 2002).

A description of different levels of assimilation or integration is used as a *descriptive* framework for the analysis. The following levels have been identified (Stiles et al., 1991; Stiles, Meshot, Anderson, & Sloan, 1992): warded off; unwanted thoughts; vague awareness (or emergence); problem statement or clarification; understanding or insight; application or working through; problem solution; and mastery (see Table 11.1) (Honos-Webb & Stiles, 1998; Varvin, 2002).

Patients may enter therapy with problems at any level of assimilation, and movement of any distance along the continuum might be considered progress.

This model implies a dialogical view on psychotherapy that is coherent with an object-relational view, seen as basically an encounter between a patient's and a therapist's inner speech. Bakhtin's concept, *responsive understanding,* appropriately describes what guides the therapist in the interaction with the patient. Briefly, this view implies that all speech, including inner speech, is addressing someone, and that the listener is inevitably drawn into this process as a second party (transference). In addition, however, there is a third party, "whose absolutely just responsive understanding is presumed" (Bakhtin, 1986, pp. 125–126, cited in Leiman, 1998), the last implying that there is always something beyond the immediate transference object. This dual nature of responsive understanding allows the message to live in the therapist without being given a final meaning but always allowing for a new meaning to appear—in due course. This is one essence of containment. The tentativeness of the conclusions in qualitative research is thus coherent with the object studied.

When analysing the patient's utterances, the following distinctions are made (see Table 11.1):

- Speaking *from* the experience: This marks the transition from the non-symbolized position, where the experience is represented mostly as bodily signs, behaviour, and so forth, to an incipient ability to formulate traces of the experience in verbal language (relating to Levels 1 and 2 of the assimilation scale).
- Speaking *about* the experience: Here the subject is beginning to establish the ability to place the experience in a time perspective and also situate him/herself in relation to different social and psychological contexts (relating to Level 3 of the assimilation scale).
- *Reflecting on* the experience: At this stage the subject is able to reflect on the emotional meaning of the experience and will be in a position where active reorganization of the self and thereby integration may be possible (relating to Levels 4 and 5 of the assimilation scale).

At each level, the listener is situated in a specific transference position, or a specific form of responsive understanding is implicitly demanded. (These distinctions in the way the utterance is organized are based on the study of the enunciation proper with enunciation analysis: Rosenbaum, 2000; Rosenbaum & Varvin, 1999, 2002a, 2002b.)

The unit of DSA is an utterance. The delimitation of the unit is flexible and may comprise a single intoned double-voiced word or narratives that are more complex (as in CCRT: Luborsky & Crits-Cristoph, 1990). Dialogical patterns and sequences may frequently be derived from the patients' self-narratives that suggest how they relate to various aspects of themselves. Dialogical patterns can also be recognized in the transference, then often mediated by non-verbal signs and metaphorical aspects of meaning in the patient–therapist discourse. The therapist's subtle countertransference feelings and fantasies may also be a source for identifying salient dialogical patterns. The following steps are taken:

1. Define subject position and explicit or implicit object positions: the "I" or self-aspect and the "you" in the dialogue.
2. Describe from what position the subject is speaking—that is, which "I" is speaking to which "you"—and which procedures (ways of relating), wishes, and fears are involved. Describe the object—that is, who/what is being addressed.
3. Follow the development of these positions through the identified sequence.
4. Specify the "I" and the "you" positions as further material is analysed. Define whether more than one position is present.
5. Make a more comprehensive picture of the "I–you scenario".
6. Go back to the beginning and specify the scenario presented at the beginning of the sequence.

Dialogical sequence analysis: identifying the central problematic experience[1]

The first step in DSA revealed the *pattern* by Mohammed shown in Figure 11.1, based on analysis of the first three sessions.

The positions with which he identified are on the left-hand side of Figure 11.1. The sequence began with the "Mohammed who can

Table 11.1
Assimilation of Problematic and Overwhelming Experiences Scale (APEOS) (revised, after Stiles et al., 1990)

0. *Warded off*

   Content is unformed; patient is unaware of the problem. An experience is considered warded off if there is evidence of actively avoiding emotionally disturbing topics (e.g. immediately changing subject raised by the therapist). Thought is vague, reflecting unformed content. At Levels 0.1 to 0.9 there may be increasing clarity but content is distorted (e.g. delusional), concrete, and there is absence of reflection.

   There may be a diffuse hostile or suspicious attitude towards the world, social withdrawal, a feeling of emptiness or hopelessness, a chronic feeling of being alert as if one is constantly being threatened, and feelings of estrangement may be signs of warded-off overwhelming experiences.

   Affect may be minimal at Level 0, reflecting successful avoidance; vague negative affect (especially anxiety) is associated with Levels 0.1 to 0.9.

   Somatization and dissociated states of mind may occur, and behaviour may be characterized by fight, flight responses, but these phenomena are not accompanied by clear thoughts relating to them or thoughts relating the experiences to an external event.

1. *Unwanted thoughts*

   Content reflects emergence of thoughts associated with discomfort. Patient prefers not to think about it; topics are raised by therapist or external circumstances. Affect is often more salient than the content and involves strong negative feelings—anxiety, fear, anger, sadness. Despite the feelings' intensity, they may be unfocused and their connection with the content may be unclear. Levels 1.1 to 1.9 reflect increasingly stronger affect and less successful avoidance.

   Somatization, dissociation, and paranoid anxieties may occur, and behaviour may be characterized by fight/flight responses, but these phenomena are accompanied by thoughts relating to them and thus represent the emergence of unwanted thoughts.

   Relations to others are disturbed in the area(s) of problematic or overwhelming experience; hostility, withdrawal, estrangement, and aggressive actions towards others may occur.

   Thinking is concrete, and the ability to apply metaphor to the problematic experience is almost nonexistent.

2. *Vague awareness*

   Patient acknowledges the existence of a problematic experience and describes uncomfortable associated thoughts but cannot formulate the problem clearly. He/she may observe how these thoughts influence behaviour and physical and mental reactions. The patient is not only speaking from the position of being subjected to adverse circumstances (internal/external) but speaks also about the traumatic or problematic experience. Metaphors are being used, and thinking is no longer only concrete.

Affect includes acute psychological pain or panic associated with the problematic thoughts and experiences. Levels 2.1 to 2.9 reflect increasing clarity of the experience's content and decreasing intensity and diffusion of affect.

3. *Problem statement/clarification*

   Content includes a clear statement of a problem—something that could be worked on. Affect is negative but manageable, not panicky. Emotions are more differentiated although mostly negative: sorrow, shame, guilt. Here concretism is almost absent, the use of metaphor is being restored, and the beginning of self-reflection is observed (that is, a reflection about the self having had the experience).

   Levels 3.1 to 3.9 reflect active, focused work towards understanding the problematic experience.

4. *Understanding/insight*

   The problematic experience is placed into a schema, formulated, understood, with clear connective links. Affect may be mixed, with some unpleasant recognitions, but with curiosity or even pleasant surprise of the "aha" sort. Past experiences are beginning to be treated as belonging to personal history (autobiographical memory).

   Levels 4.1 to 4.9 reflect progressively greater clarity or generality of the understanding, usually associated with increasingly positive (or decreasingly negative) affect.

5. *Application/working-through*

   The understanding is used to work on a problem; there is reference to specific problem-solving efforts, though without complete success. Patient may talk about considering alternatives or systematically selecting courses of action. Affective tone may be positive, businesslike. Mature depressive reactions are observed, and an ability to grieve is present (sadness, sorrow over losses).

   Thinking about past overwhelming experiences, however, is as a rule painful. The salient achievement is the ability nevertheless to "revisit" past adverse experiences and reflect on them. Definite signs of reflective function are present in the area of problematic or overwhelming experiences. Levels 5.1 to 5.9 reflect tangible progress towards solutions of problems in daily living.

6. *Problem solution*

   Patient achieves a successful solution for a specific problem. Affect is often positive, satisfied, proud of accomplishment. Relations to others are not affected by problematic or overwhelming experiences or only so to a minimal degree, and reflective function is present in relation to interpersonal relationships. Levels 6.1 to 6.9 reflect generalizing the solution to other problems and building the solutions into usual or habitual patterns of behaviour. As the problem recedes, affect becomes more neutral.

7. *Mastery*

   Patient successfully uses solutions in new situations; this generalizing is largely automatic, not salient. Affect may be positive when the topic is discussed, or there may be signs of sorrow and pain, which do not affect interpersonal behaviour significantly. Affect is positive when the topic is raised, but otherwise neutral (i.e., this is no longer something to get excited about).

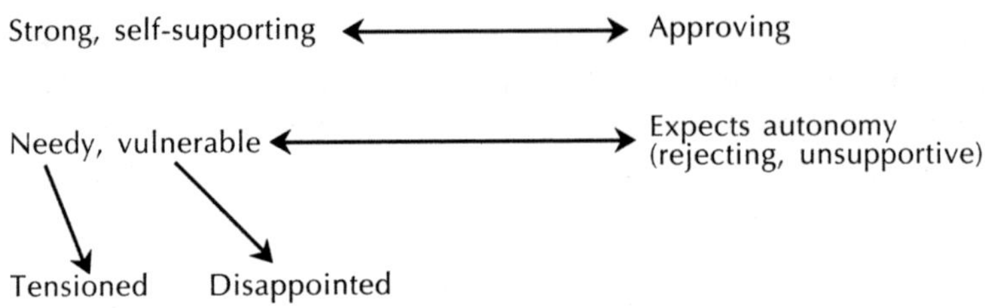

Figure 11.1

resist problems and do something for himself". The response to this position was approval that, for him, hid the conditional aspect that if needy, the others as well as he himself would become worried and disappointed. When he actually became vulnerable and in need of help, the response from others and himself was rejection. The sequence ended with disappointment and tension, perhaps as a sign of the effort to cope with and conceal helplessness.

The following example from Session 3 on the importance of not disclosing problems, for fear of making people worry and then experience rejection, may illustrate the material from which this conclusion was drawn:

MOHAMMED: yes. So always when when a [*name of country*] person
or eh comes to you eh
they're starting;
they don't they don't disappoint a person in his problem
or what happens to you.
They they they
they don't like to disappoint.
So therefore and they try to to manage to keep to keep
even some some of it in in in themselves.

THERAPIST: I see.

MOHAMMED: and not to tell.
because eh eh they like not to make eh the other person worry.

THERAPIST: I see.

MOHAMMED: yeah.

THERAPIST: so so it it may be that—when you are telling about your problems, you maybe you also think about not making me too worry.

MOHAMMED: he–he yeah yeah sometimes exactly.

[Session 3]

When talking about the prison and the torture, Mohammed conveyed the experience that when you are vulnerable, you are neglected and abused. The therapist then asked for his **feelings** related to his experience [the different styles of type indicate prosodic aspects of the voice]:

MOHAMMED: I was very bad, it's something in my;
I am feeling very bad from that.—
yes.
[*6-sec pause*]
it was a very very bad thing and,—
when I remember that things and when I think! About it—
it makes on me—I feel so so so—
I feel something that I cannot tell you.
It's really being very difficult for me
to tell you what I am feeling about that.—
I am feeling—something in my body—just coming—and—
it was very inhuman.—
and I never thought—that people can do that,
but they were doing something worse than that,
they were torturing children, and women and
[*9-sec. pause*]
they wasn't, they were not feeling ashamed of that—
they was doing everything bad.—
and the problem is,
what's you have advised me if—
what you **have advised me to do, if I see eh one of that group**
or some of that group
or some of that people who were torturing people
or who were killing people.

[Session 4]

Memories of the torture evoked feelings of helplessness, and Mohammed turned this into an active position by asking for advice—a culturally codified way of trying to resolve a problem (asking an elder, which you may do without displaying your helplessness [bold type]). The therapist responded to this according to his culture—namely, not by answering direct questions in therapy but by encouraging exploration and autonomous judgement. This then became a central theme for the next two-thirds of the session.

The transference became a power struggle and represented a repetition in the transference of the patient's problematic experience, the implicit procedural sequence being: **needing help—being rejected** or **abused.**

At the heart of his quest for advice was, as he said:

> MOHAMMED: [. . . *part of dialogue omitted* . . .]
> **so when such person eh comes! To you, and he begs! You,**
> **or he ask you something or he;**
> **and you know that he did torture**
> **on you or to your wife or to somebody else who was in /.**
> **And it is very very very very difficult situation**
> **that one even could have kill him.**
>
> [Session 4]

Here the most disastrous aspect of being helpless was revealed: that he could become similar to his torturer [bold and underlined]. At this point the therapist addressed the focus of his suffering when he affirmed the patient's worries about the violent feelings he harboured.

* * *

To sum up: In the first session, the patient reacted to the instructions given by the therapist with an appeal for help with his dilemma relating to being helpless (not included here). In Session 3 he demonstrated a culturally accepted way out of this dilemma. In Session 4 the full implication of his dilemma or conflict was revealed: his helplessness when facing his own murderous hatred when thinking of his torturers and the atrocities he had endured and what he had seen being inflicted on others. Several positions, or voices, were involved.

The problematic dialogical sequence had then to be elaborated to account for the overwhelming atrocities that he had experienced and was now re-experiencing in his tension and pain. The starting point of the analysis is now a second dialogical pattern, as shown in Figure 11.2.

The problematic dialogical pattern now contained reciprocal responses that stood in sharp contrast to the patient's ethical and social values and his view of himself as a forgiving and supportive person in relation to others' needs. The tension that he described in his first account of being rejected also assumed an elaborated mean-

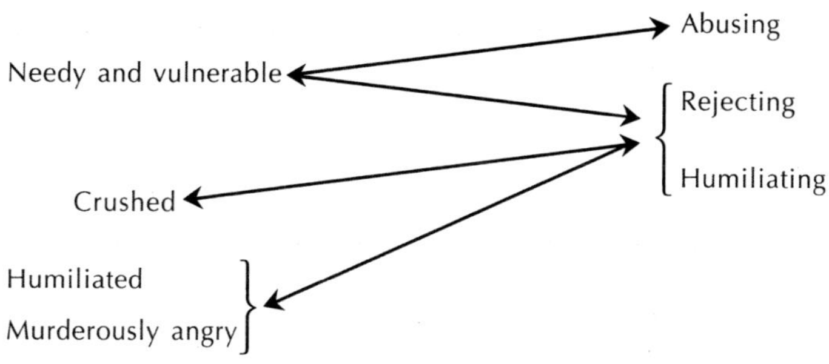

Figure 11.2

ing. It could now be regarded as a symptomatic response to the intensified conflict caused by the two incompatible dialogical patterns.

These voices could be in sharp conflict with each other, and, confronted with his murderous self or the helpless victim, he could break down, be unable to contain his feelings, and develop severe bodily reactions.

The problematic experience to be analysed with assimilation analysis could be formulated in the following way:

When faced with atrocity or thoughts and memories thereof, he would feel needy and helpless and expect rejection and humiliation, which in turn might make him feel crushed and humiliated, and this state of mind might activate another where he felt a murderous hatred.

Assimilation analysis

Assimilation analysis demonstrated how the patient achieved some integration of his problematic experience, concomitant with increased emotional differentiation, exemplified in how he was able to deal with the more complex emotions of sorrow, grief, and shame in the later part of the therapy.

The assimilation analysis comprises four steps (Honos-Webb, Stiles, Greenberg, & Goldman, 1998; Stiles, Morrison, Haw, Harper, & Shapiro, 1991; Stiles, Meshot, Anderson, & Sloan, 1992):

1. *Familiarization and indexing.* The aim was (a) to gain a thorough familiarity with the material by repeated listening to tapes and reading of transcripts, and (b) to make an index of sessions to

facilitate later retrieval of the material. This was a long therapy, and a selection of sessions had to be made. A catalogue containing the verbal and nonverbal aspects of the passages was compiled, and the topic of each passage was identified and recorded.

2. *Identifying and choosing themes.* A theme was defined as an attitude or action towards an object—that is, "a belief or feeling or evaluation or behaviour and the person(s), thing, event or situation towards which the attitude or action is expressed" (Stiles et al., 1991). These may be expressed as narratives of experiences, fantasies, memories, feelings, or bodily sensations; they are organized in dialogical sequence patterns (see above). The passages were then indexed on the basis of what the patient said and how he said it and on his reaction to interventions by the therapist. The dialogical sequence analysis demonstrated that one dominant theme in Mohammed's therapy was his relation to atrocities he had experienced and witnessed and the violent feelings he would have when confronted, either in reality or in memory, with perpetrators. Words such as "torture", "killing", "suffering", the expression "I get tensioned", "pain", "soldiers", "guards" were judged as markers for relevant passages as well as nonverbal signs signalling suffering (sighs, crying, hyperventilation, etc.).
3. *Extracting passages.* Passages concerning his relation to atrocity were selected in the following way: All passages that included the above-mentioned words or their synonyms in a context of atrocity were extracted and examined for the purposes of this analysis. The patient's relation to atrocity was a theme that was (a) prominent and important in the therapy, (b) internally coherent, and (c) illustrative of a major type of themes commonly encountered in the therapy of traumatized refugees.
4. *Describing the process of assimilation/integration.* In this step, I wrote a description of the assimilation of the theme of the problematic experience—a phenomenological account of how the theme developed and how the patient related to the problematic experience. In describing the progress of the problematic experience, I used the APEOS scale (revised version) as a descriptive framework (not, however, as an independent rating scale, which would require a very different approach to the case—cf. Field, Barkham, Shapiro, & Stiles, 1994).

I will give a short description of the assimilation process by highlighting some sequences.

First from the evaluation session: a situation where he is overwhelmed after talking about his prison experience and experiences a breakdown in the session (APEOS Level 0):

MOHAMMED: Sometimes when I am feeling these pains
I don't feel any problem in my head,
but now I am sitting here I am feeling, I am feeling
eh this pain here on my head—this place. I don't feel always.
Now I am feeling just on my part,
on this part of my head
I am feeling itching, something like itching,
some sort of unordinary feeling.

[. . . *part of dialogue omitted* . . .]

MOHAMMED: It's really in the back of the head, and this time I feel /// some sort of tension, some sort . . .

THERAPIST: Yes, you feel some sort of tension now?

MOHAMMED: Yes.

THERAPIST: Can you describe that more specific or—

MOHAMMED [*breathes heavily for 15 sec*]: I don't know, it just came //. [*breathes heavily*]
[*1-min pause*] Please can I /

THERAPIST: You want to lie down.

MOHAMMED: Yes [*breathes*].

The following sequence is from Session 30, where he tells about an episode when he became ill during a meeting with compatriots where there was intense quarrelling:

THERAPIST: I think that you are a person
who are used to people respecting each other,
you value that,
and you have experienced prison where people were not respected,
so I think you are very sensitive
for this type of interaction between people,
it makes you very angry.

MOHAMMED [*interrupts the therapist*]: Yes, yes, I became very angry
[. . . *part of dialogue omitted* . . .]
I don't remember what I said to them,
I was very sick, I was very tired, very sick,
I was tired, I was very very tired.
I have never been like that.

[Session 30]

The patient moved, in this session, towards connecting his emotions and bodily reactions with the present experiences and his past prison experiences. In assimilation terms, this corresponded to APEOS Level 2, vague awareness, moving towards Level 3, problem statement/clarification.

Session 40 showed further improvement in work with difficult experiences where the murderous anger had subsided. The theme was a young girl who had been shot:

MOHAMMED: . . . and she was talking about her situation
and and the situation in the region that she is living.
And then she often tell me that I am very sorry
she said: "I was—
somebody have shoot me—
and the bullet is in my body—
and the—
I don't know why he shoot me"
. . .

MOHAMMED: so—she was crying and she was weeping
[*12-sec pause, sighs*]

THERAPIST: It's very, it's very sad to hear
and it's very difficult to—to manage—
live with a a situation like that— + [*incomprehensible*].

MOHAMMED: mm–hm+ [*6-sec pause*] yes she was;
eh, it's very bad.
[*25-sec pause*]
it's very sad. [*crying*]
[*37-sec pause*]
it's very sad.

[Session 40]

Mohammed managed to express his sadness and contain it without being overwhelmed by affects (e.g. aggression) and/or becoming physically ill—a sign of increased mentalizing capacity and a sign that the dissociated dialogical pattern had been more integrated. When feeling helpless and needy, he did not expect rejection, abuse, or humiliation to the same extent. The second dialogical pattern was thus weakened and the first one altered. Emotion could be contained and thus become more differentiated.

This may be regarded as approaching APEOS Level 4, understanding and insight. More mature though not less difficult emotions began to dominate the scene in the later part of therapy, signifying a different relational scenario where difficult emotional states could be met by understanding.

CONCLUSION

By identifying a prominent theme, analysing its dialogical structure, and following the development through the process it was possible to analyse the scope and time-scale of the psychotherapy process comparing in-session events, usually observed on a scale of seconds or minutes, with long-term process outcome. This may then be related to post-therapy outcome (not included here). This holistic qualitative approach allowed, furthermore, for insight into specific problematic experiences typical for traumatized refugee patients, demonstrated their inner structure, and analysed how the patient dealt or coped with them. Aspects of what may be called mental survival strategies could then be identified (Varvin, 2002).

Note

1. This analysis was performed in collaboration with Mikael Leiman, PhD, University of Joensuu, Finland.

12

Preliminaries for an integration of psychoanalysis and neuroscience

Mark Solms

It is not difficult to understand why the relationship between psychoanalysis and neuroscience should interest us. Psychoanalysis is a science of the mind, and we have known since ancient times that the activities of the mind are in some intimate way connected with the tissues of the brain. This connection was established, from the start, on *clinical* grounds. Physicians through the ages have recognized that diseases of the brain—unlike those of any other organ—had immediate effects on the functions of the mind. The celebrated case of Phineas Gage, which was first reported in 1848, is classically cited in this context. A tamping rod passed through the frontal lobes of his brain, with the following results: "His physical health is good, and I am inclined to say that he has recovered . . . [but] his mind was radically changed, so decidedly that his friends and acquaintances said that he was 'no longer Gage'" (Harlow, 1868).

Observations such as these, which demonstrate that the brain and the personality are inextricable, make it clear that the object of study of psychoanalysis is somehow intrinsically connected with the object of study of neuroscience.

Freud himself recognized this fact in his neurological writings, and he continued to acknowledge it throughout his psychological writings. Nevertheless, psychoanalysis developed almost completely independently of neuroscience. We all know the reason for this: despite the fact that Freud acknowledged that "the mental apparatus . . . is also known to us in the form of an anatomical preparation" (1900a, p. 536), he nevertheless always recommended that psychoanalysts should remain aloof from neuroscience. There seems at first sight to be a contradiction in this stance, but I shall clarify Freud's position in a moment.

The mere fact that psychoanalysis and neuroscience developed separately for so long points to the reality that, notwithstanding the obvious connection between the two fields, there is a great deal that separates them. Leaving aside the philosophical complexities of the mind–body relation for present purposes, it can safely be said that, in practice, psychoanalysis and neuroscience have separate objects of study, that they bring different methods of investigation to bear on these objects, and that the knowledge that they generate is therefore of two distinct types.

This poses obvious problems for those of us who wish to forge links between these two bodies of knowledge, as can be seen from the literature that has begun to accumulate at the interface between them over the past few decades. The first investigator to explore this relationship was, of course, Freud himself. In the mid-1890s he composed a series of drafts on the subject, one of which has survived to this day in the form of a document known to us as the "Project for a Scientific Psychology" (1950 [1895]). In that work Freud attempted to translate what was known at the time about the deeper workings of the mind into the language of neurophysiology and anatomy. The method that Freud employed to achieve this translation was, as he himself acknowledged, one of "imaginings, transpositions and guesses" (Freud, 1954, p. 120). In other words, Freud relied on *speculation*. At that time the gap between the knowledge that Freud had obtained by the putative method of psychoanalytic investigation about the inner workings of the mind and the knowledge that was available to him from physiological and anatomical methods of study about the inner workings of the brain was so great that he had no choice but to fall back on speculation when trying to bridge it. This gap played no small part in Freud's eventual abandonment of his "Project" and his description of it as "a kind of aberration" (Freud, 1950a [1887–1902], p. 134). Ultimately he concluded that "in the end I may have to learn to content myself with the *clinical* explanation of the neuroses" (p. 137, emphasis added; cf. Solms & Saling, 1986). This remark about clinical explanation is pregnant with implications for our science.

It is my contention that the cause of Freud's failure to integrate his clinical findings with the neuroscience of his day was not only the paucity of neuroscientific knowledge that was available to him in the 1890s, but also the absence of a suitable *method* for relating the neurological and psychological data that *was* available. I believe, further, that despite the rapid and exponential increase in our knowledge in all branches of neuroscience, every subsequent attempt to correlate psychoanalytic and neuroscientific knowledge has stumbled on the same basic problem that Freud's did a century ago: namely, the failure to develop a valid method for relating the clinical findings of psychoanalysis with the type of knowledge that is generated by the various neurological sciences. Every investigator who has written on this subject since Freud—despite the brilliance of some of their intuitions—has relied on the same fundamental methodology that Freud did as regards the actual manner in which they correlated the two fields of inquiry—namely, speculation (e.g., Epstein, 1987, 1989, 1995; Erdelyi, 1985; Frick, 1982; Galin, 1974; Hadley, 1983, 1992; Harris, 1986; Hartmann, 1982; Heilbrunn, 1979; Hoskins, 1936; Joseph, 1982, 1992; Kokkou & Leuzinger-Bohleber, 1992; Levin, 1991; Maclean, 1962; McLaughlin, 1978; Meyersburg & Post, 1979; Miller, 1991; Negri, 1994; Olds, 1992; Ostow, 1954, 1955a, 1955b, 1955c, 1956, 1959; Palombo, 1992; Peterfreund, 1971, 1975; Reiser, 1984, 1990; Schilder, 1935; Schore, 1994; Schwartz, 1987, 1988; Stone, 1977; Winson, 1985; Zueler & Maas, 1994).

These are some of the reasons why we are now in a situation, with the sudden increase in publications in this area over the past few years, where we have a number of competing—and, in many respects, contradictory—models of the neurological organization of the deep mental functions we study in psychoanalysis, without having any rational basis for choosing between them. How are we to weigh the rival points of view? I am sure you will agree that we ought to be able to decide such questions; for, if the mind and the brain both function in regular and lawful ways and if those functions and regularities are related to each other in similarly lawful ways—as we have every reason to believe that they are—then it should be possible for us to resolve such questions in ordinary scientific ways.

My primary aim here is to introduce a method by which we can achieve this ordinary scientific task. I intend to do so, first, by relating something about where this method came from; second, how it works; and, third, by reporting very briefly some of the findings that this method is beginning to produce about how the deeper strata of the mind are organized neurologically.

In order to do that, I want first of all to go back into history, to trace the origins of psychoanalysis to a particular branch of neuroscience, and to show how the psychoanalytic method grew out of that branch; then I want to trace subsequent developments in that field in order to show that it still remains the natural point of contact between our two disciplines. In the process, I hope to be able to demonstrate that—just as we find in our clinical work—a problem that seems insolubly complex in its present, mature form frequently turns out to have a relatively simple structure when one traces it back to its origins.

To start at the beginning: Freud began his scientific career as a neuroanatomist, before, following a brief flirtation with psychopharmacology, he turned his attention to the problems of clinical neurology. By the time that Freud came to clinical neurology, it was still a very young discipline that rested almost entirely on a single method—known as *clinico-anatomical correlation*—which was carried over to the new speciality of neurology by some of the ablest practitioners of the art of internal medicine. As its name suggests, internal medicine concerned itself with the diagnosis and treatment of those diseases that, because they occur in the interior of the body, could not be apprehended directly in the living clinical case but, rather, had to be inferred from their indirect manifestations in the form of external symptoms and signs. One had to wait for the death of the patient and the pathologist's report before one could determine conclusively whether or not one's diagnosis had been correct. But with the accumulation of experience over generations regarding what sort of clinical presentation during life tended to correlate with what sort of pathological–anatomical findings at autopsy, it gradually became possible for internal physicians to recognize pathognomonic constellations of symptoms and signs, thereby to predict with reasonable accuracy what the underlying disease process was, and to conduct the treatment accordingly. This was the origin of the concept of clinical *syndromes*.

Neurology became a separate speciality of internal medicine as it became increasingly evident not only that the brain—like any other organ—was subject to its own special pathologies peculiar to its tissues, but also that damage to different parts of the brain produced a wide variety of different clinical manifestations. When Freud trained in clinical neurology in the early 1880s, this was the art that he learned: rational diagnosis and treatment of neurological diseases by the syndrome method, based on knowledge obtained by the method of clinico-anatomical correlation. In fact, we are told (Jones, 1953) that Freud was a particularly gifted practitioner of this art. He published a series of articles at the time attesting to his skill.

Because brain lesions cause mental changes, the clinico-anatomical method could be—and was—also put to another use: the *localization of mental functions.* In the early 1860s, Pierre Paul Broca demonstrated conclusively that disease in a particular part of the brain (marked A in Figure 12.1, p. 200) produced a highly characteristic mental symptom: namely, loss of speech. On the basis of this clinico-anatomical correlation, Broca localized the faculty of speech to that small part of the brain. Ten years later Carl Wernicke demonstrated that damage to a different part of the brain (region B in Figure 12.1) produced a different mental symptom—namely, loss of the capacity to *understand* spoken language—and he, too, localized that function accordingly. These two seminal discoveries were followed by a rapid series of clinico-anatomical correlations with regard to a variety of other mental functions, such as skilled movement, object recognition, and even "intelligence". On this basis a wide range of psychological faculties were localized within a mosaic of so-called centres on the surface of the hemispheres of the brain. This was the origin of a sub-speciality within the neurological sciences known as *behavioural neurology.*

We know from Freud's writings of that time that he was thoroughly versed in the methods and discoveries of this exciting new branch of science. In fact, there is abundant evidence to suggest that the clinico-anatomical localization of mental functions was a subject of special interest to him (Freud, 1888, 1891b, 1893–94). Clearly, then, Freud was aware, before he conceived of psychoanalysis, that there was a well-established method by which it was possible to correlate mental functions on a clinical basis with the functions of particular parts of the brain. But if that was the case, it raises the question of why Freud did not use this method to identify the neurological correlates of the psychological processes that he later discovered, and why we do not use it for that purpose today.

He was an unusually gifted physician, so it did not take Freud long to master the syndrome method in his diagnostic work and the clinico-anatomical method in his ongoing research. Nor did it take him long to discover the limits of this method: he soon came to the conclusion that it was, as he put it, just "a silly game of permutations" (Bernfeld, 1951, p. 214). Although it is true that the clinico-anatomical method was the only viable research technique available to the nineteenth-century neurologist interested in mental functions, it was, in fact, used in subtly different ways by two rival schools of neurology. In the Austro–German school, within which Freud was initially trained, the emphasis fell squarely on the *anatomical* side of the clinico–anatomical equation. They held that the primary aim of neurological science was not simply to recognize which syndromes correlated with which lesions but, rather, to *explain the mechanism* of the clinical phenomena—and thereby the corresponding normal mental functions—in anatomical and physiological terms. This approach reflected the broader ideals of the Helmholtz school of medicine. In the rival French school of neurology, on the other hand, the emphasis fell very much on the *clinical* side of the clinico-anatomical equation. According to this school, which collected around the personality of Charcot and the famous wards of the Salpêtrière Hospital, the primary task of neurological science was not so much to explain the various clinical pictures but, rather, to identify, classify, and *describe* them. The following quotation graphically illustrates the difference between these two ways of applying the clinico-anatomical method:

> Charcot . . . never tired of defending the rights of purely clinical work, which consists in seeing and ordering things, against the encroachments of theoretical medicine. On one occasion there was a small group of us, all students from abroad, who, brought up on German academic physiology, were trying his patience with our doubts about his clinical innovations. "But that can't be true," one of us objected, "it contradicts the Young–Helmholtz theory [of vision]." He did not reply "so much the worse for the theory, clinical facts come first" or words to that effect; but he did say something which made a great impression on us: "Theory is

> good; but it doesn't prevent things from existing." [Freud, 1893f, p. 13]

This was one of Freud's favourite anecdotes.

As is well known, during his period of study at the Salpêtrière in the mid-1880s, Freud moved from being under the direct personal influence of some of the leading figures of the Austro–German school of neurology to being under that of Charcot. This shift had a decisive influence on his thinking and, in particular, on his attitude to clinico-anatomical localization.

The reason for this shift was simple. Although the differences between the German and French schools of neurology—with the former emphasizing the anatomical and the latter the clinical side of the equation—complemented each other well with regard to most physical neurological disorders, one group of diseases—considered in the domain of neurology at the time—threw the differences between the two approaches into sharp relief. These were the neuroses, and hysteria and neurasthenia in particular, where no demonstrable lesion of the nervous system could be found at autopsy to account for the clinical symptomatology observed during the life of the patient. This posed no serious problems for the French school: Charcot simply proceeded to describe the pathognomonic clinical syndromes of hysteria and neurasthenia as he had done with countless other "nervous" diseases. As Freud wrote at the time, the neuroses were, for Charcot, "just another topic in neuropathology" (Freud 1893f, p. 20). For the German school of neurologists, on the other hand, the problem was well-nigh insoluble. How was one to explain in anatomical and physiological terms the mechanism of a clinical syndrome that had no pathological–anatomical basis? As a result, some German neurologists—Freud's teachers among them—developed elaborate speculative theories, while others simply declared that the neuroses were not fit subjects for serious scientific attention; if there was no anatomical lesion, there was no clinical syndrome.

During the crucial period that Freud studied under Charcot, this was the subject that most preoccupied him. Initially Freud became a devoted pupil of Charcot, and upon his return to Vienna he expounded his views whenever and wherever he could, much to the irritation of his old teachers. However, with increasing clinical experience and under the influence of the English neurologist John Hughlings Jackson, Freud gradually began to edge away from Charcot and to develop a viewpoint that was rather unique at the time. Charcot was content merely to describe the clinical syndromes of hysteria and neurasthenia, on the assumption that their pathological–anatomical correlates (which he believed to have a hereditary aetiology) would eventually yield to advances in micro-anatomical and other laboratory techniques. Freud, on the contrary, came to the view, at some point between 1887 and 1893, that an understanding of these clinical syndromes would never be found in pathological anatomy, or at least not via the method of clinico-anatomical correlation. He based this conclusion on two major observations that he had first made in connection with another subject in neurology, a subject that had revealed to him the limits of the clinico-anatomical method. This subject was the problem of aphasia—that is, precisely the subject to which the clinico-anatomical method had first been applied for the localization of mental functions by Broca and Wernicke some 20 or so years earlier.

Freud's critical observations were the following (Freud 1891b). He noted, first, that psychological faculties are complicated, with their own compound organization, and that they break down according to the functional logic of their own internal construction, not according to the laws of cerebral anatomy. The laws of psychological functional systems need not, therefore, have any direct relationship to the structural layout of the nervous system. For this reason, Freud concluded, psychological syndromes need both to be described and to be explained in their own psychological terms. Freud's second observation, closely related to the first, was that psychological functions are, in their essence, dynamic processes; they arise out of a complex interplay of forces between more elementary component functions, and they are constantly re-structuring and re-adapting themselves to changing circumstances. Their physiological correlates can, therefore, never be localized within discrete anatomical centres: they must be thought of as processes—the dynamic resultants of interactions between the static elements of the nervous system.

It is of crucial importance for us to note that Freud first made these observations, not with reference to hysteria or any other neurosis, but, rather, in a study of aphasia—a syndrome that can only ever occur in the context of a definite brain lesion. In other words, these were conclusions that Freud arrived at while he was still a fully fledged neurologist. This is underlined by the fact that he quickly went on to make similar observations with regard to non-psychological but equally complex functions of the brain. In his writings on the disorders of voluntary movement that occur in cerebral palsy, for example, Freud went out of his way to demonstrate that they could not be localized. In a series of monographs on the subject (1891a, 1893b, 1897), as in his book on aphasia (1891b), Freud appealed to dynamic developmental factors rather than static anatomical ones to explain the various movement disorders in terms of specific breakdowns of the complex functional system that supports them.

It was only later—between 1893 and 1900—that Freud applied these principles to psychopathology—and so psychoanalysis was born. This is a fact of critical importance, because these principles were subsequently developed and expanded within the field of neurology, and a neuroscientific method for studying the cerebral organization of mental functions was eventually established on precisely these principles. That is obviously of central importance to us in our quest for a method by which we may rejoin psychoanalysis with neuroscience.

Freud trained in the clinico-anatomical method of localizing mental functions within the Austro–German school of neurology, which emphasized the goal of physiological and anatomical explanation. Then he shifted allegiances to the French school, which emphasized the clinical side of the equation: the elucidation of pathognomonic clinical syndromes. He used this clinical-descriptive approach to make a number of highly valued contributions to neurology, in studies first of aphasia, then of cerebral palsy, and, lastly, of neuroses. In the process of doing this work, Freud rejected the clinico-anatomical method of localizing mental functions—indeed, of localizing any complex functions within circumscribed anatomical centres. He was forced to conclude that the clinico-anatomical method could only be used to localize the most elementary functions, corresponding in the mental sphere to our primary sensory modalities—of vision, hearing, taste, and so on—but that it was quite impossible to localize the neurological organization of whole mental faculties with supra-ordinate principles of organization, based on their own internal construction, which constantly changes in the process of their development and in their adaptation to unfolding circumstances. For Freud, such complex functions arose out of the dynamic interplay of a variety of more elementary functions. He concluded that we should conceive of this interplay as occurring *between* the elementary structures of the brain and therefore forego the temptation to localize them *within* those elements themselves. It was obvious to Freud, schooled as he was in the art of meticulous clinical observation, that the essential factors in the aetiology and mechanism of the neuroses arose out of complex functional dynamics of this kind and that they could therefore never be localized. This led Freud *the neurologist* to generalize the conclusions that he had reached with regard to speech and language and voluntary movement to the whole mental field and to write the following fateful words, in *The Interpretation of Dreams,* which marked the final split between psychoanalysis and the clinico-anatomical method:

> I shall entirely disregard the fact that the mental apparatus with which we are here concerned is also known to us in the form of an anatomical preparation, and I shall carefully avoid the temptation to determine psychical locality in any anatomical fashion. I shall remain upon purely psychological ground, and I propose simply to follow the suggestion that we picture the instrument which carries out our mental functions as resembling a compound microscope or a photographic apparatus, or something of the kind. On that basis, psychical locality will correspond to a point inside the apparatus at which one of the preliminary stages of an image comes into being. In the microscope or telescope, as we know, these occur at ideal points, regions in which no tangible component of the apparatus is situated. [1900a, p. 536]

What Freud retained, however, and carried over into the new field of psychoanalysis, was almost everything else that he had learned as a neurologist—that is, he continued to rely on the clinical–descriptive method of the French school of neuropathology, with its special emphasis on the careful study of the individual clinical case and the identification of regular patterns of symptoms and signs with particular pathological significance; he continued to explain the clinical phenomena in terms of underlying natural forces and energies, as he had been taught to do by his original masters in the Helmholtz school of medicine; and he continued to believe that these forces and energies were ultimately somehow describable in physical and chemical terms. All that he abandoned was the notion that psychological processes, which have complex and dynamic functional organizations, can be localized in discrete anatomical areas. Henceforth, rather than attempting to explain a clinical syndrome by correlating it with hypothetical damage to one or another anatomical region, as even Charcot did, Freud investigated the internal psychological structure of the syndrome and explained it by reference to a complex *functional system*, which he assumed to be *dynamically* represented between the elements of the brain.

That is why Freud continued to acknowledge throughout his scientific life that the model of the mental apparatus that he devised to account for his clinical observations was a provisional construct, a system of functional relations that must be represented *somehow* in the tissues of the brain, and that is why he continued to insist that we in psychoanalysis should "not mistake the scaffolding for the building", and so on. While Freud made many comments to the effect that psychoanalysis will someday be rejoined with neuroscience, he always insisted that this would not be possible until neuroscience developed a method that was capable of accommodating the complex, distributed, dynamic nature of the human mental process. As he wrote in the year of his death:

> The psychical topography that I have developed . . . has nothing to do with the anatomy of the brain, and actually only touches it at one point. [He is referring to the primary sensory modalities of the system *Pcpt.*] What is unsatisfactory in this picture—and I am aware of it as clearly as anyone—is due to our complete ignorance of the *dynamic* nature of the mental process. [Freud, 1939a (1937–39), p. 97; emphasis added]

Until that was understood, Freud insisted, psychoanalysis should continue to investigate and understand the functional organization of the mental apparatus in its own terms, using a purely clinical method, disregarding its anatomical representation.

This situates psychoanalysis in a very particular relationship to the neurological sciences. It places its fundamental assumptions and basic method within a well-established tradition in behavioural neurology, a tradition that has always been closely associated with the clinical–descriptive emphasis first promulgated by Charcot and has always rejected the notion, following Hughlings Jackson, that complex mental faculties can be concretely localized in the brain: this is the *dynamic school of neurology* that has been associated through the years with such outstanding physicians and theoreticians as Constantin von Monakow, Pierre Marie, Henry Head, Kurt Goldstein, Aleksandr Romanovich Luria, and, most recently, Jason Brown.

The influence of this branch of neuroscience has waxed and waned over the decades. Currently it is increasing enormously as functional imagery and computer simulation studies have revealed the fundamentally non-localizable and dynamic, "parallel distributed processing" that underlies all mental functioning and, indeed, all complex functions of the brain. The *clinical* emphasis of this branch of neuroscience, on the other hand, is on the wane; with the enormous strides that have been made in the use of technological auxiliary aids in medicine, the art of clinical judgement is no longer so highly valued, and the human factor in medicine is being lost. Indeed, one could say that, ironically, psychoanalysis stands together with this branch of neurology as one of the last outposts of the great clinical traditions of internal medicine.

But the important point for our purposes—looking forward rather than backward—is that Freud carried over from neurology into psychoanalysis a basic method—namely, the clinical–descriptive method, or the method of syndrome analysis, as it later came to be known—and a basic conceptualization of brain–behaviour relationships, the anti-localizationist or dynamic conceptualization that gives pride of place to psychological methods of analysing mental syndromes, regardless of whether or not those symptoms have an organic basis. This method and these basic principles have determined the object of study of psychoanalysis, the way we go about studying it, and, most important of all, the sort of knowledge that psychoanalysis generates.

Now, if we wish to integrate knowledge of this sort with knowledge about the brain, then our natural point of contact is with that branch of neuroscience which shares our basic assumptions and out of which psychoanalysis grew—that is, the dynamic school of behavioural neurology, or *neuropsychology*, as it later came to be known. If we try to relate our clinically generated psychoanalytic knowledge with knowledge about the brain generated by fundamentally incompatible methods, or by methods that Freud explicitly rejected, then we are not only confronted by the insoluble problem of having to rely on speculation, but we also have to recognize that we may be doing violence to the basic premises upon which our discipline was built. This was always Freud's most fundamental viewpoint on the matter: that there is little point in rejoining psychoanalysis with neuroscience if it means that in the process we have to abandon all that psychoanalysis stands for.

There has been a major development since Freud's death in the branch of neuroscience out of which psychoanalysis arose that, I believe, provides us with a method by which we can rejoin psychoanalysis with neuroscience in a way that is compatible with Freud's basic assumptions.

During the early 1920s, a young Russian psychologist, Aleksandr Romanovich Luria, wrote to Freud to apply for formal recognition of a new psychoanalytic society he had formed in the Eastern Russian city of Kazan. Freud granted the recognition, and a brief correspondence ensued. A few years later Luria moved to Moscow and joined the Russian Psychoanalytical Society. Over a period of about ten years, Luria conducted a wide range of psychoanalytic research, published a huge number of articles, monographs, and brief reports, and conducted clinical work in a local psychiatric hospital including—it is rumoured—the analysis of Dostoyevsky's granddaughter. Luria was drawn to psychoanalysis, he wrote, because it was the only branch of psychology that was solidly rooted in natural science and studied the living experience of real human beings.

However, the tide of political opinion soon turned against psychoanalysis in the Soviet Union, and by the early 1930s, fearing for his academic future, if not his life, Luria resigned from the Russian Psychoanalytical Society, abruptly ceased all psychoanalytic activities, and delivered a penitent speech in which he admitted to his ideological mistakes—namely, according to the Party line of that time, that psychoanalysis "biologized" human behaviour and ignored its social origins. This was a surprisingly naive remark coming from somebody with so complex an understanding of Freud's teachings, but that was not the point. Interestingly, there is evidence to demonstrate that Luria never gave up his private interest in psychoanalysis, whatever his public pronouncements. For example, in a letter he wrote to Oliver Sacks in the mid-1970s, Luria described the verbal tics of a patient with Gilles de la Tourette's syndrome as an introjection into the superego of the father's punitive voice (Oliver Sacks, personal communication, 17 March 1987).

It is also very striking, in view of the charge that psychoanalysis biologized human behaviour, to observe what Luria did next (after resigning from the Psychoanalytical Society). He went to medical school, specialized in neurology, and then immediately set about studying the mental symptoms of his neurological patients. And his first piece of research in this field—his doctoral thesis, in fact—was on precisely the same subject that had been preoccupying Freud when he had left that field some 40 years earlier: that is, the subject of aphasia.

When Luria finally published the results of his efforts in 1947, in a monograph in which he scrupulously avoided the name of Freud, he proposed a theory of the cerebral representation of language that was remarkably similar to the one that Freud had proposed in 1891 (Luria, 1970). Without going into the details here, a striking similarity can be noted between Freud's suggestion that we view the mind as a complex optical instrument in which psychic locality corresponds to an ideal point in which no tangible component of the apparatus is situated, and the following statement by Luria: "all attempts to postulate that . . . ideas could be found in single units of the brain were as unrealistic as trying to find an image inside a mirror or behind it" (1987, p. 489). However, Luria went a step further than Freud, and this represented the essential advance that he contributed to behavioural neurology, or neuropsychology, as he preferred to call it.

Luria described his approach as a "neurodynamic" one, and he used the following analogy to illustrate the principle:

> Most investigators who have examined the problem of cortical localisation have understood the term function to mean the "function of a particular tissue". . . . It is perfectly natural to consider that the secretion of bile is a function of the liver and the secretion of insulin is a function of the pancreas. It is equally logical to regard the perception of light as a function of the photosensitive elements of the retina and the highly specialised neurons of the visual cortex connected with them. [This was the type of function that Freud believed could be localized.] However, this definition does not meet every use of the term function. When we speak of the "function of respiration," this clearly cannot be understood as the function of a particular tissue. The ultimate object of respiration is to supply oxygen to the alveoli of the lungs to diffuse it through the walls of the alveoli into the blood. The whole process is carried out, not as a simple function of a particular tissue, but rather as a complete functional system, embodying many components belonging to different levels of the secretory, motor, and nervous apparatus. Such a "functional system" . . . differs not only in the complexity of its structure but also in the mobility of its component parts. [Luria, 1973, p. 27]

The same could be said of, for example, the function of digestion. Luria went on to argue that mental functions, too, can only be localized in this distributed, dynamic sense. For the purpose of identifying the different component parts that together make up the complex functional systems of the human mental apparatus, Luria devised a new method of clinico-anatomical correlation known as "dynamic localization". If one wishes to identify the neurological organization of a complex psychological function, one's first task is to find all the different ways in which that function breaks down with focal neurological disease in different parts of the brain; Luria described this first step as "qualification of the symptoms". One starts with each of the different ways in which the function under study breaks down and then carefully explores the psychological structure of each of these symptoms, identifying precisely in what way the functional system has collapsed in each case. This is done by using psychological methods of analysis in individual clinical cases.

The second step in Luria's method is called "syndrome analysis": one examines what other functions, apart from the primary function under scrutiny, are disturbed in each case. Again relying exclusively on psychological methods of investigation, one seeks to clarify the internal structure of these other, interconnected symptoms in order to learn what they have in common with the function that is the primary focus of attention. In this way a single underlying factor that can account for the full range of surface clinical manifestations can be identified.

Once one has identified the common underlying factor producing a range of psychological symptoms, one will have not only learned something about the deep psychological structure of the syndrome in question, but also identified the component function that is contributed by the part of the brain that is damaged in that syndrome—in other words, the elementary psychological function of one particular part of the brain. This is a major advance.

Once one has studied, by this method, the full series of different ways in which a complex psychological faculty breaks down with damage to each part of the brain, then one will have discovered its distributed neurological organization by identifying the parts of the brain that contribute to the complex functional system subserving that faculty as a whole and the way they do so. One will not have localized that faculty in any one part of the brain, but one will have identified the various component elements between which, by dynamic functional interaction, that psychological faculty is represented.

To my mind, this method of Luria's marks a major step forward, because it enables us to identify the neurological organization of any mental function, no matter how complex, without contradicting the fundamental assumptions upon which our own discipline was built. By this method, complex psychological functions are still understood in their own psychological terms; their dynamic nature is respected theoretically and accommodated methodologically; they are not reduced to anatomy and physiology, although their neurological distribution is laid bare; and something new is learned about their internal functional organization. As a result, a viable bridge is established between the concepts of psychology and those of anatomy and physiology and all the other branches of neurological science.

The neuropsychological method of syndrome analysis is really very simple, but I truly believe that it represents the breakthrough that Freud was waiting for: that is to say, it enables us to chart the neurological organization of everything that we in psychoanalysis know about the structures and functions of the mind.

A piece of research into the neurological organization of a mental function that is of special interest to psychoanalysis—namely, the function of dreaming (Solms, 1997)—demonstrates how this method, which, I am claiming, is the natural point of contact between psychoanalysis and neuroscience, works in practice.

Using Luria's method to study the dreams of 361 patients with neurological lesions, this research revealed that dreaming is disturbed by damage to six different parts of the brain (marked C, E, F, G, H, and J in Figure 12.1).

If the brain is damaged in regions C, E, or F—that is, in the mediobasal frontal region, or the inferior parietal region of either hemisphere—then the conscious experience of dreaming stops completely, indicating that the basic functions contributed by these three parts of the brain are fundamental to the whole process of dreaming, for when any one of them is damaged, the manifest dream is obliterated entirely. Why that should be the case is revealed through an analysis of the psychological syndrome within which the loss of dreaming is embedded.

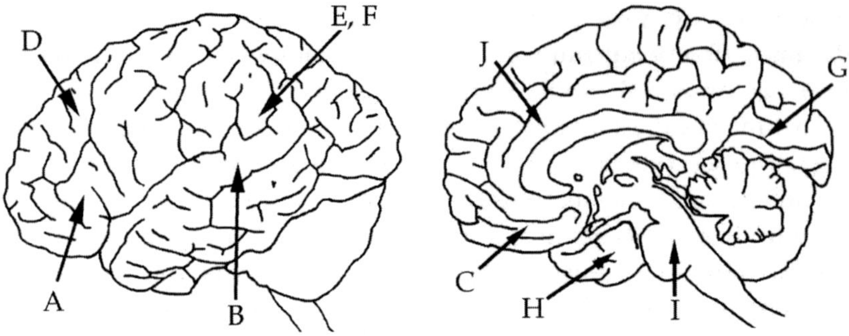

Figure 12.1. Lateral surface and medial section of the brain

Lateral surface (left panel). A: Broca's area; B: Wernicke's area; D: dorso-lateral frontal convexity; E, F: inferior parietal regions (E and F refer to the same part of the brain but on opposite hemispheres).

Medial section (right panel). C: mediobasal frontal region; G: ventral occipito-temporal region; H: temporal-limbic region; I: core brainstem region; J: frontal-limbic region.

If the brain is damaged in region G—that is, in the ventral occipito-temporal region—then the conscious experience of dreaming persists, but the patient's dreams are devoid of any visual imagery. Strange as it may seem, patients with damage to this part of the brain have completely non-visual dreams. (Cases have also been described in which only selected aspects of visual imagery are disturbed, such as, for example, colour imagery.)

If, on the other hand, damage is situated in the proximity of region H—that is, in the temporal-limbic region—and if the lesion is accompanied by a discharging focus (that is, by seizure activity), then the patient experiences recurring, stereotyped nightmares. These nightmares stop if the seizure disorder is brought under control.

Finally, if the damage is situated in region J—that is, in the frontal-limbic region—then patients experience a massive increase in the frequency of dreaming, or sometimes continual dreaming, and they have great difficulty in distinguishing between dreams and real experiences.

These symptoms, therefore, qualify the different ways in which dreaming can be disrupted by damage to the human brain. In order to discover what the cause of the breakdown of dreaming is in each of these six instances, it is necessary to study the constellation of other psychological symptoms that accompany the changes in dreaming following damage to each of these areas. This enables the investigator to isolate the elementary underlying factor that is common to all of these symptoms and is, therefore, contributed to the overall process of dreaming by the part of the brain in question.

So what are the six elementary factors that are contributed by each of these parts of the brain? Unfortunately, a description of the full richness of the psychological syndromes from which we have inferred these underlying factors is not possible in the confines of this chapter. Oversimplifying things somewhat for expository purposes, I can only say that an analysis of the psychological syndromes associated with lesions to the six areas of the brain concerned reveals the following basic factors: region C contributes a general motivational factor to mental functioning, region E a factor of quasi-spatial synthesis that is fundamental for symbolic mental operations, region F a factor of concrete spatial representation, region G a factor of revisualization that is essential for visual mental imagery, region H an emotional arousal factor, and region J a factor of selectivity, or of selective activation and inhibition, which is essential for processes such as attention, reality-testing, and judgement.

These six factors together, therefore, make up the functional system of dreaming—or, to put it differently, the process of dreaming arises out of a dynamic interaction between these six factors, which are contributed by six parts of the brain. An analysis of the special structural and functional properties of these six different brain regions, and of the dynamic relations between them, provides a basic scientific understanding of the anatomy and physiology of dreaming.

Finally, in order to arrive at a truly comprehensive account of the neurological organization of dreaming, it is also necessary to study the component functions of those regions of the brain that do *not* appear to be involved in the process of dreaming. This, simultaneously, reveals which elementary functions of the human mental apparatus are not involved in the psychological construction of dreams. Of these regions, two are of particular interest here.

Although damage to the core brainstem region, I, does severely disrupt the process of REM sleep, the conscious experience of dreaming persists in these patients, suggesting an unexpected dissociation between the physiological process of REM sleep and the conscious experience of dreams (Solms, 2000). This dissociation is confirmed by the fact that lesions in regions C, E, and F, which lead to a complete cessation of the conscious experience of dreaming, have no effect upon the physiological phenomena of REM sleep.

Region D—the dorso-lateral frontal convexity—is enormously important for the executive control of waking mental life and of voluntary motor activity. However, damage to this region has no effect at all on the conscious experience of dreams, suggesting, not surprisingly, that secondary-process thinking and volitional motor activity have very little to do with the process of dreaming.

Considering these factors together, a model of how the dynamic process of dreaming as a whole is organized in the tissues of the brain begins to emerge. On the basis of this research, I have proposed the following model, every detail of which is accessible to empirical verification by a variety of neuroscientific methods.

It appears that dreaming is stimulated by an arousal process. The most common of these is the state of neurophysiological activation—REM sleep—which occurs regularly every 90 minutes and is activated by the deep brainstem structures of region I. However, this is only one of the many arousal phenomena that may trigger the process of dreaming and it is by no means the essential one, for dreaming occurs quite normally without it. Another arousal process that can stimulate a dream is a focal discharge in the temporal-limbic region, H; this, however, being pathological, cannot be bound by the dream process and hence results in anxiety dreams or nightmares.

Another important component of the dream process is contributed by region C, which motivates appetitive interest ("libidinal interest") and channels endogenous arousal processes in the direction of volitional motor activity. An arousing stimulus only triggers the dream work proper if it engages this quasi-libidinal brain mechanism. Parts of region C also inhibit appetitive drives, and therefore, together with the selective structures of region J, they deflect the arousal process away from the executive and motor systems (D). These latter regions are inhibited during sleep, but if the brain is damaged in regions C and J, it seems that the inhibition of these motor systems breaks down, with the result that goal-directed motor activity is instituted and normal dreaming becomes impossible. This conceptualization of the process is supported by the fact that patients with damage to this region of the brain experience disturbed sleep. If the brain is damaged in region J, however, then the disturbance of inhibition is only partial, with the paradoxical result that there is an increase in dreaming and in dream-like thinking.

Next, assuming that there is a sufficient degree of frontal inhibition, the focus of the nocturnal arousal process shifts to the posterior systems of the brain, which regulate perceptual functions, and the higher spatial and symbolic operations that are based upon perception (regions E, F, and G). This, then, becomes the primary "scene of action" of the manifest dream, and it is here that the three other factors—symbolization (region E), spatial thinking (region F), and visual mental imagery (region G)—come into play. Among these, it appears that symbolization and spatial thinking play the most important role, for in their absence dreaming again becomes impossible, and the whole process breaks down. Visual mental imagery is a less important factor: the entire mental process of dreaming runs its course without it, the only difference being that the final conscious product is devoid of visual imagery. I am therefore inclined to place this factor of visual representation at the terminal end of the process of dream generation.

This overall picture suggests that dreaming is a regressive mental process, both triggered by and dependent on nocturnal states of arousal. These states are channelled and inhibited by the systems controlling goal-directed behaviour. They are deflected away from the motor systems, towards the perceptual systems. The higher perceptual systems represent the arousal process in the form of symbolic and spatial syntheses, which are projected regressively onto the lower visual zones, thus preserving the state of sleep. If, however, the nocturnal arousal process is excessive, such as occurs with seizures or defective frontal inhibition, then this sleep-protection mechanism fails, and the dreamer is disturbed, either by anxiety or by the innervation of volitional motor activity.

What Luria's method reveals about the neurological organization of dreaming is, therefore, strikingly compatible with Freud's classical theory. Also, because of the centrality of dreaming in Freud's models of the mind, it provides us with a first foothold on the anatomical and physiological representation of some crucial psychoanalytic concepts, including aspects of the libido, censorship, symbolization, topographic regression, and so on. Moreover, by identifying the specific tissues of the brain that are involved in the different psychological components of dreaming, it becomes possible to study the finer anatomical, physiological, and chemical correlates of that theory.

For example, closer analysis of the anatomical data reveals that the structures in region C that are crucial for the generation of dreams are the basal forebrain fibre pathways that connect midbrain dopaminergic nuclei with mediobasal frontal cortex (the mesocortical–mesolimbic dopaminergic pathway). This suggests that whatever this fibre pathway does is critical for the function of dreaming. These are precisely the fibres that were targeted by the modified prefrontal leucotomy procedure that was so popular in the 1950s, and there is evidence to suggest that modern antipsychotic medications act on this same pathway (Breggin, 1980). A review of the older psychosurgical literature reveals that cessation of dreaming was a common consequence of prefrontal leucotomy (Solms, 1997). Evidently, whatever it was that prevented leucotomized patients from sustaining their psychotic symptoms also prevented them from generating dreams. I am unaware of any research into the effects of modern antipsychotic medications on dreaming. However, there is evidence that dopamine agonists in general (e.g. L-dopa) stimulate excessive dreaming and that dopamine antagonists (e.g. haloperidol) suppress it (Sacks, 1985, 1990, 1991). If we review classical dream theory in the light of these findings, we have an empirical basis for linking the libidinal drive—or important manifestations thereof—with mesocortical–mesolimbic dopaminergic pathways. It is therefore not without interest that contemporary neuroscientists include these pathways in the "curiosity–interest–expectancy command systems of the brain . . . which instigate goal-seeking behaviours and an organism's appetitive interactions with the world" (Panksepp, 1985, p. 273).

The method of dynamic localization, therefore, provides psychoanalysis with a conceptual gateway to the basic neurosciences and thereby to the enormous advances in knowledge yielded in recent years by technological innovations in those fields. The potential benefits to psychoanalysis are so obvious that I need hardly enumerate them.

This brief, oversimplified example serves to illustrate how human mental functions are represented in the tissues of the brain in the form of complex functional systems that arise out of dynamic interactions between a number of elementary component parts, in the same way as an image arises out of a compound optical instrument, as Freud suggested in *The Interpretation of Dreams* (1900a). It also demonstrates that the method of syndrome analysis makes it possible to identify the component parts of the brain between which a complex mental function is distributed, and it shows the elementary contribution that each of those parts makes to the functional system as a whole. This is the scientific yield of the method that we have developed in neuropsychology over the past 60 years since the death of Freud.

Nevertheless, the research just described studied only the manifest dream process—in other words, the effects of damage to different parts of the brain upon the conscious experience of dreaming. It had to infer the underlying unconscious mechanisms from the manifest symptoms, because we cannot lay bare the unconscious structure of a psychological syndrome by examining a neurological patient at the bedside, and still less by assessing people in a neuropsychological laboratory. In order to gain more direct access to these deeper mental strata of a patient—whether or not that person has a brain lesion—we need to get to know the patient as a person within an analytic relationship in a reliable professional setting, within which we can win their confidence through tact and understanding, by analysing their resistances and then unhurriedly observing the way in which the internal determinants of the symptoms gradually unfold in the transference, and by testing the hypotheses that occur to us in this regard in the form of appropriate interpretations and observing the effects that these have upon the subsequent analytic material, and so on. In other words, we can only properly elucidate the dynamically unconscious structure of a mental symptom by means of the psychoanalytic method.

This may not be the easiest way to study a psychological syndrome, but it is the only true and reliable method when it comes to those deeper aspects of mental life that neuropsychology has left unstudied but that have always been of central concern to us in psychoanalysis: namely, the dynamically unconscious structure of the human personality. In fact, the emotional resistances that conceal the internal structures of the personality probably explain why the neurological organization of these, the most important aspects by far of human mental life, have still not been systematically explored by the method of syndrome analysis. This is the scientific contribution that I believe psychoanalysis can make to neuroscience, and this is the next step that I believe we must now take.

Ironically, we owe the development of a clinical procedure for analysing these deeper mental strata to the fact that Freud abandoned neuroscientific methods of investigation when he realized that they were—at that time—unable to accommodate the dynamic nature of human mental processes. Now, it seems, the time has come for us to re-introduce the fruits of his labours to the neuroscientific field out of which they originally grew.

What I am recommending, therefore, as I believe it will provide the essential cornerstone for a lasting integration of psychoanalysis and neuroscience, is a fully psychoanalytic investigation of patients with focal neurological lesions—in other words, charting the neurological organization of the deepest strata of the mind using a psychoanalytic version of syndrome analysis, by studying, within a psychoanalytic relationship, the deep structure of the mental changes that can be discerned in neurological patients.

Some years ago my wife and colleague, Karen Kaplan-Solms, and I began a study using precisely these methods (Kaplan-Solms & Solms, 2000). So far, we have studied the subjective life of 35 patients with focal brain lesions by taking them into psychoanalysis or psychoanalytic therapy, and colleagues in America, Austria, Sweden, and Germany are beginning to undertake similar studies. This research is starting to reveal the neurological organization of those deeper functional systems that can only be reached via the psychoanalytic method of investigation, showing not only that it is now possible, using the methods that I have described, to elucidate the neurological organization of the deepest mental functions that we have traditionally studied in psychoanalysis using purely psychopathological material, but also that this is a worthwhile way to proceed. In doing so, although I do not wish to underestimate the enormity of the task before us, I believe that we will be able to gradually integrate psychoanalysis and neuroscience, on a solid clinical basis, in a way that is beneficial to both fields, without ignoring any of the valuable lessons that the pioneers of psychoanalysis fought so long and hard to learn.

13

Two pathways towards knowing psychoanalytic process

Norbert Freedman, Richard Lasky, & Marvin Hurvich

At a 1996 meeting of the House of Delegates of the IPA, the issue of the appropriate database for defining analytic process was debated within the Committee on Analytic Specificity. The question was: "What is specific about the nature and consequences of analytic process?" In spite of wide theoretical divergences, the group agreed fairly readily on a broad outline.

What had at first seemed to be incompatible views were reshaped into a position statement that included four points: (1) any effort at validation must be rooted in the history of psychoanalytic clinical thought; (2) the evaluation of process should originate in the subjective and intuitive judgement of the engaged and experiencing analyst; (3) evaluation should be corroborated by consultants using the time-honoured methods of peer review and supervision; and (4) only then would these essentially clinical procedures receive external validity through the study of recorded texts. This ideal prescription was accepted by the house. These recommendations were internalized and incorporated into our IPTAR Research Program.

From the IPTAR Program of Research in Psychoanalysis, New York City.

With this in mind, we addressed the question, "Can psychoanalytic process be defined empirically?" with a design we have called "sequential specification". This approach is documented in our evaluation of the recorded psychoanalysis of Mrs P, a married woman with two children. The ensuing material is based on 54 sessions from the third year of analysis.

A vision of psychoanalytic process: oscillation between integration and destabilization

No study of analytic process can be carried out without the prior statement of one's theoretical frame. We have been guided by the hypothesis that process always involves variations in the organization of psychic structure. It is based on the view that controlled regression, the ability of the working ego to tolerate unmanageable tension states, is a precondition for assimilating experiences not previously held in consciousness. More specifically, we have pursued the notion that psychoanalytic process entails "transformation cycles": recurrent shifts in mental organization within sessions, between sessions, or within phases in the course of analytic treatment.

Process, then, always entails variability. It does not take place in stasis but in the encounter with novel mental forces. At points of polarization it assumes the shape of clusters. In the literature, we can find many types of polarization. Here we focus on one, to us, crucial form: namely, the contrast between integration and destabilization.

We have chosen the abstract terms "*A*" and "*Z*" to designate the polarities of "integration" and "destabilization", respectively. These abstract terms were selected for two reasons: (1) because the opposite of integration suggests more than only destabilization (and the opposite of destabilization also suggests more); and (2) so as to avoid an evaluative designation—that is, so *A* or *Z* do not simply mean "good" or "bad". To be sure, a clinical course marked by redundancy, by only *A* or only by *Z*, must be clinically unproductive. However, rhythmic alternation of *A* and *Z* may well be the condition through which psychic work proceeds. Furthermore, *A* and *Z* are not independent psychic entities: they are always reciprocally dependent upon each other, for *A* tends to rely upon *Z* and *Z* may well be embedded in *A*.

In much of the material that follows, we hope to show that a psychoanalytic process is defined by the alternation of *A* qualities and *Z* qualities—within sessions, between sessions, and within phases of the course of psychoanalytic treatment. This view advances the concepts of integration and destabilization as organizing constructs.

The method of sequential specification: from immediacy of clinical experience to objective confirmation

Sequential specification appears to be the appropriate term for our project, which aims at capturing the specificity of analytic work. Our procedures start with the basic database: recorded treatment sessions conducted within the frame of the psychoanalytic method. The inquiry then moves systematically from intuitive observations (Pass 1), to confirmation (Pass 2), to specification and contextualization (Pass 3), and then to external validation (Pass 4). It is a method in which a single session undergoes evaluation through those four successive passes.

Pass 1: Capturing the immediacy of the session—the clinical scan. The analyst (on tape) describes the session: "The patient was extremely anxious at first, she saw her dilemma, and I sensed what she wanted from me, I felt I knew her . . ." or "The session didn't seem to go anywhere; the material was chaotic, I felt attacked and irrelevant."

These are the kinds of thoughts and feelings that may permeate an analyst's consciousness just after the patient has left the room. These five-minute reflections by the analyst become the subject for translation and interpretation, pointing to the presence of *A* and *Z* valences.

Pass 2: Inside the analytic session. Was it really an *A* session, or a *Z* session, as described by the analyst? This is our query as we appraise the impressions gathered by the initial clinical scan. At this point, two consultants working independently listen to and read the transcripts of the recorded session. They immerse themselves in the matrix of feelings, actions, and interactions and then seek to determine whether, from their perspective, this is an *A* or a *Z* session. This is the next move towards specificity.

Pass 3: Specifying changes in mental functioning. Once more two consultants listen to and read the entire session, this time working together. They listen much the way a supervisor might—on the lookout for shifts in mental functioning. In this pass we seek to affect the transition, from the fact that change in mental functioning seems to have taken place to how such change is being deployed. This step in the method is explicitly qualitative and intuitive. We eschew submitting this process to the rigours of quantification.

Pass 4: A computer-generated program of discourse analysis. The typed transcripts of criterion sessions are submitted to evaluate the saliency of referential activity, as well as the use of affect words, and those indicative of reflectivity. The measures are guided by a computer-assisted program developed in the frame of Bucci's multiple code theory (1997); more recent methodological innovations (using computerized analysis) have been introduced by Maskit, Bucci, and Roussos (2003), which we have used in this project.

Two pathways towards psychoanalytic knowing

Each of the passes represents an effort in the direction of defining the broad constructs of integration and destabilization. It is also clear that each pass contributes in distinct ways. Indeed, there may be two paths towards knowing analytic process: Passes 1, 2, and 4 represent one mode. Here we find a reliance on quantification—a linear, empirical description of psychic events, readily susceptible to consensual agreement. This mode might be termed a nomothetic mode of knowing. Pass 3, in contrast, relies on qualitative analysis and the synthesis of convergent events by an intersubjectively engaged listener (Lasky, Freedman, & Hurvich, 2002). We may term this an ideographic and psychoanalytic interpretive mode of knowing.

The quantitative–qualitative contrast is drawn even more sharply by the comparison of Passes 3 and 4. In Pass 4, the computer-generated assessment of discourse is highly reliable and has a track record of clinical application. Most importantly, it yields scores reflecting the use of word frequencies that are not dependent upon clinical judgement. These measures are rooted in a cognitive linguistic source of knowledge, relatively remote from clinical psychoanalytic thought. Pass 3, on the other hand, not only is qualitative but relies on a view of apprehending meaning that stresses a series of multidimensional events, occurring concurrently in rapid succession, governed by primary-process thought, and operating at varying levels of consciousness. Here meaning is synthesized by the experienced and experiencing analytic listener.

This comparison reaches the heart of the concern of the present volume. Yes, there is a pluralism of the differing sciences—and we are grateful to Leuzinger-Bohleber (2002a, 2002b), both for her pointed critique of the illusion of a unified science and for her affirmation of the divergent paths towards knowing. More important yet is her assertion that the sciences differ in method, quality of experience, and truth-value. It is precisely these kinds of distinctions that are implied in our various passes. While there is pluralism of the sciences, of greater relevance to psychoanalytic research is the reliance on different scientific models in the pursuit of validity. Then, what matters is the interrelationship between these different sources of knowing, their redundancy, complementarity, even contradictions, which often divide our analytic enterprise.

Portraits from two sessions in the analysis of Ms P

Session 257, an A session, opens with a characteristic scheduling ritual within which a transference conflict is embedded. Ms P goes on to describe the effects of giving her analysis priority over her husband and their relationship. She begins to muse in the session about how the analyst excites her in a way her husband does not. She articulates how her relationship with the analyst feels like an affair, and she reveals a sexual fantasy in which she and the analyst are making love, groins pressed against one another, and a lack of satisfaction because the analyst has no penis. Then, following an intervention by the analyst, a headache, tearful silences, and a state of confusion ensue; this lasts for 10 minutes. In this state of transitory crisis, the patient expresses a wish that the session were not almost over. She then returns to less conflictually encumbered work on the material, going on to describe sexual fantasies about her chiropractor. At the end of this hour she delivers a kind of analytic *coup de grace*, commenting on how the power of her fantasy life takes over her capacity for objective thinking and feeling and even her ability to relate and function, as well. The tape recording runs out before the session ends, indicating that the analyst has extended the hour.

Session 245, a Z session, begins with the repetitive scheduling ritual. Ms P reports feeling lifeless, depressed, and upset. She is unable to go beyond the naming of these affects. She describes critical thoughts about the analyst, focusing on body parts rather than ideas and feelings about their relationship. She follows this with a venomous description (and an explicitly stated hatred) of her body. She anticipates a visit from her parents and communicates it as a factual event. With each shift one expects that she will see how they are linked, but she simply reports as if these were merely changes of subject. She next enters into a highly obsessional description of a house she and her husband may buy, and this continues until the end of the session. In this phase, covering roughly the last 80% of the hour, she occasionally refers to the analyst, her family, her childhood, and her conflicts. This goes nowhere, because the patient, as at the beginning of the session, treats her experiences as facts to be reported, not to be reflected upon. The analyst seems unable to move deeper herself and collaborates with the patient by asking factual questions or making factual comments about the house.

Now we would like to show how these divergent modes of mental organization distilled in these portraits are played out through three distinct methodological approaches that form the substance of this report.

Distinguishing between A and Z sessions: a quantitative/empirical approach

The successive evaluation of the criterion sessions from their respective vantage points told much about the psychological functions associated with *A* and *Z* sessions. The quantitative findings are contained in a separate report (Freedman, Lasky, Bucci, & Hurvich, 2002). Here we sketch out the highlights of our findings.

Pass 1: Evaluating the analyst's scan. Our method enabled us to evaluate the analyst's immediate impressions in quantitative terms. The scans were presented to experienced clinical judges, and they were able to discern (qualitatively) central organizing themes defining *A* and *Z* attributes. Thus, when the analyst in her scan reported the patient to show reflective functioning, to tolerate contradictory ideas and feelings, to maintain psychic distance from raw experience, to show active psychic participation, and also when the analyst found herself listening and relating empathically—then a tilt towards *A* was rated. When the analyst's scan described the patient to reveal labile and stormy affects, helpless or hopeless object relations, disturbed/disorganized thinking, concrete or repetitive thinking, and also when subjectively the analyst felt bored and recognized countertransference enactments within herself—then a rating of *Z* was indicated. Each of the 54 sessions was given two ratings, on a 10-point scale: one rating for *A* qualities and one for *Z* qualities. The scans could be rated with very high reliability. From the 54 scans, 16 were selected as criterion sessions for further study.

Pass 2: Was it really an A or Z session? With the Pass 2 analysis we enter into the analytic session itself and ask the question: "Was it really an *A* or a *Z* session?" Through listening now to the actual audio recording of the entire session (rather than just the analyst's scan), we are in a position to broaden our inquiry. We can consider not just the integrative or non-integrative functions within the patient, but, by considering the words of both participants, we can ask how well they are in tandem with each other. Our perspective on *A* or *Z* has become decidedly more interactional. A substantial correlation between consultants' perception and judgement of the analyst's scan was found. In fact, in a majority of the 16 sessions we noted perfect agreement.

Nevertheless, there were noteworthy exceptions, and these divergences of judgement between the analyst's and the consultants' perception are of particular clinical interest. They became a major vehicle for the scrutiny of the interplay of the patient's transference and the analyst's countertransference. These instances of analyst–consultant discrepancies derived from quantitative analysis offer a fruitful opportunity for further clinical qualitative examination and explanation.

Pass 4: Analyzing spoken language in A or Z sessions The typed transcripts of the 16 criterion sessions were subjected to an evaluation of referential activity, emotionality, and reflectivity. The work was guided by computer-assisted linguistic procedures developed in the context of the theory of multiple coding and the referential process. Computer dictionaries, which were developed as an outgrowth of this theory, enabled us to arrive at highly reliable scores, so that we were in a position to determine which were the *A* and *Z* sessions, now in terms of saliences of word frequencies for each of the three categories mentioned.

The yield was congruent with expectations. The analyst scan characterized by *A* qualities was related to referential activity, and it was not related to affectivity or reflectivity. However, what was unexpected was the joint effect of both affect and reflection. These two variables taken together revealed a strong correlation with the *A* or *Z* character of a given session.

Conclusions

We have now completed the task of defining the properties of integrative and destabilized sessions, which we have arbitrarily termed *A* and *Z*. The constructs of *A* and *Z* were enlarged through a perusal of these successive observations. From the clinical scan we were led to believe that these functions reside primarily within the patient. From the consultant's work, we learned about differential patterns pointing to distinct transference–countertransference constellations. In the computer analysis of spoken language, we found reciprocal activity carried out by each member of the dyad. Hence, we now understand that the constructs of *A* and *Z* encompass mental activity in both members of the analytic couple.

Finally, we have given further specificity to the construct of integration. Particularly noteworthy is the contribution of language measures based on multiple code theory. *A* was not correlated with affectivity alone, nor with reflectivity, but we did note a powerful interplay between the two. This redefinition of integration will play a major role in our psychoanalytic understanding of integration.

Distinguishing phases of A and Z activity inside the analytic session: a quantitative/qualitative approach

Now that we have shown systematic oscillations between *A* and *Z* sessions occurring in the course of analytic treatment and have specified their respective properties, we wish to inquire whether this variation is recapitulated in the course of single, perhaps crucial sessions. Such a recapitulation will tell us much about process.

The "A–Z–A" Zones. When we re-examined the distribution of *A* and *Z* sessions, we noted not only oscillations, but also entire zones of *A* and *Z* activity. Furthermore, the zones followed an *A–Z–A* sequence. We selected three sessions as salient representatives of this sequence. These sessions were the arena in which we further pursued this more detailed study of process.

The envelopes of psychoanalytic intervention. We next developed a method aimed at identifying critical juncture points within a session, which we call "envelopes of psychoanalytic intervention" (EPI). EPI evaluates the manner in which a patient resolves or makes use of the analyst's intervention. The envelope has three components: the antecedent, the intervention proper, which can be verbal or non-verbal, and the consequent. Each envelope can be identified as having properties pointing in the direction of *A* or *Z*.

The trajectory of sessions. Here we encounter the crucial qualitative test underlying the *A–Z–A* proposition—namely, that even in an integrative session we can find the onset of destabilization to be followed by a return to integration. In what follows, we give the event sequence from selected envelopes, starting with an *A* envelope, a subsequent *Z* envelope, and a final *A* envelope, as observed in Session 257. The initial *A* envelope depicts a libidinal transference, the analyst's ability to receive it, and the patient's elaborating with new material. However, in the subsequent *Z* envelope the patient appears blocked and self-critical and takes recourse in somatization. Finally, in the consequent *A* envelope, we can note a return to reflective functioning through a shared explicit transference communication.

Computer-generated analysis of the envelopes. We examine the hypothesis that the distinct modes of resolving the interventions at critical junctures in Session 257 are also reflected in the measures of computer-generated language. This is a complex and detailed analysis, but a very encouraging pattern emerged—namely, that in the envelopes marked by *A* activity, which includes the patient's ability to use what the analyst had offered, referential activity and the combined effect of both emotion tone and reflectivity are salient. Conversely, in the *Z* zone, this pattern of relationship has broken down. This is precisely what we have observed at the macro level, when *A* sessions were compared with *Z* sessions. In other words, the properties between *A* and *Z* in their relation to referential activity were recapitulated when critical zones within the session were scrutinized.

Conclusions

The notion of zones of mental functioning defined by phases of integration and destabilization, both between and within sessions, has extended our understanding of process. Through delineating the *A–Z–A* transformation cycles on both macro and micro levels, we have affirmed the crucial role of destabilization as a precursor of reintegration, both between and within sessions. Furthermore, the study of shifts of mental functioning taking place within criterion sessions has given shape to our understanding of destabilization. We noticed that in the *Z* session the destabilization was more pervasive, more intense, and longer in duration. In the *A* session it was transitory and appeared as zonal activity. Indeed, there seems to be one kind of integration, but there may well be two kinds of destabilization, and who knows how many kinds, through which the capacity for mental cohesiveness is lost.

A psychoanalytic interpretation of A and Z

Addressing, now, the issue of the two paths towards psychoanalytic knowing, we have established that in the course of a mainstream (i.e. contemporary Freudian) psychoanalysis systematic shifts in mental functioning occur, and through the method of sequential specification we noted congruence first between sessions and now also within sessions. We might say: "Hooray, it all correlates, it is all convergent." Alternatively, we may reflect and ask: "What does it all say about the meaning of *A* and *Z*?" In other words, can it all be explained within the frame of cognitive–linguistic theory?

We would like to take a different, additional, considerably more complicated path. We want to explore whether and how these observations can be described along the lines of contemporary Freudian psychoanalytic thought. In this we follow the line of research inquiry suggested by Leuzinger-Bohleber (2002a, 2002b), which stresses the plurality of sciences, with its emphasis on method, modes of experiencing, and truth value. The psychoanalytic mode of knowing entails an empathic intersubjective participation in the events of the analytic situation. This approach rests on the ability to discern rapid shifts in levels of mental functioning, often involving varying states of consciousness governed by primary-process ideation, and the truth value is dependent upon a particular—in this case a mainstream, or contemporary, Freudian—psychoanalytic frame.

Whereas it is important to reaffirm the gains derived from the quantitative empirical observations thus far, from an interpretive psychoanalytic perspective these observations are regarded as external, perhaps not touching the depth of psychic life. In short, the empirical analysis points to the fact that something has happened, and it has done so reliably. Now we are prepared to go further and explore its psychoanalytic meaning. In this juxtaposition from the "that" to the "what", we may well find the contrast between quantitative and qualitative methodology.

We shall turn to exploring the psychoanalytic interpretive meaning of *A* and *Z* in the context of a destabilized session: Session 245. Whereas in the integrated session—Session 257 (*A*)—we noted an orderly *A–Z–A* sequence, for the destabilized session—Session 245 (*Z*)—the profile was a jagged one. While there were sporadic moments of integrative activity, this was short-lived. The whole configuration between *A* and *Z* envelopes was the reverse for the *A* session. All this points to a set of phenomena with which we have become increasingly impressed—namely, there are two qualities of *Z*: one embedded in the context of an integrated *A* session and the other in the context of a destabilized *Z* session.

A scrutiny of our units in Session 245 (*Z*) reveals strands of uninterrupted speech, exclusion of the analyst, as well as unproductive silences. There are affect explosions and, also, obsessive reflection on externals. While implicitly involved with the analyst, Ms P does not really speak to her, as her reflections are in the service of problem solving rather than as affect experiences related to transference. She just could not bring her thoughts together, and, also, the analyst was not functioning as an object for resolution. Limitations of space prevent an elaboration of our Pass 3 methodology, which is presented elsewhere (Lasky, Freedman, & Hurvich, in preparation).

There is yet another way to describe this disjunction—one that André Green regards as part of the work of the negative. We were delighted to discover in Green's *The Fabric of Affect in Psychoanalytic Discourse* (1997) the fact that he distinguishes different configurations of impasse in analytic work, which he terms Type 1 and Type 2. These judgements about difficult sessions are drawn from his private practice, and, for this reason alone, only he can speak with great authority. They are also presented in the form of "caricatures" of sessions and, as such, are presented with a great deal of vividness. Green's Type 1 and Type 2 offer most interesting similarities to kinds of destabilization, transitory or pervasive regression. In general terms, Green's Type 1 seems to match our notion of pervasive *Z*, whereas, with some modification, his Type 2 resembles aspects of our *Z* as embedded in an *A* session. Green's "Types" are useful for two reasons: they suggest a complementarity to our cognitively verified psychoanalytic observations, yet they are housed within a fabric of unconscious fantasies.

In his Type 1 caricature of a session in which a favourable outcome does not take place, the speech is stifled and monotonous, often not allowing for interruptions; when there are silences, they are leaden. There is also an emphasis on current realities. "Thought as thought" is absent in the organization of discourse. The most striking apparent overlap of the two spheres of inquiry is the lack of coordination between affect and representation, which we have stressed all along. However, what Green means by affect is quite different from the idea that affect is primarily measured through spoken language.

But now Green's account is suffused with the recognition of the unconscious counterpart. While speech may be stifled, Green would also emphasize that this apparent withdrawal signifies the sense of overwhelming presence. We must not think that the stuck transference is decathected; on the contrary, it is hyper-cathected. The analyst is felt to be ever-present and is experienced as "an iron lung that enables survival outside". The accompanying countertransference may exhaust the ability for empathy, leading to a situation in which the analyst seeks to extract herself from the transferential quagmire. The analyst is as much a prisoner of the patient as the patient is of his or her own body.

CONCLUSION: Beyond correlations

All psychoanalytic research is embedded in psychoanalytic theory, as was this effort. This was a study of a recorded psychoanalysis, conducted within the frame of a contemporary Freudian method and implemented through four distinct and successive sources of observation. We advanced the hypothesis that transformation cycles are the organizers of analytic process, and that these are manifest in recurrent oscillations of states of integration and destabilization during crucial phases of an analysis. Each of the four modes of observation supported this expectation. Yet what was the gain from this enterprise?

This question leads us back to the issue of the pluralism inherent in psychoanalytic knowing. Whereas we started this study with four perspectives, there are really only two that matter, and these two are considered to hold quite opposite approaches to the generating of psychoanalytic concepts. There is the opposition of a quantitative, nomothetic perspective grounded in cognitive and linguistic science; and there is the qualitative, clinical, ideographic perspective, which has its roots in interpretive psychoanalytic knowing. Each of these perspectives has offered discrimination between our criterion sessions, and yet we ask ourselves what the contribution of each is to an understanding of mental functioning. Here we shall borrow a phrase from Hartmann and ask what are the mutual, facilitating, and contradictory influences that are brought to bear on analytic knowledge. Hence, we would like to examine the complementarity, the facilitation, and the contradictions derived from these two sources.

It is our impression that psychoanalytic knowledge is not only complemented but is facilitated by empirical, quantitative observations. The idea of mutual influences suggests that one mode of knowing has a discernible impact upon the other. Indeed, psychoanalysis needs and is benefited by empirical research.

Our quest to understand clinical material is often beset by multiple meanings. When we are faced with manifold choices, as we saw in the definition of integration or destabilization, the empirical data offered us both a selective confirmation of what appeared to be relevant in a given context and a disconfirmation of what appeared to be irrelevant. Here is an instance of the generative (not replicative) impact of empirical research. Indeed, it succeeded in helping to shape the definition of organizing psychoanalytic constructs.

Second, the unfolding of the analytic process also depends on the identification of critical-event structures. We have situated such moments in the envelopes of psychoanalytic intervention: interaction as process, not determinant or cure. We found these structures to be precursors of subsequent developments, such as regression or repair. Here empirical research that is both quantitative and qualitative offers an additional arena—one for the evaluation of alternative clinical strategies.

Third, clinical practice is often confronted by divergences in analyst and patient subjectivity: "Was it a negative transference on the part of the patient?" / "Was it a countertransference on the part of the analyst?" Our observations of divergences were most evocative, especially the confirmation through language analysis, which helped us to pinpoint the effects of the analyst's countertransference. Stated in another way, empirical research elucidates the decisive role of the analyst's unconscious subjectivity.

Having said all this, let us now state the role of interpretive psychoanalytic knowing. Here we affirm that the quality of mental functioning that appears in the ideographic context of the session is rooted in the history of the subject. Interpretive psychoanalytic knowing diminishes the pull towards abstractions and universals. It relies on the power of the evocative metaphor, and it is the heart of (or, one might say, it *is*) our analytic work.

Earlier we spoke of the complementarity of the two ways of knowing, which are based upon correlations. But now we shall speak of phenomena beyond correlations, for correlations do not imply identity. Once again, we ask: "What does psychoanalytic interpretive research give us that quantitative research does not?" We have noted that quantitative empirical research tells us that an event has occurred. Interpretive analytic research tells us what it is that happened.

In the interpretive analytic mode of knowing, we seek to encompass a synthesis of psychic forces that make for change in mental functioning. This involves the apprehension and containment of simultaneously interacting psychic events, occurring at various levels of consciousness in an intersubjective matrix. This can only be achieved through intuitive listening, which relies upon an internal, not an external, frame of reference.

Through quantitative analysis we identified certain constituents of mental functioning. Through qualitative analysis, we were brought face to face with evocative metaphors. We hear André Green's voice offering the metaphoric synthesis: "You want me to be a life support" or, citing a desymbolizing patient, "I don't want to hear you, and I have shit in my ears." It is this metaphoric synthesis that pulls together in one intuitive grasp the essence of the many levels of consciousness and the balance of conflicting forces.

Quantitative empirical research, with its emphasis on the observable, stresses the immediacy of psychic events. While most analysts pay homage to the fact that the past is recapitulated in the here-and-now, what is missing is the vision of historic man. The contextualization of psychic events from the vantage point of this historic perspective is the hallmark of the interpretive psychoanalytic mode of knowing.

Psychoanalytic research must aim for spheres of knowledge that reach beyond correlation. The cognitive or linguistic investigators will continue to create and discover computer dictionaries that match the evocative metaphor, the moments of change or historical vision. These will be not only confirmatory, but generative in their own right. Then the analytic interpreter will find—as we did in the "two kinds of *Z*"—new patterns, new elaborations, new metaphors: and thus *la Ronde* of psychoanalytic research will continue. It is not only a dialogue between two modes of knowing, it is also a dialectic. It is this transition from dialogue to dialectic that is at the heart of this volume.

14

Psychoanalysis and science: some remarks on demarcation and legitimation

Folkert Beenen

Several years ago, my attention was drawn to an article by a Dutch author (Derksen, 1994) that presented some interesting thoughts about the early development of psychology as an official academic discipline in the Netherlands. Thinking about our ongoing discussions on the scientific status of psychoanalysis as such and of the need for evidence-based research data to prove the effectiveness and efficiency of psychoanalytic treatment, I thought it worth the effort to apply some of Derksen's ideas to our discipline, in order to put the actual issues into a developmental–historical perspective.

Let us start with the observation that every scientific discipline, in addition to producing (new) knowledge, also constantly "produces" itself—that is, in society much energy has to be put into survival activities that are not unlike the Darwinian principle of "survival of the fittest" in nature. One can think of fund-raising, of recruiting enough and suitable/promising students and teachers, and of adequate accommodation, to mention only a few of many concrete tasks the discipline has to fulfil in order to guarantee its material future.

A prerequisite for being successful in reaching these concrete goals is to have a clear own identity as a discipline. It is a basis for acceptance by the outside world and furnishes the profession with the necessary authority.

Identity requires, first of all, a certain amount of consensus within the discipline itself, among its membership. Production and reproduction of the discipline's identity is mainly accomplished via constant internal discussion of basic issues and via the collective and personal narratives around the discipline and through which new student members are introduced to the field.

A well-known debate of the last decade on the identity of psychoanalysis (as discussed by Wallerstein and many others) has been the question: "one psychoanalysis or many?" Whether the answer is "one" or whether it is "many", everyone in the field realizes the importance of ultimate consensus on this issue for the sake of a clear identity of psychoanalysis.

After the strategy of working towards internal clarity, the next task with which we are confronted is the demarcation of psychoanalysis in relation to adjacent (academic) disciplines and towards other activities and entities in society—for instance, religious belief and the Church. Gieryn (1983) introduces this strategy as "boundary work", by which he means that in essence all the boundaries around a discipline are no more and no less than historical constructions and reconstructions by the discipline itself.

Within and between the disciplines, the true object for research and the proper definition of the way the central problems have to be investigated are a constant source of discussion and disagreement. Attempts to solve this constant struggle by simply trying to postulate that each discipline studies its "own" object, a specific and delimited part of the truth, do not fit with reality. Neither does the idea that, although two disciplines may focus on the same object of investigation, they do so by way of clearly different questions and methods. Unfortunately, the differences are relative and the object of (inter-) disciplinary discussion, instead of being unambiguous and absolute.

In other words, there is no tenable justification for the idea of the disciplines as just "natural kinds" of entities, characterized by a few given unique and immanent criteria. An artificial attempt to introduce sharp discontinuity into the continuum of reality is deemed to fail.

All this means that concept research is really at the heart of the matter in psychoanalysis, if it is to create and maintain an individual identity as a specific discipline.

Moreover—and this is not unimportant—concept research fits in very well with clinical practice. To paraphrase Freud, it is, in my experience, the royal road to rouse interest in systematic scientific inquiry in practising clinicians. In the late 1980s and early 1990s, the Dutch Psychoanalytic Society organized a common effort to study one psychoanalytic concept extensively every year. The task was to consider how psychoanalysis defines and applies concepts like "(mental) health", "the psychoanalytic process", "structural change", "sublimation", and so on. To answer such a question, several lines of approach, varying from clinical case studies to empirical pilot studies on the subject, were chosen. However, at the heart of the activities in all cases was an extensive comparative study of the literature, focusing on clarifying the essential meaning of the concept and also illuminating the bottlenecks and fundamental controversies around it in the psychoanalytic community. This literature search resulted in what could be seen as a conceptual meta-study, comparable to other well-known empirical meta-studies. It was such collectively executed and mutually discussed conceptual meta-studies that, in the end, raised the interest of clinicians in more systematic (empirical) research and also made them aware of the need for that type of activity. The whole project created the soil for cooperation and subsequent collaboration within the framework of some empirical studies we executed.

Apart from boundary work in relation to the adjacent disciplines—especially the life sciences focusing on the human being, as is the case with psychoanalysis—it is of the utmost importance to demarcate the discipline from non-scientific knowledge, from everyday views and beliefs. To keep the status of a scientific discipline, psychoanalysis will constantly have to make it evident that its knowledge and methods are substantially different from the know-how and methods of lay people—and I think most of us realize that in our domain, that of the human psyche, these boundaries often are far from self-evident.

So it's a hard day's work for psychoanalysis to acquire and maintain the status of a scientific discipline and the material and non-material advantages inherent in this—like autonomy, the right to handle its own business without outside interventions.

On the other hand, one of the main dangers we have to be aware of when we try to distinguish psychoanalysis as a science from common everyday knowledge is creating too great a distance between ourselves and "normal life", resulting in an ivory-tower position, for in that case society would, sooner or later, evaluate our profession as irrelevant.

This means that the two criteria mentioned—that is, building and maintaining an individual identity in the field of scientific disciplines and creating internal consensus—have to be accompanied by a third one: showing convincing evidence for societal relevance of the activities of psychoanalysis.

This third task in maintaining the discipline asks for a strategy of its own, particularly one that creates alliances in the sphere of influence in the society around us. Put in terms of boundary work, one also could say that many such activities consist of regulating relationships with "the rest of the world".

The basic set-up is, again and again, one of two (warring) parties, one on each side of the border, that have to try to reach agreement as to the exact borderline. For psychoanalysis, this means, first of all, that we will have to convince the other party of the fact that as lay people in our specific field, they are not licensed to join in the scientific discussion of psychoanalytic experts and their methods. This does not mean, of course, that the boundary is permanent and static. On the contrary, at any given moment the exact boundaries are the result of constant dynamic interaction and communication with "the other side". Only then can the recognition of the actual border be maintained and adaptations and changes in it be made on the basis of mutual agreement.

Having acquired scientific autonomy up to at least a certain degree, the next question is how we can legitimate that status. Shapin (1990) distinguishes two basic strategies for a science to try to accomplish this aim. Historically, up to the middle of the nineteenth century, the legitimacy of the autonomy of science in relation to the rest of society was rooted in the thesis that science serves Faith, in the sense that scientific discoveries again and again show God's celebrity.

In the second half of the nineteenth century, the new conception of a secularized science arose. The legitimacy of such a science was primarily based not on its moral (religious) quality, but far more on its pragmatic meaning for society—that is, the practical value it delivered to society.

Psychoanalysis is one of the most thorough answers in a long tradition since the ancient Greeks to the question of the relativity of human knowledge: knowledge is indeed human knowledge, which means that it is determined not just by the characteristics of the observed objects, but just as much by the characteristics of the observing mind. Instead of, like the old philosophers, constantly searching for the real truth behind the things—that is, beyond science—psychology in general, and psychoanalysis in particular, try to disentangle the nature and laws of the human psyche, of our thinking mind and of our feeling and acting as human beings. This brings into focus the fundamental influence of subjective factors on the production of human knowledge, next to the significance of objective quantities.

So, in the tradition of the development of scientific knowledge, psychoanalysis is the discipline that has brought its very own "structure of the world" and has presented this new form of knowledge to the outside world, the public. And as the basic content of the psychoanalytic knowledge is not best suited to show the world God's celebrities, it has to prove unequivocally its practical value to society in order to become accepted. In fact, we are still in the thick of it, trying convince the sceptical public—people who have many critical questions and objections to our views—of the correctness and appropriateness of the structure we offer them.

It should at least be the case that we put a great deal of energy into this legitimation process. But on the issue of the need for legitimation towards society as well as on the strategies that should be used in executing these activities, it seems that the analytic community is quite diversified in its opinions.

Could it be that the majority of psychoanalysts are not really aware of the fundamental legitimation problem of psychoanalysis? Or, even worse, that they actively resist the idea of the need for psychoanalysis to prove its legitimacy to the outside world? There is no simple answer to these questions, of course, but I will not be the only one who has observed quite a great deal of ignorance, of trivializing, of arrogance also in our circles, easily leading to the harmful ivory-tower position of psychoanalysis.

There also seems to be a substantial group of colleagues who are characterized by quiet resignation as to these issues. They simply do not want to bother themselves with questions at a macro level: they have undergonc a long, intensive, and expensive education as psychoanalysts, and now they "just want to do their job", earn their money, and so on.

A third attitude to the issues under consideration is found in the subgroup who consider themselves the real psychoanalysts. They are very aware of the importance of societal acceptance of psychoanalysis, but they deem themselves to be the chosen ones to execute and apply psychoanalysis without being distracted and disturbed by its survival struggles. Responsibility for the latter they delegate to a small group of colleagues—a private army that they expect to win the battle for them.

So, the next question is: what are the chances of winning, and what is the best strategy?

A small group of scientists–psychoanalysts have tried to advance the legitimacy of psychoanalysis by presenting it as an empirical science that can be tested according to generally accepted scientific criteria. It may be true that lay people in daily life also occupy themselves with psychology and even psychoanalysis, but by analogy to the natural sciences, systematic empirical research makes the difference between the knowledge of the public and the scientific learning of the psychoanalyst. The effectiveness of this strategy is largely based on the move to bring psychoanalysis under the topography of the exact sciences. So it acquires also the legitimate status of the exact sciences—a fact that should convince the public domain of the right of psychoanalysis to exist.

An additional argument towards the lay world concerns the complexity of the psyche. It may be true that the public does, indeed, have substantial intuitive knowledge about the psyche and its mechanisms, but to bring all the material into a significant and meaningful structure and to situate this in a larger context asks for a science—that is, psychoanalysis.

Moreover, it is implicitly evident that the science we are presenting here has its own identity, with clear boundaries to the "other" exact natural sciences. After all, the natural sciences have inanimate things as their object of investigation, whereas psychoanalysis focuses on the "anima", the psyche. The latter also implies a clear boundary with physiology. Of course, demarcation from psychology nevertheless remains a problem that cannot be tackled by this strategy. It is even more problematic that psychology itself uses the very strategy to legitimate itself, and it claims to be much more of an exact empirical science than psychoanalysis.

Not only for this reason, but also because they judge it too high a price for psychoanalysis to join the exact sciences in order to acquire legitimacy in society, another movement in the psychoanalytic community has strong doubts about this strategy. This group is especially worried about the danger of selling the soul of psychoanalysis to the "devil" of the natural sciences. The human psyche constantly gets into tight corners in modern society, and psychoanalysis is the discipline of choice to oppose this tendency and to show that we need a more humanistic and spiritual way of dealing with the psyche and psychic problems: a very specific approach that psychoanalysis can offer to mankind and that can have great practical and spiritual value for society. So here the main issue is one of moral value and not (yet) one of scientific standards. Psychoanalysis is promoted as a counterbalance to the influence of the unidirectional materialism of the natural sciences in society.

Although sympathetic and inspiring in principle, this strategy is not without its hazards. In its strong reaction against the reductionism and materialism of the natural sciences there is a real danger that the movement itself also develops a (too) one-sided view and, as a consequence, overshoots the scientific mark of psychoanalysis. It was a well-considered choice by Freud to "naturalize" the psyche by means of a systematic approach based on the methods of the natural sciences in order to strip the concept of its supernatural connotations and classify it in the domain of the sciences. His message to the world was: look, human behaviour and the mechanisms and structure of the human psyche are in the end as determined and understandable as the phenomena in the material world around us. Precisely from this starting point it was possible to develop a treatment method that both fulfils scientific standards and has great practical value as well and can, therefore, open the way to autonomy and legitimacy of our discipline.

My personal opinion is that psychoanalysis cannot and should not renounce this basis as created by Freud. First of all, this means that we have to acquire the relevant knowledge of the modern empirical scientific findings regarding the psychic functioning of the human being. But merely acquiring the knowledge does not suffice. We will also have to integrate this knowledge into our theories, into the definitions of our basic concepts, and, ultimately, in positive adaptations in our clinical work. By participating in multidisciplinary, psychoanalytically inspired research projects—or, perhaps even better, by taking the lead in designing and executing such projects ourselves—the psychoanalytic community can strengthen the scientific identity of the profession and thereby also consolidate and increase its social standing.

In addition, the fact remains, of course, that psychoanalysis has also introduced, and can still introduce, specific moral values into society. To contribute to that aim is a most honourable motive on the part of many a practising psychoanalyst. But at the same time we have to beware promoting a new secularized religion that neglects and trivializes the scientific argument; this would make Freud turn in his grave and mark the beginning of the definitive decline of psychoanalysis as a scientific discipline and as a respected profession.

To conclude, returning to the legitimacy strategies for psychoanalysis: to have and execute more than one approach can, in principle, increase the chances to reach the goals set. At the same time we will, however, have to keep a sharp eye on the possible fundamental questions and differences in opinion that are behind the different strategies, and the degree to which we have arrived at internal consensus about the identity of our discipline. The danger is real that each separate strategy will present a fundamentally different picture to the outside world. It goes without saying that, next to giving rise to a great deal of tension within the discipline, this would lead without doubt to a very undesirable lack of clarity and confusion in the outside world, substantially reducing the chances of reaching the goals of demarcation and legitimacy.

It is, therefore, of the utmost importance for psychoanalysis to address forcefully the internal dialogue on and between the different positions and opinions, in order to be able to operate on a common base represented by a good-enough internal consensus. At the same time, good-enough in this case does not at all mean that we should make frenetic efforts to hide fundamental, still unsettled issues about which we are all concerned. Discussions, differences in opinion, and more or less existential uncertainties are characteristic of the developmental dynamics of a discipline, and, provided they are supported by sufficient and sufficiently clear basic consensus, they can, in the end substantially contribute to the impression that psychoanalysis is a dynamic, strong, and autonomous scientific discipline.

APPENDIX

SUMMARY OF ADDITIONAL STUDIES PRESENTED AT THE PLURALISM OF SCIENCES CONFERENCE

Frankfurt, 26–29 September 2002

1. The combination of psychoanalytic and non-psychoanalytic research methods in a representative, multiperspective follow-up study of psychoanalyses and psychoanalytic long-term therapies

Marianne Leuzinger-Bohleber, Ulrich Stuhr, Bernhard Rüger, & Manfred Beutel

One characteristic profile of this large study of a representative sample (n = 401) of all the former patients who had finished their psychoanalyses or psychoanalytic therapies with analysts of the German Psychoanalytic Association, 1990–93, is the attempt to combine and to contrast genuinely psychoanalytic research methods with non-psychoanalytic instruments of comparative psychotherapy research. Therefore the clinical psychoanalytic research method (e.g. trying to understand the conscious and the unconscious communication of a patient in a psychoanalytic situation with an analyst—by observation of transference–countertransference reactions, dreams, slips of the tongue, etc.) was applied in follow-up interviews with 129 former patients of experienced psychoanalysts. Psychoanalytic supervisions and psychoanalytic research groups were additional research instruments. The findings gained by these psychoanalytic instruments were compared and contrasted to those gained via non-psychoanalytic instruments (questionnaires, tests, socioeconomic data, analyses of the costs in the mental health services, etc.). We also compared the results gained by quantitative instruments with those gained by a number of qualitative ones. This multiperspective approach enabled us to achieve a variety of interesting and challenging insights into the long-term outcome of psychoanalytic treatments as well as a critical reflection of methodological and epistemological perspectives of clinical and extra-clinical research in psychoanalysis (see, e.g., Leuzinger-Bohleber, Stuhr, Rüger, & Beutel, 2003; Leuzinger-Bohleber & Target, 2002.) (This study was awarded the Research Prize of the International Psychoanalytical Association, 2003.)

2. The combination of psychoanalytic and sociological research strategies in an interdisciplinary study on the history of individual and institutional conflicts with adolescent school dropouts

Thomas von Freyberg & Angelika Wolff

In this interdisciplinary study clinical psychoanalytic research methods (psychoanalytic interviews with adolescents) are compared with sociological research strategies analysing, for example, the institutional history of these school dropouts. The results of the two independent research procedures are then combined and lead to a fascinating opportunity for discussing intrapsychic conflicts of these severely traumatized adolescents and their connection and interrelation with conflicts in their outside (institutional) reality.

3. Psychoanalytic expert validation in a transgenerational study: love after Auschwitz

Kurt Grünberg

In this study a systematic psychoanalytic expert validation helped to understand unconscious dimensions in the love relations of second-generation Jews in Germany after the Shoah. These findings were compared with the results of other procedures (questionnaires, content analyses). Kurt Grünberg discussed in detail how "independent" raters in one part of his studies were unconsciously involved via unreflected countertransference reactions on the emotionally extremely difficult subject of the transgenerational transmission of trauma in families of victims of the Holocaust, compared with the situation of sons and daughters of persecutors and bystanders in Germany. According to his experience, these involvements can only be discovered by applying psychoanalytic research instruments.

4. Psychoanalytic contributions to a social phenomenology of aggression: case study as method

Karola Brede, Sylvia Thomas, Heike Westenberger-Breuer, & Dietmar Wetzel

The research project explored a type of employee whose work centres on communicative activities. This type is drawn towards the perceived and somewhat realized freedom for personal development and professional capabilities, but to a certain extent ignores the personal and social risks associated with professional relationships of power and subordination. It is assumed that reconciling communicative equality with power and subordination leads to conflict-prone connotations of aggression. It is also assumed that aggression will become visible primarily in its social manifestations—that is, in socially coded patterns, which are to be described. These manifestations are not primarily the aggressiveness of behaviour but condoned competition and hidden meanings.

So far, interviews have been conducted with 14 participants coming from the banking, high-tech, and insurance sectors.

After the conclusion of the case study, the participants will be given psychoanalytic feedback. In addition, we are trying to contrast the results of our individual case studies with the assessments of an Assessment Center that the individual participants make available to us.

We keep a research diary. Various workshops will take place with entrepreneurial experts (workers' committee members, human resource experts, trade unionists) and psychoanalysts as well as social scientists from the Rhein–Main area.

5. Changes of dreams in psychoanalysis: one example of conceptual research

   Heinrich Deserno, Susanne Doell, Marianne Leuzinger-Bohleber, & Ulrich Moser

Following the model of dream generation by Moser and Zeppelin (1996), dreaming is conceptualized as a special simulated micro-world among others, carrying out cognitive–affective regulation guided by the principles of security and involvement. A model-derived coding system is under evaluation and validation for the purpose of being used in psychotherapy process research showing changes in relationship models, in affect regulation, and in problem solving. Basic elements of the coding system, which is based on results of empirical research and integrated concepts, are the fields of position, movement, and interaction, as well as the interruptions that form the dream sequences. Comparing coded dreams from different stages in treatment and linking them to relevant phenomena other than the transference will be important to the assessment of change.

6. Qualitative versus quantitative methods in psychotherapy research

   a. Individual versus standardized: adequate research strategies for psychoanalytic therapies

   Michael von Rad, Dorothea Huber, & Günther Klug

The authors demonstrate the dialectic relationship between individual versus standardized measurement devices using the paradox of equivalence and the aptitude–treatment interaction research paradigm to illustrate the necessity of a more differentiated approach in comparative psychotherapy research. They discuss, furthermore, the problem of mode-specific, individualized outcome measurement strategies, viz. scales of psychological capacities (SPC) and goal-attainment scaling (GAS), in contrast to standardized, non-specific measures like the symptom checklist (SCL 90-R). The authors advocate that adequate research strategies have to grasp specific effects in order to understand the unique in a patient and a therapy.

b. "*Verstehende Typenbildung*": a qualitative instrument for psychoanalytic psychotherapy research?

Ulrich Stuhr

The author first states that he wants to prevent any misunderstanding: an enlightened qualitative research strategy should not hinder a reasonable quantitative approach, while, at the same time, unspecific, uncontrolled qualitative research approaches should not be promoted. (A real overview of scientific qualitative research can be found in Denzin & Lincoln, 1994; Frommer & Rennie, 2001.)

Faced with a sort of research boom in the IPA, he asks himself why old procedures and empirical research styles are being used now, years too late. Research into psychoanalysis is unquestionably necessary; but why, half a century after Rogers and Truax, do we still need metric scales to illustrate psychotherapeutic processes!?

Scepticism, a philosophical root of empirical science, is also necessary in qualitative research. Especially in qualitative research, we must be prepared to accept that "ugly facts can kill beautiful theories". We therefore need a research method for our field that is suitable for the symbolic interactions between people, but also—as Bachrach, Galatzer-Levy, Skolnikoff, and Waldron (1997), for instance, formulated—one that produces a formalized but specifically psychoanalytic method. For this reason, in Hamburg over several years we have developed, or further developed, a method—so-called understanding type formation—based on ideas from Max Weber and Uta Gerhardt.

In science we know the nomothetic approach, aiming for generally applicable laws, and the ideographic approach, which serves to gain insight into individual cases. Understanding type formation attempts to place itself between these two positions, much the way psychoanalysis as a science tried to position itself as either natural science or hermeneutics, then as "both", and, finally, as "neither". Type formation by comprehension shows the link between nomothetic and ideographic procedures, as it is possible to be closely oriented towards the object or the individual case, but also to be able to make statements directed beyond the individual case. The four steps of formation by understanding are discussed in the paper.

c. The relationship episodes "Type X": a modified CCRT-Analysis

Stephan Hau, Eike Brech, & Heinrich Deserno

Psychoanalytic psychotherapy research tries to evaluate transference processes. The CCRT method developed by Lester Luborsky claims to depict transference patterns in relationship episodes reported by the patient. Unfortunately, the CCRT method focuses only on features of the transference, indicating the occurrence of inappropriate repetitive relationship patterns. Modern concepts understanding transference neurosis as a new compromise formation, developed by both the patient and the analyst in the here-and-now of the session (actualization), are not taken into consideration, nor are possible changes to this pattern as a result of the progressive course of treatment.

The authors introduce a new type of relationship episode (therapist type-X) in order to register the actualization of transference processes in the here-and-now of the analytic session, especially within phases of interactions following interventions by the analyst—that is, the focus lies on the development of and change in transference patterns.

7. Neuropsychoanalysis

a. Psychoanalytic treatments of patients with a hemi-neglect

Neuropsychoanalysis Group Frankfurt–Cologne/Mark Solms

The members of the Neuropsychoanalysis group Frankfurt–Cologne (F. Dick, R. Kennel, M. Leuzinger-Bohleber, H. G. Metzger, K. Roeckerath, H. J. Rothe, H. Schultz, & L. V. Strauss) are psychoanalysts and neuropsychologists, and some of them are neurologists as well. We are studying a group of patients suffering from a hemi-neglect syndrome. We have treated seven patients psychoanalytically, studying the influence of the stroke and the localized brain damage on self and identity of these patients, on transference–countertransference phenomena, and so forth. Analysing the seven single case studies, the following aspects seem to be important: individual biography, object relations, self-development, subjectivity, and identity. In this paper, first hypotheses are discussed trying to bridge our clinical observations with epistemological questions concerning the basic mind–body problem.

b. fMRI studies in psychotherapy research

Manfred Beutel

The tremendous progress in the cognitive neurosciences has a high relevance for the development of psychoanalytic theory and practice. Neuroscience provides empirical biological approaches useful for the investigation of psychoanalytic models. In the panel, the current state of functional neuroimaging techniques, selected paradigms, and collaborative studies going on in New York and Giessen were briefly reviewed, along with findings relevant for psychotherapy research. Engaging psychoanalysts and neuroscientists in a dialogue may help to re-establish a solid position of psychodynamic theory and treatments in contemporary medicine, to bridge the division between "psychological" and "somatic" treatments, and to gain insights into the mind–brain relationship.

c. A fMRI study of dream processes: a challenge to Freud's dream theory?

Stephan Hau, Michael Russ, Marianne Leuzinger-Bohleber, & Mark Solms

Freud's dream theory has often been rejected by experimental dream researchers. Dreaming was seen as a product of the "auto-activated brain–mind" (Hobson).

Nevertheless, recent neuro-scientific data seem broadly compatible with psychoanalytic dream theory. An arousal stimulus causes activation of the motivational systems of the brain. As access to motor systems is blocked, the process of activation takes a regressive course. Perceptual systems that serve memory and abstract thinking are activated, as well as the perceptual system that serves concrete imagery. As the reflective systems are inactivated, no reality testing can take place, and the imageries are taken for reality.

However, these findings were gained by applying syndrome analysis to patients with brain lesions. In a fMRI study, dream processes and sleep processes are investigated with sound subjects. Performance of this kind of research leads to many technical problems when EEG data and fMRI data are registered at the same time. In addition, methodological problems have to be focused: is there any gain for psychoanalytic theory out of this interdisciplinary dialogue?

d. Psychoanalytic treatment of children in a coma

Tamara Fischmann, Wilfried Schneider, & Manfred Sauer

The authors discuss the possibilities of treating patients in a state of altered consciousness. By referring to sleep research and the fact found there that non-consciously perceived material will be processed preconsciously and remembered (Leuschner), the question whether the same can be assumed for coma is raised. It is suggested that this should be studied by taking the following questions into consideration: (1) What influence does an early start to psychotherapy have upon recovery from children in coma? (2) Are there changes in physiological parameters as a result of a familiar relationship offered under the consideration of the medication given? Methodologically, the question arises as to how this can be measured. Which variables can be used to prove an effect on intervention? A pilot study concentrating foremost on physiological parameters is under way.

REFERENCES AND BIBLIOGRAPHY

Adler, A. (1912) Preface. In: C. Furtmueller, *Psychoanalyse und Ethik*. Munich: Reinhardt, 1912. (English edition: In: P. E. Stepansky, *In Freud's Shadow: Adler in Context*. Hillsdale, NJ: Analytic Press, 1983.)

Albani, C., Blaser, G., Jones, E., Thomä, H., & Kächele, H. (2001). Amalie X im Lichte des "Psychotherapie-Prozess Q-Sort" von E. Jones. In: U. Stuhr, M. Leuzinger-Bohleber, & M. Beutel (Eds.), *Langzeit-Psychotherapie: Perspektiven für Therapeuten und Wissenschaftler* (pp. 215–224). Stuttgart: Kohlhammer.

Althusser, L. (1974). *Philosophie et philosophie spontanée des savants*. Paris: Editions F. Maspero.

Ameisen, J. C. (1996). The origin of programmed cell death. *Science, 272*: 1278–1279.

Anzieu, D. (1959). *L'auto-analyse de Freud et la découverte de la psychanalyse, Vol. 3*. Paris: PUF.

Arbeitskreis OPD (Eds.) (1998). *Operationalisierte Psychodynamische Diagnostik: Grundlagen und Manual*. Bern: Huber.

Argelander, H. (1968). Der psychoanalytische Dialog. *Psyche, 22*: 325–339.

Argelander, H. (1970a). *Das Erstinterview in der Psychotherapie*. Darmstadt: Wissenschaftliche Buchgesellschaft.

Argelander, H. (1970b). Die szenische Funktion des Ichs und ihr Anteil an der Symptom- und Charakterbildung. *Psyche, 24*: 325–345.

Argelander, H. (1974). Über psychoanalytische Kompetenz. *Psyche, 28*: 1063–1076.

Argelander, H. (1977). Diskussionsbeitrag zu P. Fürstenaus Arbeit "Die beiden Dimensionen des psychoanalytischen Umgangs mit strukturell ich-gestörten Patienten. Ein Beitrag zur Erweiterung der psychoanalytischen Praxeologie". *Psyche, 31*: 208–215.

Argelander, H. (1979). *Die kognitive Organisation psychische: Geschehens. Ein Versuch zur Systematisierung der kognitiven Organisation in der Psychoanalyse.* Stuttgart: Klett-Cotta.

Bachrach, H. M., Galatzer-Levy, R., Skolnikoff, A., & Waldron, S. (1991). On the efficacy of psychoanalysis. *Journal of the American Psychoanalytic Association, 39*: 871–916.

Bachrach, H. M., Galatzer-Levy, R., Skolnikoff, W., & Waldron, S. (1997). Über die Wirksamkeit der Psychoanalyse. In: M. Leuzinger-Bohleber & U. Stuhr (Eds.), *Psychoanalysen im Rückblick: Methoden, Ergebnisse und Perspektiven der neueren Katamneseforschung* (pp. 285–319). Gießen: Psychosozial Verlag.

Bakhtin, M. M. (1986). *Speech Genres and Other Late Essays.* Austin, TX: University of Texas Press.

Baranger, W. (1980). Acerca del concepto psicoanalítico de objeto. In: W. Baranger, E. del Campo, R. Z. de Goldstein, E. C. Merea, J. M. Mom, B. Resnicoff, L. Ricón, E. Romano, & B. A. Schutt, *Aportaciones al concepto de objeto en psicoanálisis* (pp. 130–152). Buenos Aires: Ed. Amorrortu.

Berenstein, I. (2001). The link and the other. *International Journal of Psycho-Analysis, 82*: 141–149.

Bernardi, R. (2002). The need for true controversies in psychoanalysis. *International Journal of Psycho-Analysis, 83*: 851–873.

Bernfeld, S. (1951). Sigmund Freud, MD. 1882–1885. *International Journal of Psycho-Analysis, 32*: 204.

Binswanger, L. (1942). *Grundformen und Erkenntnis menschlichen Daseins* (2nd edition). Zürich: Max Niehans Verlag, 1953.

Binswanger, L. (1947). *Ausgewählte Vorträge und Aufsätze, Vol. 1.* Bern: A. Francke.

Binswanger, L. (1955). *Erinnerungen an Sigmund Freud.* Bern: Francke Verlag.

Bion, W. R. (1992). *Cogitations.* London: Karnac.

Bleichmar, H. (2003). "Conceptual Paper on Depression." Presented at the Joseph Sandler Research Conference on Depression, London, 8 March.

Bonomi, C. (1994). Why have we ignored Freud the "Paediatrician"? *Cahiers psychiatriques génevois* (Special Issue): 55–99.

Bornstein, M. (1989). Methodology in psychoanalytic research (Special Issue). *Psychoanalytic Inquiry, 9* (2).

Breggin, P. (1980). Brain disabling therapies. In: E. Valenstein (Ed.), *The Psychosurgery Debate.* San Francisco, CA: W. H. Freeman.

Bucci, W. (1997). Patterns of discourse in "good" and troubled hours: A multiple code interpretation. *Journal of the American Psychoanalytic Association, 45*: 155–187.

Bürgin, D., & von Klitzing, K. (1995). Prenatal representations and postnatal interactions of a threesome (mother, father, baby). In: J. Bitzer & M. Stauber (Eds.), *Psychosomatic Obstetrics and Gynaecology* (pp. 185–191). Bologna: Monduzzi Editore.

Canestri, J. (1993). The logic of Freudian research. In: D. Meghnagi (Ed.), *Freud and Judaism* (pp. 117–129). London: Karnac.

Canestri, J. (1999). Psychoanalytic heuristics. In: P. Fonagy, A. M. Cooper, & R. S. Wallerstein (Eds.), *Psychoanalysis on the Move* (pp. 201–217). London: Routledge.

Canestri, J. (2001). "Changing Scientific Ideals and Idols in the History of Psychoanalysis." Psychanalyse en Europe, Fédération Européenne de Psychanalyse, Bulletin 55.

Cardona, G. R. (1976). *Introduzione all'etnolinguistica.* Bologna: Il Mulino.

Cardona, G. R. (1987). *Introduzione alla sociolinguistica.* Torino: Loescher.

Carnap, R. (1938). Logical foundation of the unity of science. In: O. Neurath, R. Carnap, & Ch. Morris (Eds.), *International Encyclopedia of Unified Science.* Chigago, IL: University of Chicago Press.

Carruthers, P., & Boucher, J. (Eds.) (1998). *Language and Thought: Interdisciplinary Themes.* Cambridge: Cambridge University Press.

Cassirer, E. (1977). *Philosophie der symbolischen Formen.* Darmstadt: Wissenschaftliche Buchgesellschaft.

Colby, K. M., & Stoller, R. J. (1988). *Cognitive Science and Psychoanalysis.* Hillsdale, NJ: Lawrence Erlbaum Associates.

Cooper, D. (1986). Some limitations on therapeutic effectiveness: The "burnout syndrome" in psychoanalysts. *Psychoanalytic Quarterly, 55*: 576–598.

Cremerius, J. (1984). *Vom Handwerk des Psychoanalytikers: Das Werkzeug der psychoanalytischen Technik, 2 Bde.* Stuttgart: Frommann-Holzboog.

Denzin, N. K., & Lincoln, J. S. (Eds.) (1994). *Handbook of Qualitative Research.* Thousand Oaks, CA: Sage.

Derksen, M. (1994). De muren van het lab: De demarcatie van de vroege Nederlandse psychologie. *Kennis en Methode, 2* (3): 250–264.

Devereux, G. (1967). *Angst und Methode in den Verhaltenswissenschaften.* Munich: Hanser, 1972.

Dewey, John (1982). *Reconstructions in Philosophy.* Carbondale, IL: Southern Illinois University Press.

Dreher, A. U. (2000). *Foundations for Conceptual Research in Psychoanalysis,* London: Karnac.

Edelman, G. M. (1992). *Bright Air, Brilliant Fire: On the Matter of the Mind.* New York: Basic Books.

Edelson, M. (1995). Can psychotherapy research answer this psychotherapist's questions? In: E. Kaiser (Ed.), *Psychoanalytisches Wissen* (pp. 114–138). Opladen: Westdeutscher Verlag.

Elias, N. (1983). *Engagement und Distanzierung: Arbeiten zur Wissenssoziologie, Vol. 1*, ed. M. Schröter. Frankfurt a/M: Suhrkamp.

Eliot, T. S. (1940). *Four Quartets.* London: Faber and Faber.

Epstein, A. (1987). The phylogenesis of the "ego" with remarks on the frontal lobes. *American Journal of Psychoanalysis, 47*: 161–166.

Epstein, A. (1989). Associations and their nature: A foundation of psychosomatic science. *Journal of the American Academy of Psychoanalysis, 17*: 463–473.

Epstein, A. (1995). *Dreaming and Other Involuntary Mentation: An Essay in Neuropsychiatry.* Madison, CT: International Universities Press.

Erdelyi, M. (1985). *Psychoanalysis: Freud's Cognitive Psychology.* New York: W. H. Freeman.

Etchegoyen, R. H. (1986). *The Fundamentals of Scientific Technique.* London: Karnac.

Federn, E. (2001). "Kann man Psychoanalyse lernen?" Paper presented at Honorary Degree ceremony, Universität Kassel, 27 November.

Ferenczi, S. (1927). *Bausteine der Psychoanalyse* [The Fundamentals of Psychoanalysis]. Berne: Hans Huber Verlag, 1964.

Ferenczi, S., & Rank, O. (1924). *The Development of Psychoanalysis: On the Mutual Relation between Theory and Practice.* New York: Nervous and Mental Disease Pub. Co, 1925; New York: Dover, 1956.

Feyerabend, P. (1975). *Against Method: Outline of an Anarchistic Theory of Knowledge.* London: New Left Books.

Field, S. D., Barkham, M., Shapiro, D. A., & Stiles, W. B. (1994). Assessment of assimilation in psychotherapy: A quantitative case study of problematic experiences with a significant other. *Journal of Counseling Psychology, 41*: 397–406.

Fischer, G. (1995). Die Transformation von Beziehungsschemata in der psychoanalytischen Langzeitbehandlung. In: E. Kaiser (Ed.), *Psychoanalytisches Wissen* (pp. 240–265). Opladen: Westdeutscher Verlag.

Fleck, L. (1935). *Genesis and Development of a Scientific Fact*, ed. T. J. Trenn & R. K. Merton. Chicago, IL, & London: University of Chicago Press, 1979.

Follesdal, D. (1999). Mind and meaning. *Philosophical Studies, 94* (no. 1–2/ May): 139–149.

Fonagy, P. (1998). "The Outcome of Psychodynamic Therapy: The Work of the Anna Freud Centre." Paper presented to the Department of Psychosomatic Medicine and the Munich Psychoanalytic Institute, 2 October, pp. 1–39.

Fonagy, P. (Ed.) (1999). *An Open Door Review of Outcome Studies in Psychoanaly-*

sis. London: International Psychoanalytical Association, Research Committee.

Fonagy, P. (2001). Saisir les orties à pleines mains ou pourquoi la recherche psychanalytique est tellement hésitante. *Revue Française de Psychanalyse (Courants de la psychanalyse contemporaine)*: 265–283.

Fonagy, P., Gergely, G., Jurist, E. L. J., & Target, M. (2002). *Affect Regulation, Mentalization and the Development of the Self*. New York: Other Press.

Fonagy, P., & Moran, G. S. (1991). Understanding psychic change in child analysis. *International Journal of Psycho-Analysis, 72*: 15–22.

Fonagy, P., Moran, G. S., Edgcumbe, R., Kennedy, H., & Target, M. (1993). The roles of mental representations and mental processes in therapeutic action. *Psychoanalytic Study of the Child, 48*: 9–48.

Fonagy, P., & Target, M. (1995). Understanding the violent patient: The use of the body and the role of the father. *International Journal of Psycho-Analysis, 76*: 487–502.

Fonagy, P., & Target, M. (2000). Playing with reality, III: The persistence of dual psychic reality in borderline patients. *International Journal of Psycho-Analysis, 81* (5): 853–874.

Fonagy, P., Target, M., Steele, H., & Steele, M. (1998). *Reflective Function Manual*. London: University College London.

Freedman, N., Lasky, R., Bucci, W., & Hurvich, M. (2002). "Transformation Cycles as Organizers of Analytic Pprocess: The Method of Sequential Specification." Paper presented at the annual meeting of the Rappaport–Klein Study Group, Autin Riggs Center at Stockbridge, MA.

Freedman, N., Lasky, R., & Hurvich, M. (2000). "Transformation Cycles as Organizers of Analytic Process. A Method of Sequential Specification." Paper presented to the Annual Meeting of the Collaborative Analytic Multicenter Programs (CAMP), December.

Freedman, N., Ward, R., & Lasky, R. (2003). "The Envelopes of Psychoanalytic Intervention Manual." Presented at the Scientific Meeting of the Program of Research in Psychoanalysis, IPTAR.

Freedman, N., Ward, R., Lasky, R., & Hurvich, M. (2002). "The Envelopes of Psychoanalytic Intervention Manual." Program of Research in Psychoanalysis, IPTAR.

Freud, S. (1877b). Beobachtungen über Gestaltung und feineren Bau der als Hoden beschriebenen Lappenorgane des Aals. *Sitzungsber. Akad. Wiss. Wien (Math.-Naturwiss. Kl.), 75* (1): 419–431.

Freud, S. (1879a). Notiz über eine Methode zur anatomischen Präparation des Nervensystems. *Zbl. med. Wiss., 17* (26): 468.

Freud, S. (1888). Aphasia. In: M. Solms & M. Saling (Eds.), *A Moment of Transition: Two Neuroscientific Articles by Sigmund Freud*. London: Karnac, 1990.

Freud, S. (1891a) (with Rie, O.). *Klinische Studie über die halbseitige Cerebrallähmung der Kinder. Beiträge zur Kinderheilkunde, Vol. 3,* ed. M. Kassowitz. Vienna: Moritz Perles.

Freud, S. (1891b). *On Aphasia: A Critical Study.* London: Imago.

Freud, S. (1893b). *Zur Kenntniss der cerebralen Diplegien des Kindesalters (im Anschluss an die Little'sch Krankheit.* Vienna: Deuticke.

Freud, S. (1893f). Charcot. *S.E., 3.*

Freud, S. (1893–94). Amnesie und Aphasie. In: A. Bum & M. Schnirer (Eds.*), Diagnostiches Lexikon für praktische Ärzte.* Vienna: Deuticke.

Freud, S. (1897). *Infantile Cerebral Paralysis.* Miami, FL: Miami University Press.

Freud, S. (1897a). Die infantile Cerebrallähmung, ed. H. Nothnagel. *Specielle Pathologie und Therapie, 9,* Vienna.

Freud, S. (1900a). *The Interpretation of Dreams. S.E., 4–5.*

Freud, S. (1906a). My views on the part played by sexuality in the aetiology of the neuroses. *S.E., 7.*

Freud, S. (1907a). *Delusions and Dreams in Jensen's "Gradiva". S.E., 9.*

Freud, S. (1909b). Analysis of a phobia in a five-year-old boy. *S.E., 10.*

Freud, S. (1910c). *Leonardo da Vinci and a Memory of His Childhood. S.E., 11.*

Freud, S. (1913j). The claims of psycho-analysis to scientific interest. *S.E., 13.*

Freud, S. (1914d). On the history of the psycho-analytic movement. *S.E., 14.*

Freud, S. (1915). *Übersicht der Übertragungsneurosen: Ein bisher unbekanntes Manuskript.* Frankfurt: S. Fischer Verlag, 1985.

Freud, S. (1915c). Instincts and their vicissitudes. *S.E., 14.*

Freud, S. (1916–17). *Introductory Lectures on Psycho-Analysis. S.E., 15–16.*

Freud, S. (1917d [1915]). A metapsychological supplement to the theory of dreams. *S.E., 14.*

Freud, S. (1918b [1914]). From the history of an infantile neurosis. *S.E., 17.*

Freud, S. (1919c). A note on psycho-analytic publications and prizes. *S.E., 17.*

Freud, S. (1919j [1918]). On the teaching of psycho-analysis in universities. *S.E., 17.*

Freud, S. (1922a). Dreams and telepathy. *S.E., 18.*

Freud, S. (1922d). Prize offer [included in 1919c]. *S.E., 17.*

Freud, S. (1925b). Letter to the Editor of the *Jüdische Presszentrale, Zurich. S.E., 19.*

Freud, S. (1926e). *The Question of Lay Analysis. S.E., 20:* 183–250.

Freud, S. (1927a). Postscript to *The Question of Lay Analysis. S.E., 20.*

Freud, S. (1933a [1932]). *New Introductory Lectures on Psycho-Analysis. S.E., 22:* 251–258.

Freud, S. (1934b [1930]). Preface to the Hebrew translation of *Totem and Taboo. S.E., 13.*

Freud, S. (1939a [1937–39]). *Moses and Monotheism. S.E., 23.*

Freud, S. (1940a [1938]). *An Outline of Psycho-Analysis. S.E., 23.*

Freud, S. (1941d [1921]). Psycho-analysis and telepathy. *S.E., 18.*

Freud, S. (1941e [1926]). Address to the members of the *B'nai B'rith. S.E., 20.*

Freud, S. (1950 [1892–1899]). Extracts from the Fliess papers. *S.E., 1.*

Freud, S. (1950 [1895]). A project for a scientific psychology. *S.E., 1.*

Freud, S. (1950a [1887–1902]). *The Origins of Psycho-Analysis.* New York: Basic Books, 1954.

Freud, S. (1960a). *Letters 1873–1939,* trans. T. Stern & J. Stern, ed. E. L. Freud. New York: Basic Books, 1961.

Freud, S. (1965a). *A Psycho-Analytic Dialogue: The Letters of Sigmund Freud and Karl Abraham.* London: Hogarth Press.

Freud, S. (1989a [1871–81, 1910]). *Jugendbriefe an Eduard Silberstein 1871–1881,* ed. W. Boehlich. Frankfurt a/M: Fischer Verlag.

Freud, S. (1993). *The Complete Correspondence of Sigmund Freud and Ernest Jones 1908–1939,* ed. R. A. Paskauskas. Cambridge, MA: Belknap Press of Harvard University Press.

Freud, S., & Binswanger, L. (1992). *The Freud–Binswanger Correspondence* , ed. G. Fichtner. New York: Other Press, 2003.

Freud, S., & Ferenczi, S. (1996). *The Correspondence of Sigmund Freud and Sandor Ferenczi, Vol. 2 (1914–1919).* Cambridge, MA: Harvard University Press/Belknap Press..

Freud, S., & Ferenczi, S. (2000). *The Correspondence of Sigmund Freud and Sandor Ferenczi (1920–1933), Vol. 3.* Cambridge, MA: Harvard University Press..

Freud, S., & Fliess, W. (1985). *The Complete Letters of Sigmund Freud to Wilhelm Fliess* (1887–1904), trans. J. M. Masson. Cambridge, MA: Harvard University Press/Belknap Press.

Frick, R. (1982). The ego and the vestibulo-cerebellar system: Some theoretical perspectives. *Psychoanalytic Quarterly, 51*: 93.

Frommer, J., & Rennie, D. (Eds.) (2001). *The Methodology of Qualitative Psychotherapy Research.* Berlin: Pabst.

Fürstenau, P. (1977a). Die beiden Dimensionen des psychoanalytischen Umgangs mit strukturell ich-gestörten Patienten: Ein Beitrag zur Erweiterung der psychoanalytischen Praxeologie. *Psyche, 31*: 197–207.

Fürstenau, P. (1977b). Stellungnahme zu dem Diskussionsbeitrag von Hermann Argelander und zu den Anmerkungen von Wolfgang Loch. *Psyche, 31*: 361–365.

Gadamer, H. G. (1960). *Truth and Method.* New York: Crossroad Publishing, 1974.

Gadamer, H. G. (1967). *On the Scope and Function of Hermeneutical Reflection.* Berkeley, CA: University of California Press, 1976.

Gadamer, H. G. (1971). Replik zu Hermeneutik und Ideologiekritik. In: *Gesammelte Werke II* (pp. 251–275). Tübingen: Mohr Siebeck, 1990.

Galin, D. (1974). Implications for psychiatry of left and right cerebral specialization: A neurophysiological context for unconscious processes. *Archives of General Psychiatry, 31*: 572.

Gay, P. (1988). *Freud: A Life for Our Time.* New York & London: W. W. Norton.

George, C., Kaplan, N., & Main, M. (1985). "The Adult Attachment Interview." Unpublished manuscript, Department of Psychology, University of California at Berkeley.

Gieryn, T. F. (1983). Boundary work and the demarcation of science from non science: Strains and interests in professional ideologies of scientists. *American Sociological Review, 48*: 781–795.

Giorello, G. (1976). Introduction. In: I. Lakatos, *Proofs and Refutations: The Logic of Mathematical Discovery.* Cambridge: Cambridge University Press.

Glover, E. (1954). The indications for psycho-analysis. *Journal of Mental Science, 100*: 393–401.

Goodman, N. (1972). *Problems and Projects.* Indianapolis & New York: Bobbs-Merrill.

Goodman, N. (1978). *Ways of Worldmaking.* Indianapolis & Cambridge: Hackett Publishing.

Green, A. (1991). Méconnaissance de l'inconscient. In: R. Dorey (Ed.), *L'inconscient et la science.* Paris: Dunod.

Green, A. (1997). *The Fabric of Affect in the Discourse of Psychoanalysis.* Madison, CT: International Universities Press.

Green, A. (2002). *Time in Psychoanalysis,* trans. Andrew Weller. London: Free Association Books.

Green, A., Botella, S., Botella, C., & Guignard, F. (1997). *Pulsions, représentations, langage: Théorie et clinique psychanalytiques,* ed. M. Pinol-Douriez. Paris: Delachaux et Nieslé.

Green, A., & Wallerstein, R. (1996). Controversy. *Newsletter of the International Psychoanalysis, 5*: 10–21.

Grubrich-Simitis, I. (1981). Siegfried Bernfeld: Historiker der Psychoanalyse und Freud-Biograph. *Psyche, 35*: 397–434.

Grubrich-Simitis, I. (1986). Six letters of Sigmund Freud and Sandor Ferenczi on the interrelationship of psychoanalytic theory and technique. *International Review of Psycho-Analysis, 13*: 259–277.

Grubrich-Simitis, I. (2000). Metamorphosen der Traumdeutung. In: J. Starobinski, I. Grubrich- Simitis, & M. Solms (Eds.), *Hundert Jahre Traumdeutung von Sigmund Freud* (pp. 49–100). Frankfurt: Fischer Taschenbuch Verlag.

Grubrich-Simitis, I. (2002). How Freud wrote and revised his *Interpretation of Dreams*: Conflicts around the subjective origins of the book of the century. *Psychoanalysis and History, 4* (2): 111–126.

Gullestad, S., & Killingmo, B. (2001). "Relational Scenarios." Unpublished manuscript.

Habermas, J. (1968). *Knowledge and Human Interest.* London: Heinemann, 1972.

Habermas, J. (1970). *On the Logic of Social Sciences.* Cambridge, MA: MIT Press, 1988.

Habermas, J. (2000). Nach dreißig Jahren: Bemerkungen zu "Erkenntnis und Interesse". In: S. Müller-Dohm (Ed.), *Das Interesse der Vernunft: Rückblicke auf das Werk von Jürgen Habermas seit "Erkenntnis und Interesse"* (pp. 12–22). Frankfurt: Suhrkamp.

Hacking, I. (1983). *Representing and Intervening.* Cambridge: Cambridge University Press.

Hadley, J. (1983). The representational system: A bridging concept for psychoanalysis and neurophysiology. *International Review of Psycho-Analysis, 10*: 13.

Hadley, J. (1992). The instincts revisited. *Psychoanalytic Inquiry, 12*: 396–418.

Hampe, M. (2000). Pluralismus der Erfahrung und Einheit der Vernunft. In: M. Hampe & M.-S. Lotter (Eds.), *"Die Erfahrungen, die wir machen, sprechen gegen die Erfahrungen, die wir haben." Über Formen der Erfahrung in den Wissenschaften* (pp. 27–39). Berlin: Duncker, Humblot.

Hampe, M., & Lotter, M.-S. (Eds.) (2000). *"Die Erfahrungen, die wir machen, sprechen gegen die Erfahrungen, die wir haben." Über Formen der Erfahrung in den Wissenschaften. Series Erfahrung und Denken. Schriften zur Förderung der Beziehungen zwischen Philosophie und Einzelwissenschaften, Vol. 86.* Berlin: Duncker, Humblot.

Hanson, N. R. (1958) *Patterns of Discovery.* Cambridge: Cambridge University Press.

Hardt, M., & Negri, A. (2000). *Empire: The New World Order.* Cambridge, MA: Harvard University Press.

Harlow, J. (1848). Passage of an iron rod through the head. *Boston Medical Surgery Journal, 39*: 389–393.

Harlow, J. (1868). Recovery from the passage of an iron bar through the head. *Massachusetts Medical Society Publications, 2*: 329–347.

Harris, J. (1986). *Clinical Neuroscience: From Neuroanatomy to Psychodynamics.* New York: Human Sciences.

Hartmann, E. (1982). From the biology of dreaming to the biology of the mental. *Psychoanalytic Study of the Child, 37*: 303–335.

Hartmann, H. (1952). The mutual influences in the development of ego and id. *Psychoanalytic Study of the Child, 7*: 9–30.

Heilbrunn, G. (1979). Biologic correlates of psychoanalytic concepts. *Journal of the American Psychoanalytic Association, 27*: 597–626.

Hermanns, L., & Schröter, M. (1992a). Felix Gattel (1870–1904): Freud's first pupil. Part I. *International Review of Psycho-Analysis, 19*: 91–104.

Hermanns, L., & Schröter, M. (1992b). Felix Gattel (1870–1904): Freud's first pupil. Part II. *International Review of Psycho-Analysis, 19*: 197–208.

Holzhey, H. (2001). Flug und Fall der Seele—Philosophische Reflexionen in anthropologischer Absicht. In: U. Stuhr, M. Leuzinger-Bohleber, & M. Beutel (Eds.), *Langzeit-Psychotherapie. Perspektiven für Therapeuten und Wissenschaftler* (pp. 17–37). Stuttgart: Kohlhammer.

Honos-Webb, L., & Stiles, W. B. (1998). Reformulation of assimilation analysis in terms of voices. *Psychotherapy, 35*: 23–33.

Honos-Webb, L., Stiles, W. B., Greenberg, L. S., & Goldman, R. (1998). *Assimilation Analysis of Process-Experiential Psychotherapy: A Comparison of Two Cases.* New York & London: Guilford Press.

Horowitz, M. J. (1981). *States of Mind: Analysis of Change in Psychotherapy.* New York: Plenum.

Hoskins, R. (1936). An endocrine approach to psychodynamics. *Psychoanalytic Quarterly, 5*: 87–107.

Jeannet-Hasler, M. (2002). *Thérapie contre la théorie? Les enjeux d'un concours.* Paris: PUF.

Jones, E. (1953). *Sigmund Freud: Life and Work, Vol. 1.* London: Hogarth Press.

Jones, E. (1955). *Sigmund Freud. Life and Work, Vol. 2.* London: Hogarth Press.

Jones, E. (1957). *Sigmund Freud. Life and Work, Vol. 3.* London: Hogarth Press.

Jones, E. E. (2001). Interaktion und Veränderung in Langzeittherapien. In: U. Stuhr, M. Leuzinger-Bohleber, & M. Beutel (Eds.), *Langzeit-Psychotherapie: Perspektiven für Therapeuten und Wissenschaftler* (pp. 224–238). Stuttgart: Kohlhammer.

Joseph, R. (1982). The neuropsychology of development: Hemispheric laterality, limbic language, and the origin of thought. *Journal of Clinical Psychology, 38*: 4–33.

Joseph, R. (1992). The limbic system: Emotion, laterality and unconscious mind. *Psychoanalytic Review, 79*: 405–456.

Jung, C. G. (1912). *Psychology of the Unconscious: A Study of the Transformations and Symbolisms of the Libido. A Contribution to the History of the Evolution of the Thought.* Princeton, NJ: Princeton University Press, 1992. [*Symbols of Transformation. Collected Works, Vol. 5.* London: Routledge & Kegan Paul, 1967.]

Kächele, H. (1992). Psychoanalytische Therapieforschung. *Psyche, 3*: 259–285.

Kantrowitz, J. L., Katz, A. L., Paolitto, F., Sashin, J., & Solomon, L. (1987). Changes in the level and quality of object relations in psychoanalysis: Follow-up of a longitudinal prospective study. *Journal of the American Psychoanalytic Association, 35*: 23–46.

Kaplan-Solms, K., & Solms, M. (2000). *Clinical Studies in Neuro-Psychoanalysis.* London: Karnac.

Kemper, W. (1947). *Die Seelenheilkunde in unserer Zeit: Ihre Entwicklung, ihr Stand, ihr Anspruch, ihre Aufgaben.* Stuttgart: Ernst Klett.

Kernberg, O. (1972). Final report of the Menninger Foundation's psychotherapy research project: Summary and conclusions. *Bulletin of the Menninger Clinic, 36*: 181–195.

Kernberg, O. (1980). *Internal World and External Reality.* New York: Jason Aronson, 1985.

Kiesler, D. J. (1966). Some myths of psychotherapy research and the search for a paradigm. *Psychological Bulletin, 65*: 110–136.

Killingmo, B. (1992). Issues in psychoanalytic research. *Scandinavian Psychoanalytic Review, 15*: 37–57.

Kokkou, M., & Leuzinger-Bohleber, M. (1992). Psychoanalysis and neurophysiology: A look at case material from the two theoretical perspectives. An interdisciplinary understanding of some basic psychoanalytic concepts. In: M. Leuzinger-Bohleber, H. Schneider, & R. Pfeifer (Eds.), *"Two Butterflies on My Head." Psychoanalysis in the Interdisciplinary Dialogue* (pp. 133–179). Berlin: Springer Verlag.

Krause, R. (1992). Die Zweierbeziehung als Grundlage der psychoanalytischen Therapie. *Psyche, 46*: 588–612.

Kuhn, T. S. (1962). *The Structure of Scientific Revolutions.* Chicago, IL: University of Chicago Press.

Kuhn, T. S. (1977). *Die Struktur wissenschaftlicher Revolutionen.* Frankfurt: Suhrkamp.

Kurthen, M. (1998). Intentionalität und Sprachlichkeit in Psychoanalyse und Kognitionswissenschaft. *Psyche, 52* (9–10): 850–884.

Kustadt, L. (2001). Ongoing discussion of Allan Hobson. *Neuro-Psychoanalysis, 3*: 85–100.

Lakatos, I. (1976). *Proofs and Refutations: The Logic of Mathematical Discovery.* Cambridge: Cambridge University Press.

Laplanche, J., &. Pontalis, J. B. (1973). *The Language of Psychoanalysis.* London: Karnac.

Lasky, R., Freedman, N., & Hurvich, M. (2002). *What We Listen for Matters: An Approach to Qualitative Analysis of Analytic Process.* Manuscript in preparation.

Lear, J. (1995). The shrink is in. In: M. Leuzinger-Bohleber & U. Stuhr (Eds.), *Psychoanalysen im Rückblick* (pp. 92–106). Gießen: Psychosozial Verlag, 1997.

Leclaire, S. (1972a). Visit of Prof. Serge Leclaire of the Freudian School of Paris to the Asociación Psicoanalítica del Uruguay (August). *Vol. 1: Seminars.* Unpublished.

Leclaire, S. (1972b). Visit of Prof. Serge Leclaire of the Freudian School of Paris to the Asociación Psicoanalítica del Uruguay (August). *Vol. 2: Clinical Seminars.* Unpublished.

Leiman, M. (1998). Words as intersubjective mediators in psychotherapeutic discourse: The presence of hidden voices in patient utterances. In: M. Lähteenmäki & H. Dufva (Eds.), *Dialogues on Bakhtin: Interdiciplinary Readings* (pp. 105–116). Jyväskylä: University of Jyväskylä, Centre for Applied Language Studies.

Leuzinger-Bohleber, M. (1995). Die Einzelfallstudie als psychoanalytisches Forschungsinstrument. *Psyche, 49* (5): 434–481.

Leuzinger-Bohleber, M. (1998). Nachträgliches Verstehen eines psychoanalytischen Prozesses: Einige einführende Überlegungen zu einem pluralistischen, modellzentrierten Erkenntnisprozeß. In: M. Leuzinger-Bohleber, W. Mertens, & M. Koukkou (Eds.), *Erinnerung von Wirklichkeiten: Psychoanalyse und Neurowissenschaften im Dialog. Vol. 2: Folgerungen für die psychoanalytische Praxis* (pp. 36–96). Stuttgart: Klett Cotta.

Leuzinger-Bohleber, M. (2000). Psychoanalyse—Erfahrungswissenschaft des Unbewussten. In: M. Hampe, & M.-S. Lotter (Eds.), *"Die Erfahrungen, die wir machen, sprechen gegen die Erfahrungen, die wir haben." Über Formen der Erfahrung in den Wissenschaften* (pp. 145–168). Berlin: Duncker, Humblot.

Leuzinger-Bohleber, M. (2002a). "Psychoanalytic Research and the Pluralism of the Sciences." Paper presented to the British Psychoanalytical Society.

Leuzinger-Bohleber, M. (2002b). Quelques remarques critiques illustrées par un suivi représentatif de psychoanalyses et thérapies psychoanalytiques de longue durée. *Bulletin de la Société Psychoanalytique de Paris, 63*: 157–175.

Leuzinger-Bohleber, M. (2003). "Discussion of David Taylor's Paper on Depression from a Perspective of Conceptual Research in Psychoanalysis." Joseph Sandler Research Conference on Depression, London, 8 March.

Leuzinger-Bohleber, M., Deserno, H., & Hau, S. (Eds.) (in press). *Pluralität und Einheit der Wissenschaften: Die Psychoanaytische Methode zwischen klinischer, konzeptueller und empirischer Forschung.* Stuttgart: Kohlhammer.

Leuzinger-Bohleber, M., & Pfeifer, R. (2002). Remembering a depressive primary object: Memory in the dialogue between psychoanalysis and cognitive science. *International Journal of Psycho-Analysis, 83*: 3–33.

Leuzinger-Bohleber, M., & Stuhr, U. (Eds.) (1997). *Psychoanalysen im Rückblick. Methoden: Ergebnisse und Perspektiven der neueren Katamneseforschung.* Gießen: Psychosozial Verlag.

Leuzinger-Bohleber, M., Stuhr, U., Rüger, B., & Beutel, M. (2002). *"Forschen und Heilen" in der Psychoanalyse: Ergebnisse und Berichte aus Forschung und Praxis.* Stuttgart: Kohlhammer.

Leuzinger-Bohleber, M., Stuhr, U., Rüger, B., & Beutel, M. (2003). How to study the "quality of psychoanalytic treatments" and their long-term effects in patients' well-being: A representative, multi-perspective follow-up study. *International Journal of Psycho-Analysis, 84*: 263–290.

Leuzinger-Bohleber, M., & Target, M. (Eds.) (2002). *Outcomes of Psychoanalytic Treatment: Perspectives for Therapists and Researchers.* London: Whurr.

Levin, F. (1991). *Mapping the Mind: Intersection of Psychoanalysis and Neuroscience.* Hillsdale, NJ: Analytic Press.

Lewin, K. (1981). Der Übergang von der aristotelischen zur galileischen Denkweise in Biologie und Psychoanalyse. In: *Wissenschaftstheorie, Vol. 1: Kurt Lewin—Werkausgabe,* ed. C.-F. Graumann. Bern/Stuttgart: Klett-Kotta.

Lindner, R. (2003). "Biografie und Psychodynamik suizidaler Männer—Studien zur Diagnostik in psychoanalytisch orientierten Psychotherapien." Dissertation, University of Hamburg, Department of Medicine.

Loch, W. (1965). *Voraussetzungen, Mechanismen und Grenzen des psychoanalytischen Prozesses.* Bern: Huber.

Loch, W. (1972). *Zur Theorie, Technik und Therapie der Psychoanalyse.* Frankfurt: S. Fischer.

Loch, W. (1974). Der Analytiker als Gesetzgeber und Lehrer. *Psyche, 28*: 431–460.

Loch, W. (1975). *Über Begriffe und Methoden der Psychoanalyse.* Bern: Huber.

Loch, W. (1977). Anmerkungen zum Thema Ich-Veränderungen, Ich-Defekte und psychoanalytische Technik. *Psyche, 31*: 216–227.

Loch, W. (1986). *Psychoanalytische Perspektiven.* Stuttgart: Hirzel.

Lorenzer, A. (1970). *Sprachzerstörung und Rekonstruktion.* Frankfurt: Suhrkamp.

Lorenzer, A. (1981). *Das Konzil der Buchhalter. Die Zerstörung der Sinnlichkeit. Eine Religionskritik.* Frankfurt a/M: Fischer.

Lorenzer, A. (1983). Sprache, Lebenspraxis und szenisches Verstehen in der psychoanalytischen Therapie. *Psyche, 37*: 97–115.

Lorenzer, A. (1985). Das Verhältnis der Psychoanalyse zu ihren Nachbardisziplinen. *Fragmente, 14* (15): 8–22.

Lorenzer, A. (2002). *Die Sprache, der Sinn, das Unbewußte: Psychoanalytisches Grundverständnis und Neurowissenschaften,* ed. U. Prokop. Stuttgart: Klett-Cotta.

Luborsky, L., & Crits-Cristoph, P. (1990). *Understanding Transference: The CCRT Method.* New York: Basic Books.

Luria, A. (1970). *Traumatic Aphasia: Its Psychology, Syndromes and Treatment.* Paris & The Hague: Mouton.

Luria, A. (1973). *The Working Brain: An Introduction to Neuropsychology.* Harmondsworth: Penguin.

Luria, A. (1987). Mind and brain: Luria's philosophy. In R. Gregory (Ed.), *The Oxford Companion to the Mind.* Oxford: Oxford University Press.

Maclean, P. (1962). New findings relevant to the evolution of the psychosexual functions of the brain. *Journal of Nervous & Mental Diseases, 135*: 289–301.

Maskit, B., Bucci, W., & Roussos, A. (2002). "The Discourse Attribute Analysis Program: Parameters and Problems." Paper presented at the International Meeting of the Society for Psychotherapy Research, Santa Barbara, CA.

Maskit, B., Bucci, W., & Roussos, A. (2003). *Capturing the Flow of Verbal Interactions: The Discourse Attribute Analysis Program.* Manuscript submitted for publication.

McLaughlin, J. (1978). Primary and secondary process in the context of cerebral hemispheric specialization. *Psychoanalytic Quarterly, 47*: 237–266.

Meyersburg, H., & Post, R. (1979). An holistic developmental view of neural and psychological process: A neurobiologic-psychoanalytic integration. *British Journal of Psychiatry, 135*: 139–155.

Mijolla, A. de (1996). Un adolescent bien tranquille: Sig(is)mund Freud, 1870–1876. *Les Cahiers du Collège International de l'Adolescence, 1*: 231–267.

Mijolla, A. de (2002). *Dictionnaire International de la Psychanalyse* (2 vols.). Paris: Calmann-Levy.

Mijolla, A. de (2003). *Freud, fragments d'une histoire: Qui êtes-vous Sigmund Freud?* Paris: PUF.

Miller, L. (1991). *Freud's Brain: Neuropsychodynamic Foundations of Psychoanalysis.* New York & London: Guilford Press.

Moore, B. E., & Fine, B. D. (Eds.) (1990). *Psychoanalytic Terms and Concepts.* New Haven, CT, & London: The American Psychoanalytic Association and Yale University Press.

Morin, E. (1977–2001). *La méthode, Vols. 1–5.* Paris: Le Seuil.

Moser, U. (1992). Two butterflies on my head, or, why have a theory in psychoanalysis? In: M. Leuzinger-Bohleber, H. Schneider, & R. Pfeifer (Eds.), *"Two Butterflies on My Head." Psychoanalysis in the Interdisciplinary Dialogue* (pp. 29–47). New York: Springer.

Moser, U., & Zeppelin, I. von (1996). *Der geträumte Traum: Wie Träume entstehen und sich verändern.* Stuttgart: Kohlhammer.

Moser, U., Zeppelin, I. v., & Schneider, W. (1991). *Cognitive-Affective Processes: New Ways of Modeling.* Berlin: Springer.

Müller-Braunschweig, C. (1947). Prolegomena zum Grundriß einer praktischen und theoretischen Tiefenpsychologie. *Psyche, 1*: 189–205.

Müller-Braunschweig, C. (1954). Zur Methodik und Technik in der Praxis der Psychoanalyse. *Psyche, 7*: 676–688.

Negri, R. (1994). *The Newborn in the Intensive Care Unit: A Neuropsychoanalytic Model.* London: Karnac.

Nielsen, H. B. (1995). Seductive texts with serious intentions. *Educational Researcher, 24* (1): 4–12.

Nunberg, H., & Federn, E. (1962–75). *Minutes of the Vienna Psychoanalytic Society*. New York: International Universities Press.

Olds, D. (1992). Consciousness: A brain-centred, informational approach. *Psychoanalytic Inquiry, 12*: 419–444.

Orange, D., Atwood, G., & Stolorow, R. (1997). *Working Intersubjectively: Contextualism in Psychoanalytic Practice*. Hillsdale, NJ: Analytic Press.

Ostow, M. (1954). A psychoanalytic contribution to the study of brain function: 1. The frontal lobes. *Psychoanalytic Quarterly, 23*: 317.

Ostow, M. (1955a). A psychoanalytic contribution to the study of brain function: 2. The temporal lobes: 3. Synthesis. *Psychoanalytic Quarterly, 24*: 383.

Ostow, M. (1955b). Behavior correlates of neural function. *American Scientist, 43*: 127–133.

Ostow, M. (1955c). Psychic contents and processes of the brain. *Psychosomatic Medicine, 17*: 396–406.

Ostow, M. (1956). Psychoanalysis and the brain. *Acta Medica Orientalia, 15*: 167–176.

Ostow, M. (1959). The biological basis of human behavior. In A. Arieti (Ed.), *American Handbook of Psychiatry*. New York: Basic Books.

Palombo, S. (1992). Connectivity and condensation in dreaming. *Journal of the American Psychoanalytic Association, 40*: 1139–1159.

Panksepp, J. (1985). Mood changes. In: P. Vinken, G. Bruyn, & H. Klawans, *Handbook of Clinical Neurology, 45*: 271–285.

Peirce, C. S. (1877). The fixation of belief. *Popular Science Monthly, 12*: 1–15. Reprinted in: P. P. Wiener (Ed.), *Values in a Universe of Chance: Selected Writings of Charles S. Peirce* (pp. 91–112). Garden City, NY: Doubleday 1958.

Perelman, Ch., & Olbrechts-Tyteca, L. (1958). *Traité de l'argumentation: La nouvelle réthorique*. Brussels: Editions de la Université de Bruxelles, 1983.

Perron, R. (1999). Part 2: Epistemological and methodological background. Section A: Reflections on psychoanalytic research problems—the French-speaking view. In: P. Fonagy (Ed.), *An Open Door Review of Outcome Studies in Psychoanalysis*. London: International Psychoanalytical Association, Research Committee.

Perron, R., et al. (2002). La question de la recherche en psychanalyse/sur la psychanalyse. Dossier. *Bulletin de la Société Psychanalytique de Paris, 64*: 147–190.

Peterfreund, E. (1971). Information systems and psychoanalysis: An evolutionary biological approach to psychoanalytic theory. *Psychological Issues, 7* (1 & 2, Monograph): 25–26.

Peterfreund, E. (1975). New general theoretical frame of reference for psychoanalysis. *Psychoanalytic Quarterly, 44*: 534.

Petroni, A. M. (1993). Conventionnalisme, découverte scientifique et sociologie de la connaissance. In: R. Boudon & M. Clavelin (Eds.), *Le relativisme est-il résistible? Regards sur la sociologie des sciences*. Paris: PUF, 1994.

Popper, K. R. (1934). *Logik der Forschung*. Tübingen: J. C. Mohr. (English edition: *The Logic of Scientific Discovery*. London: Hutchinson, 1959.)

Popper, K. R. (1972). *Objective Knowledge: An Evolutionary Approach*. Oxford: Clarendon Press.

Quine, W. V. O. (1951). Two dogmas of empiricism. In: *From a Logical Point of View*. Cambridge: Cambridge University Press.

Raguse, H. (1998). Psychoanalytische Hermeneutik—Weltanschauung oder Regelkorpus? *Psyche, 52*: 648–703.

Rank, O. (1924). *The Trauma of Birth*. London: Routledge & Kegan Paul.

Reicheneder, J. G. (1985). "Zum Konstitutionprozess der Psychoanalyse." PhD Thesis, Freie Universität Berlin.

Reiser, M. (1984). *Mind, Brain, Body: Toward a Convergence of Psychoanalysis and Neurobiology*. New York: Basic Books.

Reiser, M. (1990). *Memory in Mind and Brain: What Dream Imagery Reveals*. New York: Basic Books.

Rheinberger, H.-J. (2000). Dimensionen der Darstellung in der Praxis des wissenschaftlichen Experimentierens. In: M. Hampe & M.-S. Lotter (Eds.), *"Die Erfahrungen, die wir machen, sprechen gegen die Erfahrungen, die wir haben." Über Formen der Erfahrung in den Wissenschaften* (pp. 235–246). Berlin: Duncker, Humblot.

Rickert, H. (1926). *Kulturwissenschaft und Naturwissenschaft*. Tübingen: Mohr.

Rickert, H. (1929). *Die Grenzen der naturwissenschaftlichen Begriffsbildung. Eine Einleitung in die historischen Wissenschaften*. Tübingen: Mohr.

Ricoeur, P. (1979). The model of the text: Meaningful action considered as a text. In P. Rabinow & W. M. Sullivan (Eds.), *Interpretive Social Science: A Reader* (pp 73–101). Berkeley, CA: University of California Press. (Original work published in 1971.)

Ricoeur, P. (1991a). Construing and constructing: A review of "The Aims of Interpretation" by E. D. Hirsh. In: M. J. Valdés (Ed.), *Reflection and Imagination: A Ricoeur Reader* (pp. 195–199). New York & London: Harvester Wheatsheaf.

Ricoeur, P. (1991b). What is a text? Explanation and understanding. In: M. J. Valdés (Ed.), *Reflection and Imagination: A Ricoeur Reader* (pp. 43–64). New York & London: Harvester Wheatsheaf.

Rosenbaum, B. (2000). *Tankeformer og talemåder*. Danmark: Multivers.

Rosenbaum, B., & Varvin, S. (1999). "The Breaking Down of the Mind: Trauma in a Psychosemiotic Perspective." Paper presented at the 30th Annual Meeting of the Society for Psychotherapy Research, Braga, Portugal, June.

Rosenbaum, B., & Varvin, S. (2002a). The enunciation of exiled and traumatized persons: A model and its application. In: S. Varvin & T. Stajner-Popovic (Eds.), *Upheaval: Psychoanalytic Perspectives on Trauma*. Belgrade: IAN.

Rosenbaum, B., & Varvin, S. (2002b). "The Influence of Extreme Traumatisation on Body, Mind and Social Relations." Unpublished manuscript.

Roth, A., & Fonagy, P. (1996). *What Works for Whom? A Critical Review of Psychotherapy Research*. New York & London: Guilford Press.

Rubovits-Seitz, P. (2001). *The Interpretive Process in Clinical Practice: Progressive Understanding and Communication of Latent Meaning*. London: Jason Aronson.

Sachs, H. (1944). *Freud: Master and Friend*. Cambridge, MA: Harvard University Press.

Sacks, O. (1985). *The Man Who Mistook His Wife for a Hat*. London: Duckworth.

Sacks, O. (1990). *Awakenings* (2nd revised edition). New York: Harper Collins.

Sacks, O. (1991). Neurological dreams. *MD Magazine* (February): 29–32.

Salner, M. (1989). Validity in Human Science research. In: S. Kvale (Ed.), *Issues of Validity in Qualitative Research* (pp. 47–71). Lund: Studentlitteratur.

Samarango, J. (1997). *All the Names*. London: Harvill Press.

Sandler, J. (1962). The Hampstead Index as an instrument of psychoanalytic research. *International Journal of Psycho-Analysis, 43*: 287–291.

Sandler, J. (1983). Reflections on some relations between psychoanalytic concepts and psychoanalytic practice. *International Journal of Psycho-Analysis, 64*: 35–45.

Sandler, J. (Ed.) (1987). *From Safety to Superego: Selected Papers of Joseph Sandler*. London: Karnac.

Sandler, J., & Dreher, A. U. (1996). *What Do Psychoanalysts Want? The Problem of Aims in Psychoanalytic Therapy*. London: Routledge.

Sandler, J., Dreher, A.U., Drews, S., Fischer, R., Klüwer, R., Muck, M., Vogel, H., & Will, C. (1987). *Psychisches Trauma: Ein Konzept im Theorie-Praxis-Zusammenhang*. Dossiers, Frankfurt a/M: Sigmund-Freud-Institute.

Sandler, J., & Sandler, A.-M. (1983). The "second censorship", the "three box model" and some technical implications. *International Journal of Psycho-Analysis, 64*: 413–425.

Sandler, J., Sandler, A.-M., & Davies, R. (Eds.) (2000). *Clinical and Observational Psychoanalytic Research: Roots of a Controversy*. London: Karnac.

Schepank, H. (1995). *BSS—Der Beeinträchtigungs-Schwere-Score*. Göttingen: Beltz-Test.

Scheunert, G. (1956). Einige Entwicklungstendenzen der neueren psychoanalytischen Ich-Psychologie. *Psyche, 10*: 29–40.

Scheunert, G. (1959). Zum Problem der Gegenübertragung. *Psyche, 13*: 574–593.

Schilder, P. (1935). Psycho-analysis of space. *International Journal of Psycho-Analysis, 16*: 274–295.

Schneider, G. (2003). Die Zukunft? Plädoyer für eine atopische Grundhaltung in der Psychoanalyse mit einem Exkurs zu Melvilles Bartleby. *Psyche-Z. Psychoanal., 57*: 226–250.

Schore, A. (1994). *Affect Regulation and the Origin of the Self: The Neurobiology of Emotional Development.* Hillsdale NJ: Lawrence Erlbaum Associates.

Schottlaender, F. (1952). Das Problem der Begegnung in der Psychotherapie. *Psyche, 6*: 494–507.

Schröter, M. (1989). Freud und Fliess im wissenschaftlichen Gespräch: Das Neurasthenieprojekt von 1893 [A Scientific Dialogue between Freud and Fliess: The Research Project on Neurasthenia]. *Jahrbuch der Psychoanalyse, 22.* (French version: Un dialogue scientifique entre Freud et Fliess. Le projet d'étude sur la neurasthénie (1893). *Rev. internat. histoire psychanal., 2*: 109–146.)

Schwartz, A. (1987). Drives, affects, behavior—and learning: Approaches to a psychobiology of emotion and to an integration of psychoanalytic and neurobiologic thought. *Journal of the American Psychoanalytic Association, 35*: 467.

Schwartz, A. (1988). Reification revisited: Some neurobiologically filtered views of "psychic structure" and "conflict". *Journal of the American Psychoanalytic Association, 36* (Suppl.): 359–385.

Sellars, W. (1963). Empiricism and the philosophy of mind. In: *Science, Perception and Reality.* London: Routledge & Kegan Paul.

Sennett, R. (1998). *Der flexible Mensch: Die Kultur des neuen Kapitalismus.* Berlin: Berlin Verlag.

Shapin, S. (1990). Science and the public. In: R. C. Olby, G. N. Cantor, J. R. R. Christie, & M. S. J. Hodge (Eds.), *Companion to the History of Modern Science* (pp. 991–1007). London: Routledge.

Simon, H. (1973). Does scientific discovery have a logic? In: *Models of Discovery and Other Topics in the Methods of Science.* Dordrecht & Boston, MA: Reidel, 1977.

Solms, M. (1995). New findings on the neurological organisation of dreaming: Implications for psychoanalysis. *Psychoanalytic Quarterly, 64*: 43–67.

Solms, M. (1997). *The Neuropsychology of Dreams: A Clinico-Anatomical Study.* Mahwah, NJ: Lawrence Erlbaum Associates.

Solms, M. (2000). Dreaming and REM sleep are controlled by different brain mechanisms. *Behavioral and Brain Sciences, 23*: 843-850.

Solms, M., & Saling, M. (1986). On psychoanalysis and neuroscience: Freud's attitude to the localizationist tradition. *International Journal of Psycho-Analysis, 67*: 397.

Sperber, D., & Wilson, D. (1998). The mapping between the mental and the public lexicon. In: P. Carruthers & J. Boucher (Eds.), *Language and Thought: Interdisciplinary Themes.* Cambridge: Cambridge University Press.

Steiner, R. (1994). The Tower of Babel, or, After Babel in contemporary psychoanalysis. *International Journal of Psycho-Analysis, 75* (5–6): 883–903.

Stekel, W. (1911). *Die Sprache des Traumes: Eine Darstellung der Symbolik und Deutung des Traumes in ihren Beziehungen zur kranken und gesunden Seele für Ärtze und Psychologen.* Munich & Wiesbaden: J. F. Bergmann.

Stepansky, P. E. (1983). *In Freud's Shadow: Adler in Context.* Hillsdale, NJ: Analytic Press.

Stern, D., Sander, L., Nahum, J., Harrison, A., Lyons-Ruth, K., Morgan, A., Bruschweiler-Stern, N., & Tronick, E. (1998). Non-interpretive mechanisms in psychoanalytic therapy. *International Journal of Psycho-Analysis, 79*: 903–921.

Stiles, W. B. (2001). "The Assimilation Model: Theory and Theoretical Developments." Paper presented at the Ohio SPR Meeting, April.

Stiles, W. B., Elliott, R., Llewelyn, S. P., Firth-Cozens, J. A., Margison, F. R., Shapiro, D. A., & Hardy, G. (1990). Assimilation of problematic experiences by clients in psychotherapy. *Psychotherapy, 27*: 411–420.

Stiles, W. B., Meshot, C. M., Anderson, T. M., & Sloan, W. W. J. (1992). Assimilation of problematic experiences: The case of John Jones. *Psychotherapy Research, 2*: 81–101.

Stiles, W. B., Morrison, L. A., Haw, S. K., Harper, H., & Shapiro, D. A. (1991). Longitudinal study of assimilation in exploratory psychotherapy. *Psychotherapy Assimilation, 28*: 195–206.

Stiles, W. B., & Shapiro, D. A. (1994). Disabuse of the drug metaphor: Psychotherapy process-outcome correlations. *Journal of Consulting and Clinical Psychology, 62* (5): 942–948.

Stone, M. (1977). Dreams, free association, and the non-dominant hemisphere: An integration of psychoanalytical, neurophysiological and historical data. *Journal of the American Academy of Psychoanalysis, 5*: 255–284.

Stuhr, U., Leuzinger-Bohleber, M., & Beutel, M. (Eds.) (2001). *Langzeit-Psychotherapie: Perspektiven für Therapeuten und Wissenschaftler.* Stuttgart: Kohlhammer.

Sulloway, F. (1979). *Freud—Biologist of the Mind.* London: Burnett.

Target, M. (2002). The problem of outcome in child psychoanalyis: Contribution from the Anna Freud Centre. In: M. Leuzinger-Bohleber & M. Target (Eds.), *Outcomes in Psychoanalytic Treatment* (pp. 252–264). London: Whurr.

Taylor, D. (2003). "Thinking, Ideomotor Mental Action and Depression as a Psychosomatic Illness." Paper presented at the Joseph Sandler Research Conference, London, 7 March.

Theunissen, M. (1977). *The Other: Studies in the Social Ontology of Husserl, Heidegger, Sartre, and Buber*. Cambridge, MA: MIT Press, 1984.

Thomä, H. (1981). *Schriften zur Praxis der Psychoanalyse: Vom spiegelnden zum aktiven Psychoanalytiker*. Frankfurt: Suhrkamp.

Thomä, H. (1983). Erleben und Einsicht im Stammbaum psychoanalytischer Techniken und der "Neubeginn" als Synthese im "Hier und Jetzt". In: S. O. Hoffmann (Ed.), *Deutung und Beziehung. Kritische Beiträge zur Behandlungskonzeption und Technik in der Psychoanalyse* (pp. 17–43). Frankfurt: S. Fischer.

Thomä, H., & Kächele, H. (1985). *Lehrbuch der psychoanalytischen Therapie, Vols. 1, 2*. Berlin: Springer. English edition: *Psychoanalytic Practice*. Berlin: Springer, 1992/1995.

Toulmin, S. E. (1958). *The Uses of Argument*. Cambridge: Cambridge University Press, 1969.

Toulmin, S. E. (1983). *Kritik der kollektiven Vernunft*. Frankfurt a/M: Suhrkamp.

Toulmin, S. E. (1986). Self psychology as a "postmodern" science. *Psychoanalytical Inquirer, 6* (3): 459–477.

Trendelenburg, F. A. (1840). *Logische Untersuchungen*. Berlin: Bethge.

van Eemeren, F. H., Grootendorst, R., Jackson, S., & Jacobs, S. (1993). *Reconstructing Argumentative Discourse*. Tuscaloosa & London: University of Alabama Press.

Varvin, S. (2002). "Mental Survival Strategies after Extreme Traumatisation." PhD thesis submitted to the University of Oslo, Medical Faculty, Oslo.

Varvin, S., & Stiles, W. B. (1999). Emergence of severe traumatic experiences: An assimilation analysis of psychoanalytic therapy with a political refugee. *Psychotherapy Research, 9* (3): 381–404.

Von Klitzing, K., Simoni, H., & Bürgin, D. (1999). Child development and early triadic relationships. *International Journal of Psycho-Analysis, 80*: 71–89.

Vygotsky, L. S. (1934). *Thought and Language*. Cambridge, MA: MIT Press, 1962.

Wachholz, S., & Stuhr, U. (1999). The concept of ideal types in psychoanalytic follow-up research. *Psychotherapy Research, 9* (3): 347–351.

Waldron, S., Scharf, R. D, Crouse, J., Firestein, S. K., Burtun, A., & Hurst, D. (2001). Das Richtige zur richtigen Zeit sagen—Psychoanalytische Interventionen von guter Qualität führen zu sofortiger Patientenproduktivität. In: U. Stuhr, M. Leuzinger-Bohleber, & M. Beutel (Eds.), *Langzeit-Psychotherapie: Perspektiven für Therapeuten und Wissenschaftler* (pp. 277–313). Stuttgart: Kohlhammer.

Wallerstein, R. S. (1986). *Forty-two Lives in Treatment: A Study of Psychoanalysis and Psychotherapy*. New York & London: Guilford Press.

Wallerstein, R. S. (1989). Follow-up in psychoanalysis: Clinical and research values. *Journal of the American Psychoanalytic Association, 37*: 921–941.

Wallerstein, R. S. (2001). The generations of psychotherapy research: An overview. In: M. Leuzinger-Bohleber & M. Target (Eds.), *Outcomes of Psychoanalytic Treatment: Perspectives for Therapists and Researchers*. London: Whurr.

Weizsäcker, C. F. von (1988). *Der Aufbau der Physik*. Munich: Deutscher Taschenbuch Verlag.

Whitehead, A. N. (1898). *Treatise on Universal Algebra*. Cambridge: Cambridge University Press.

Whitehead, A. N. (1929). *The Function of Reason*. Princeton, NJ: Princeton University Press.

Whitehead, A. N. (1938). *Modes of Thought*. Cambridge: Cambridge University Press.

Widlöcher, D. (2001). "Presidential Address." Presented at the Conference of the International Psychoanalytical Association, Nice, August.

Williams, B. (2002). *Truth and Truthfulness: An Essay in Genealogy*. Princeton, NJ: Princeton University Press.

Winson, J. (1985). *Brain and Psyche: The Biology of the Unconscious*. Garden City, NY: Anchor & Doubleday.

Zueler, M., & Maas, J. (1994). An integrated conception of the psychology and biology of superego development. *Journal of the American Academy of Psychoanalysis, 22*: 195–209.

INDEX

AAI coding, *see* Adult Attachment Interview (AAI) coding
abduction, concept of [Peirce], 138
Aberastury, A., 132
Abraham, K., 37
acting out, 15
Adler, A., 89
Adorno, T., 63, 74
Adult Attachment Interview (AAI) coding, 163–165, 167
affect(s), 112
  role of in session, 131
after-effect (after-wardness [Laplanche]), 42
Age of Enlightenment, 32
Albani, C., 19
Althusser, L., 143
Ameisen, J. C., 42
analysis, assimilation (AA), 171–183
analytic process, research on, 103
Analytic Process Scale, 19
Anderson, T. M., 171, 179
Anna Freud Centre, 150, 161, 165
Anna Freud Foundation, 155
Anna O [Breuer], 86
anthropological–psychoanalytic thinking, 65–71
anti-realism, 138, 139
anxiety neurosis, 86, 87
APEOS, *see* Assimilation of Problematic and Overwhelming Experiences Scale
aphasia, Freud's research on, 84, 191, 192, 197
apoptosis, 42
Arbeitskreis OPD, 120, 121
Argelander, H., 74–76, 79
artificial intelligence programs, 138
assimilation:
  analysis (AA), 171–183
    steps of, 179–181
  levels of, 171
Assimilation of Problematic and Overwhelming Experiences Scale (APEOS), 174–175, 180–83
asthenia, 84
Atlan, H., 43
attachment:
  patterns, 19
  research, 111

attachment (*continued*):
security, evaluation of, 153, 154
theory, 41, 149–167
and life narratives, 163–164
Atwood, G., 64
Aulagnier, P., 37
auto-aggressive behaviour, 111
auxiliary ego, analyst as, 162

Bachelard, G., 9
Bachrach, H. M., 19, 235
Bacon, F., 8, 9, 10, 138
Baginsky, A., 85
Bakhtin, M. M., 172
Balint, M., 71, 73, 78
Baranger, M., 127
Baranger, W., 127, 130
Barkham, M., 180
Beenen, F., xiii, 23, 222–229
behavioural neurology, 188, 194, 197
dynamic school of, 195
Berenstein, I., 64
Berlin Psychoanalytic Institute, 65, 91
Bernardi, R., xiii, 21, 125–136
Bernays, M., 84
Bernfeld, S., 189
Beutel, M., 231, 232, 237
Bick, E., 42
Binswanger, L., 67–70, 78, 89, 90
Bion, W. R., xxii, 30, 40, 73, 127
on communication in psychoanalysis, 147
hypothesis of vertices, 37
"no memory and no desire", 23
on "public-ation", 148
on scientists' attitude to psychoanalysis, 34
Blaser, G., 19
Bleger, J., 127
Bleichmar, H., 21
body:
concept of, 131
–mind problem, 40
Bohleber, W., xiii, 6, 17, 63–80, 146
Bohr, N., 27
Bonaparte, M., 95
Bonomi, C., 86
Borch-Jacobsen, M., 32
Borderline Group, 161
borderline personality disorder(s), 39, 79
countertransference in, research on, 38–40
vs. neuroses, 166
Bornstein, M., 11
Boston Institute Project, 151
Boucher, J., 146
"boundary work" [Gieryn], 223–225
Bowlby, J., xxi
brain:
diagram, 200
lesion, 205
Brech, E., 236
Brede, K., 233
Breggin, P., 204
Brentano, F., 82, 131
Breuer, J., 86
Broca, P. P., 188, 191
Brown, J., 194
Brücke, E. W. von, 83, 84, 85
Buber, M., 67, 68, 70
Bucci, W., 210, 212
Bürgin, D., xiv, 1–25, 19

Canestri, J., xiv, 17
Cardona, G. R., 146
Carnap, R., 47
Carrington, H. H. L., 93–94
Carruthers, P., 146
Cassirer, E., 47, 49
CCRT-Analysis, 236
censorship, 145, 203
cerebral palsy, 192
chaos theory, 7
Charcot, J.-M., 85, 189, 190, 191, 194
child(ren):
analysis, long-term follow-up study, 149–167
concepts of, 144
sexual theories of, 42
Claus, K., 82, 83
clinical–descriptive method, 193, 195
clinical research, 15–25, 30, 32, 110
attachment theory, 149–167
vs. conceptual research, 20–25
on countertransference in

borderline personality disorders, 38–40
definition of, 4
diagrammatic representation of, 16–20
vs. empirical research, 20–25, 30
psychological, Freud's stage of, 81, 86–88
value of, 28, 38–40
clinical syndromes, concept of, 187
clinical thought, 18
Green, 28–30
psychoanalytic, 207
clinico-anatomical correlation, 187–188
clinico-anatomical method, 191–193
of localizing mental functions, 188–189, 192
cocaine, Freud's studies on, 81, 84, 85, 88
cognition, 112
of existence, 70
cognitive development, 143, 144, 146
cognitive–linguistic theory, 217
cognitive science, xxi, xxii, 22, 112
coherence, 46, 47, 51, 54, 60, 169
criteria, external, 170
system, 104
coherentism, 46, 48
Colby, K. M., 20
communication:
intrapsychic latent content of, 37
pathologies, 77
problems of, 110
psychoanalytic [Bion], 147
computer simulation, examination of complex psychoanalytic theories via, 20, 22, 195
concepts:
analytic meaning content of, 112
research on, 103–108
conceptual research, 30, 143, 150, 157, 234
vs. clinical research, 20–25
vs. conceptual reflection, 117
concept of, 109–124
definition of, 4
vs. empirical research, 20–25, 119, 123–124
experimentally tested psychoanalytic concepts, 22
formally validated psychoanalytic concepts, 21
hypothesis-generating, 166
integrative, 21
qualitative, 119
value of, 39–40
constructivism, 63, 139
containment, 172, 221
contemplation vs. technical skill, 46, 51–54
Cooper, D., 136
countercathexis, 29
countertransference, 114, 213, 218, 220
analyst's use of, 70
in borderline personality disorders, research on, 38–40, 39
concept of, 121
Racker, 127
development of, research on, 103
dialogical patterns in, 173
hermeneutic concept of [Loch], 72–74
in latency period, study of, 100
Lorenzer on, 77
related to transference, 29
unconscious processes shown in research on, 15
see also transference–countertransference: process
Cremerius, J., 78
Crews, F., 32
Crits-Cristoph, P., 173
cultural theory, 10, 122

Darwin, C., 35, 83, 222
Davidson, D., 148
da Vinci, Leonardo, 82
death drive/instinct, 41, 108
concept of, 105
decathexis, 29
deductive science, 47
deep-interview technique, 129
defence(s):
dynamics of, research on, 103
primitive, 150
psychoneurosis of, 87

defensive processes, 77
demarcation of psychoanalysis from other sciences, 222–229
Denzin, 235
depression:
  conceptual research on, 21
  study of, 101
depth-psychological anthropology, 66
depth psychology, 7, 42, 66
Derksen, M., 222
Descartes, R., 8, 33
descriptions in qualitative research, 168
Deserno, H., 24, 234, 236
destabilization vs. integration, 208, 220
Devereux, G., 8
Dewey, J., 51
dialogic hypercomplexity, 44
dialogical sequence analysis, 171–183
dialogues, in qualitative research, 168
Diatkine, G., 146
Dick, F., 236
Didier-Vincent, J., 43
Dilthey, W., 13, 69
discourse analysis, 210
Doell, S., 234
Donnet, J.-L., 29
dopamine agonists, 204
dopamine antagonists, 204
Dora [Freud's case of], 88
Dostoyevsky, F. M., 196
DPV follow-up study, 153, 156
dream(s), 14, 43, 53, 82
  interpretation of, 49, 52
  navel of [Freud], 95
  -reporting, 58
  theory, Freud's, 19, 22, 30, 93
  unconscious processes manifest in, 15
dreaming, function of, neurological organization of, 199–206
Dreher, A. U., xiv, 10, 20–22, 109–124, 143, 150
drive(s), 112
  dynamics of, research on, 103
duality, constitutive primacy of, 68
Dutch Psychoanalytic Society, 224
dynamic school of behavioural neurology, 195
dynamic unconscious, 121
  interpretation of, 150

eating disorders, 111
Ebner, F., 67
Edelman, G. M., 35–36, 43
Edelson, M., 24
Edgcumbe, R., 151
ego:
  -disorders, structural, 79
  function, 150
    deficits in, 161
  -psychology, 38, 39, 65–72, 76
Einstein, A., 27
Eissler, K. R., 78
Elias, N., 86
eliminative inductivism, 129
Eliot, T. S., 44
Emde, R., 42
emotion(s), 112
emotionality, 214
empathy, 219
Empedocles, 35
empirical research, 18, 151, 217
  vs. clinical research, 20–25, 30
  vs. conceptual research, 20–25, 30, 119, 123–124
  creative relevance of, 53
  definition of, 4
  hypothesis-testing, 166
  problems of, 40–44
  qualitative, 220
  quantitative, 3, 4, 119, 120, 219–221
  systematic, value of, 227
  value of, 219
empiricism, 4, 9, 10, 13, 51
  logical, 13, 16
  neo-, 147, 148
encounter, 75, 172
  concept of, 64–65
    philosophical–psychotherapeutic, 67–71
Engels, F., 143
English Middle Group, 71
Enlightenment, 56, 57, 58, 61
  Age of, 32

enumerative inductivism, 129
enunciation analysis, 173
"envelopes of psychoanalytic intervention" (EPI), 215
EPF Working Party on Theoretical Issues, 147
epigenesis, 41
epistemic values, 13
epistemology, 11, 31, 40, 43, 46, 138, 145
Epstein, A., 186
Erdelyi, M., 186
Eros/Thanatos, 105
Etchegoyen, R. H., 130
European Psychoanalytic Federation, Working Party on Theoretical Issues, 147
evaluation, 18, 207–209, 212, 214
  of alternative clinical strategies, 220
  data, 118
  of medication vs. psychotherapy, 6
  of process, 207
  session, 181
evenly suspended attention, 75
evidence-based research data, 222
expert validation, 21
extra-clinical (empirical) research, 5, 15–25, 110, 111, 118
  vs. clinical research, diagrammatic representation of, 16–20
  off-line, 17
  see also empirical research

Faimberg, H., 17
falsificationist hypothetical–deductive method, 147
Federn, E., 10, 89, 91
Ferenczi, S., xxii, xxiii, 37, 88, 89, 91, 93, 94, 96, 141
Feyerabend, P., 33, 54
Field, S. D., 180
Fillion, D., 155
Fine, B. D., 115
First World War, 10, 91
Fischer, G., 24
Fischmann, T., 238
Fleck, L., 9
Fleischl-Marxow, E., 85
Fliess, W., 10, 29, 85–88, 93, 96
Fluss, E., 82
fMRI study(ies) of dream processes, 237
Follesdal, D., 13
follow-up study, long-term, child analysis, 149–167
Fonagy, P., xiv, xx, 17–19, 22, 32, 37, 40–44, 126, 129, 146
  attachment theory, 19, 41, 149–167
  IPA Research Committee, 3, 36
  study of development, 42
forgetting, in dealing with Nazi past, 78–80
free association, 36, 52, 58, 79, 131
Freedman, N., xv, 18, 19, 207–221
free-floating attention, 23, 37
French structuralism, 40
Freud, A., 37, 150, 151, 152, 158
  Anna Freud Centre, 150, 161, 165
  Anna Freud Foundation, 155
  –Klein, Controversial Discussions, 39
Freud, S. (*passim*):
  anatomo–pathological investigations of, 84, 85, 191
  biological thinking of, 29
  on body–mind problem, 40
  Breuer and Anna O, 86
  classical theory of, 203
  clinical accounts of, 166
  clinico-anatomical method of localizing mental functions, 188–189, 192
  conception of time, 42–43
  dream theory of, 30, 237
  drive theory of, 39
  dynamic developmental factors applied to psychopathology, 192
  evolution of thought of, xxiv
  "Freud-bashing", 5–6
  Gradiva, Jensen's, 90
  interest in occultism, 93–94
  The Interpretation of Dreams, The, 30, 89, 95, 96, 193, 205
  "Little Hans", 152
  models of the mind, 203
  move from work on physiology to psychology, 30

Freud, S. (*continued*):
"naturalization" of psyche, 228
natural science based on interpretation, 126
psychoanalysis and neuroscience, integration of, 184–206
on psychoanalytic cure, 100
psychoanalytic research, 81, 88–94
history of, 81–96
research of:
laboratory, period of, 81–86
method of, 104
as observation of empirical facts, 126
on psychic activity, 26–29
psychological clinical, period of, 81, 86–88
strategy of, ethics of, 140
"scientific fantasies", 145, 147
study of neurasthenia, 86, 87, 190, 191
work of, meaning of Jewishness in, 140–142
Freudian cultural criticism, 4
Freudian dream theory, PET and fMRI studies of, 19
Freudian School of Paris, 128
Freyberg, T. von, 232
Frick, R., 186
Frommer, 235
fundamentalism, 46, 48
Fürstenau, P., 79

Gadamer, H. G., 11, 63, 70–73, 76
Gage, P., 184
Galatzer-Levy, R., 19, 235
Galin, D., 186
Garma, A., 132
Gattel, F., 87, 88
Gay, P., 95, 141
George, C., 163
Gergely, G., 151
Gerhardt, U., 235
German DPV Follow-up Project, 151
German Idealism, 13, 67
German Psychoanalytic Association, 66, 79, 231
German Romanticism, 66
Germany:
National Socialist past of, 65
psychoanalytic clinical theory in, after 1945, 63–80
Gestalt principle, 75
Gieryn, T. F., 223
Gilles de la Tourette's syndrome, 196
Giorello, G., 139
Glover, E., 151
Goldman, R., 179
Goldstein, K., 194
Goodman, N., 47, 53
Gradiva, Jensen's, Freud's study of, 90
Green, A., xv, 4, 22, 24, 26–44, 218, 221
Greenberg, L. S., 179
Grootendorst, R., 127
Grossman, W., 38
Grubrich-Simitis, I., 10, 89, 141
Grünbaum, A., 33, 47
Grünberg, K., 232
Gullestad, S., 171

Habermas, J., 47, 49, 63, 70, 71, 76, 77
Hacking, I., 51
Hadley, J., 186
Hampe, M., xv, 8, 10, 13, 14, 15, 45–62
Hampstead Clinic, 160
Hampstead Index Project, 116, 120, 150, 154
Hampstead Working Group, 117
Hanson, N. R., 138
Hardt, M., 2
Harlow, J., 184
Harper, H., 179
Harris, J., 186
Hartmann, E., 186
Hartmann, H., 219
Hartmann, N., 66
Hau, S., 24, 236, 237
Haw, S. K., 179
Head, H., 194
Heidegger, M., 67, 68, 70, 73
Heilbrunn, G., 186
Heisenberg, W. K., 27
Helmholtz, H. L. F. von, 85, 189, 193
Heraclitus, 29
Hermanns, L., 88

hermeneutical science, psychoanalysis as, 49
hermeneutic experience, 70
hermeneutics, 47, 97, 126, 147, 169
of corporeality, 76–78
depth, 77
and natural science, 63–80
philosophical, 71–72
heuristics, 139, 145, 146
historical context of discovery, 9
Hitschmann, E., 88
Hobson, A., 30, 237
hologrammatic hypercomplexity, 44
Holton, G., 27
Holzhey, H., 8
Honos-Webb, L., 172, 179
Horkheimer, M., 63, 74
Horowitz, M. J., 17
Hoskins, R., 186
Huber, D., 234
humanities vs. natural sciences, 11
human mind, computer metaphor for, 121
Hurvich, M., xv, 18, 19, 207–221
Husserl, E. G. A., 70
hypercomplexity, 43
hypothesis(es):
broad, 107
-generating research, 166
meaning of term, 28
research on, 103–108
-testing research, 166
hysteria, 111, 190, 191

idealization, in dealing with Nazi past, 78–80
identity:
of psychoanalysis as discipline, 222
psychoanalytic, 23, 79, 113
ideographic and psychoanalytic interpretive mode of knowing, 210
incestuous wishes, 157
"increasing equilibration" [Piaget], 104
Independent Group of the British Society, 38
inductivism:
eliminative, 129
enumerative, 129
infant(s):
observation, 42, 43
research, 40, 64, 111
infantile neurology, 85
infantile neuropathology, 84, 85
infantile sexuality, 87
inference, 46
inductive, 138
inner world, conscious and unconscious processes of, 112
insight, 78
instinct, death, 41, 105, 108
Institute of Physiology, Vienna, 83
institutions, analytic, relationship with, 133
integration vs. destabilization, 208, 220
International Psychoanalytical Association (IPA), xxii, 3, 4
Congress:
1910: Nuremberg, 89
1922: Berlin, 91
1985: Hamburg, 3
1999: Santiago de Chile, 3
2001: Nice, 3, 64
House of Delegates, Committee on Analytic Specificity, 18–19, 207
Research Advisory Board, xx, 3, 155
Research Committee, xx, 1, 3
research culture within, 3, 4, 22, 23, 38, 117
controversy within, 43
Research Subcommittee for Conceptual, Clinical, Epistemological and Historical Research, 4, 18, 24, 25
standing research committee, 36
interpretation(s), 72–74, 106, 131, 170, 205, 209
as analytic method, 72
essential, 79
Binswanger on, 69
in child psychotherapy, 100
dream, 52

interpretation(s) (*continued*):
  Eissler on, 78
  evaluation of, 38
  Loch on, 73
  Lorenzer on, 77
  of negation, 105, 108
  psychoanalysis as natural science based on [Freud], 126
  and qualia, 36
  research on, 102
  Ricoeur, 170
  transference, 102, 107
  of transference–countertransference processes, 64
  truthfulness of, evaluation of, 14, 114
Interpretation of Dreams, The [Freud], 30, 89, 95, 96, 193, 205
Interpretative Phenomenological Analysis (IPA), 155, 156, 167
interpretive psychoanalytic knowing, 219, 220
intersubjectivism, 63–64
intersubjectivity, 12, 15, 16, 18, 29, 47, 69, 156
  in psychoanalytic research, 15–24
introjection, 131, 196
IPA, *see* International Psychoanalytical Association
IPTAR Research Program, 207

Jackson, J. H., 190, 194
Jackson, S., 127
Jacobs, S., 127
Jacques, E., xxi
James, H., 34
James, W., 34
Jeannet-Hasler, M., 91
Johnson, V. E., 89
Jones, E., 83, 85, 89, 94, 96, 188
Jones, E. E., 19
Joseph, R., 186
Jouvet, M., 30
Jung, C. G., 89, 93
Junktim, 5
  research ["*Junktim-Forschung*"], 14–16, 18
Jurist, E. L. J., 151

Kächele, H., 3, 6, 19, 78
Kantrowitz, J. L., 151
Kaplan, N., 163
Kaplan-Solms, K., 206
Katz, A. L., 151
Kemper, W., 66
Kennedy, H., 151
Kennel, R., 236
Kepler, J., 27
Kernberg, O., 3, 38, 79, 112, 151
Kiesler, D. J, 11
Killingmo, B., 18, 171
Klein, G., xxi
Klein, M., 37, 40, 127, 132
  –A. Freud, Controversial Discussions, 39
Kleinian psychoanalytic theory, 38, 79, 80, 127, 128, 129, 131
Klug, G., 234
Knöpfmacher, W., 82
knowing, interpretive psychoanalytic, 219, 220
Kohon, G., 38
Kohut, H., 127
  self-psychology, 39, 79
Kokkou, M., 186
Koller, C., 84
Krafft-Ebing, R. von, 87
Krause, R., 19
Kuhn, T. S., 9, 33, 111, 112, 129, 148
Kurthen, M., 10
Kustadt, L., 30

Lacan, J., xxi, 30, 33, 37, 40, 104, 127, 128, 131, 147
Lagache, D., xxi
Lakatos, I., 33, 139
language:
  interior and external, 144
  supra-communicative view of, 146
Laplanche, J., 21, 42, 115, 170
Lasky, R., xv, 18, 19, 207–221
Lear, J., 5, 77
Leclaire, S., 128, 130, 131
legitimation, of psychoanalysis as science, 222–229
Leiman, M., 171, 172, 183
Lenin, V. I., 143
Leuschner, W., 238

Leuzinger-Bohleber, M., xiii, xv, 1–25, 53, 151, 153, 157, 186, 211, 217, 231–237
Levin, F., 186
Lewin, K., 49
Liberman, D., 127
libidinal interest, 202
libido, 203
life narratives and attachment theory, 163
"Little Hans" [Freud], 152
localization of mental functions, clinico-anatomical method of, 188–189, 192
Loch, W., 72–74, 78, 79
Loden, S., 167
logical empiricism, 13, 16
logical positivism, 11, 47
logic of mathematical discovery, 139
Lorenzer, A., 12, 76–78
Lotter, M.-S., 8, 10
Luborsky, L., 173, 236
Ludwig, K., 83
Luria, A. R., 194, 196–199, 203
Lutenberg, J., 38

Maas, J., 186
Maclean, P., 186
Mahler, M., 42
Main, M., 163
Marie, P., 194
Marx, K., 143
Maskit, B., 210
Masters, 89
Matalon, B., 139
mathematical discovery, logic of, 139
Max Kassowitz Institute, Vienna, 85
McLaughlin, J., 186
meaning vs. significance [Ricoeur], 169
Mecacci, L., 143, 144
medical models in psychoanalysis, 29–30
Meltzer, D., 127
memories of childhood:
  of "rejecting" adults, 165
  of "secure" adults, 164
Menciskaja, N. A., 144
Menninger Project, 151
mental functioning, systematic shifts in, 216
mental functions, localization of, clinico-anatomical method of, 188, 189, 192
mental health care, evidence-based, 154
mental survival strategies, 183
  after extreme traumatization, 169–183
mentalization, 152
mentalizing capacity, 183
mentalizing processes, 19
Meshot, C. M., 171, 179
Metzger, H. G., 236
Meyersburg, H., 186
Meynert, T. von, 84
"Michael E" [case study] child analysis, long-term follow-up study of, 157–162, 166
Midgley, N., 155, 167
Mijolla, A. de, xvi, 10, 21, 27, 81–96, 106, 115
Miller, L., 186
Milner, M., 37
Mitscherlich, A., 66
Moebius-strip model [Lacan], 131
"moments of meeting", 64
Monakow, C. von, 194
Moore, B. E., 115
Moran, G. S., 151
Morin, E., 43, 44
Morrison, L. A., 179
Moser, U., 15, 20, 22, 234
mother–baby relationships, 100
Ms P [case study], 211–212
Müller-Braunschweig, C., 66, 67
multiple code theory, 210

narrative(s), 63
  in qualitative research, 168
  "of self", 156
narrative plausibility, 61
nasal reflex neuroses, 87
natural science(s), 5, 11–13, 47, 121, 126, 196, 227, 228
  unidirectional materialism of, 228
negation, concept of, 105, 108
negative, work of [Green], 218

negative therapeutic reaction, research on, 103
Negri, A., 2
Negri, R., 186
neo-empiricism, 147, 148
neo-Kantian school, 47, 48, 66
neurasthenia, 86, 87, 190, 191
neurobiology, xxi, 40
neurological organization of dreaming, 199
neurology:
  Austro–German school, 189, 190, 192
  behavioural, 188, 194, 195, 197
  dynamic school of, 194
  French school, 189, 190, 192, 193
Neuropsychoanalysis Group Frankfurt–Cologne, 236
neuropsychology, 195, 197, 205
neurosciences, 112, 204
  imaging procedures in, 111
  and psychoanalysis, integration of, 184–206
neurosis(es), 8, 38, 49, 60, 67, 68, 77, 80, 88, 90, 152, 157, 190–193
  anxiety, 86, 87
  clinical explanation of [Freud], 186
  nasal reflex, 87
  transference, research on, 103
Newton, I., 27
Nielsen, H. B., 169, 171
Nunberg, H., 89, 91

object relation, 64, 72, 73, 157
  helpless or hopeless, 213
  primary, 161
  theory, 29, 38, 39, 71–73, 78
observational psychoanalytic research, 32
occultism, Freud's interest in, 93–94
oedipal conflict, 150
  revival of during adolescence, 100
Oedipus complex, 31, 85, 90
Olbrechts-Tyteca, L., 127
Olds, D., 186
ontology, 67
Orange, D., 64
Ostow, M., 186
outcome studies, 132, 150, 151

Palombo, S., 186
Panksepp, J., 204
Paolitto, F., 151
parallel distributed processing, 195
pathognomonic clinical syndromes, 190, 192
pathology, meaning of concept, 50
patient populations, as focus of research, 100–102
Peirce, C. S., 42, 52, 138
Perelman, Ch., 127
Perron, R., xvi, 4, 10, 17, 22, 43, 97–108
personality, human, dynamically unconscious structure of, 205
personality disorder(s):
  borderline, 79
    study of, 38
  narcissistic, 79
  severe, treatment of, 79, 80
Peterfreund, E., 186
Petroni, A. M., 138
Pfeifer, R., 22
phallic inadequacy, 157
phenomena in qualitative research, 169
philosophical anthropology, German, 67–80
philosophy, 3, 37, 58
  Brentano's, 131
  of communicative action [Habermas], 63
  of dialogue, 67
    socio-ontological, 65
  of language and of linguistics, 146
  neo-Kantian, 66
  post-analytic, 148
  and psychoanalysis, 66
  of psychoanalysis, 46
  of science, 8, 12, 13, 45–62, 143
    postmodernism, 54
    pragmatic turn in, 51
  subject, 64
  transcendental, 67
Piaget, J., 104, 144
Pichon Rivière, E. J., 127
plausibility, narrative, 61

Pontalis, J.-B., 21, 115, 170
Popper, K. R., 9, 33, 52, 122, 137–139, 145–146, 148
Post, R., 186
postmodernism, 54
pragmatic validation, 170
preconscious, 142, 143
  role of, 145
primal phantasies, 42
primal scene, 157
primary process ideation, 217
primitive defences, 150
Prochiantz, A., 43
projection(s), 131
  reciprocal, 4
psychic activity as progression and regression, 42
psychoanalysis (*passim*):
  development of, in Río de la Plata region, 127
  legitimacy strategies for, 222–229
  and neuroscience, integration of, 184–206
psychoanalytic field, concept of, 127
psychoanalytic identity, 23, 79, 113
psychoneurosis, 87
psychopathology:
  application of dynamic developmental factors [Freud], 192
  childhood, later effects of, 152
  and reflective capacities, 151
psychopharmacology, Freud's study of, 84, 187
psychotherapeutic dialogue, 169
"publication" [Bion], 148
Putnam, H., 148

Q-sort techniques, 19
qualia assumption [Edelman], 35–36
qualitative analysis, 210, 221
  and clinical case report, 168–183
qualitative methodology, 165
qualitative research, 17, 155, 156, 166, 168–183, 172
  quantitative empirical research, 120, 220, 221
  on patient who suffered extreme traumatization, 168–183
quantitative research, 36, 37, 151, 220
Quine, W. V. O., 51, 148

Racker, H., 127
Rad, M. von, 234
Raguse, H., 75
Randomized Controlled Trials (RCTs), 6
Rank, O., 91, 92
Rapaport, D., xxi
rationality, 28, 29, 50, 54–61
  coherentist theory of, 60
  higher-order, 55
  instrumental, 55
recursive hypercomplexity, 44
referential activity, 214
reflective capacities, and psychopathology, 151
reflective function, 175, 213, 215
  evaluation of, 129, 153
reflectivity, 214
reflexivity, 56
regression, 42, 208, 218, 220
  topographic, 203
Reich, W., 89
Reichenbach, H., 137, 138
Reiser, M., 186
REM sleep, 201–202
repetition compulsion, 42
repression, 61, 77
research:
  clinical, *see* clinical research
  conceptual, *see* conceptual research
  dissemination, 170
  empirical, *see* empirical research
  extra-clinical, *see* extra-clinical (empirical) research
  in vs. *on* psychoanalysis, 97–108
  intersubjectivity in, 15–24
  observational, 32
  quantitative, xx
resistance, 205
responsive understanding [Bakhtin], 172
Rheinberger, H.-J., 53
Rickert, H., 47, 48
Ricoeur, P., 47, 49, 169, 170, 171
Rie, O., 86
Roeckerath, K., 236

Rogers, 235
Rolland, J.-C., 38
Rosenbaum, B., 173
Rosenzweig, F., 67
Rosenzweig, S., 95
Roth, A., 126
Rothe, H. J., 236
Roussos, A., 210
Rubovits-Seitz, P., 11
Rüger, B., 231, 232
Russ, M., 237
Russian Psychoanalytical Society, 196

Sachs, H., 95
Sacks, O., 196, 204
Saling, M., 186
Salner, M., 171
Salpêtrière Hospital, 189, 190
Samarango, J., 171
Sander, L., 64
Sandler, A.-M., 142
Sandler, J., 3, 10, 32, 115, 116, 120, 128, 133, 142, 143, 145, 150
  psychoanalytic concept research, 20
Sapir, E., 143
Sashin, J., 151
Sauer, M., 238
"scenic function of the ego" [Argelander], 75
"scenic understanding":
  Argelander, 74–75
  Lorenzer, 76–78
Schachter, A., 155
Scheunert, G., 70
Schilder, P., 186
Schneider, G., 23
Schneider, W., 20, 238
Schore, A., 186
Schottlaender, F., 68
Schröder, E., 27
Schröter, M., 85, 86, 88
Schultz, H., 236
Schwartz, A., 186
science(s) (*passim*):
  deductive, 47
  history of, 6–12
  natural, 11
    and hermeneutics, 63–80
  philosophy of, 8, 45–62
  pluralism of (*passim*)
  positivist, 170
  unified, 6–12
  unity of, 2
"scientific fantasies" [Freud], 145, 147
screen memories, 75
Secret Committee, 94
self-knowledge, 56
self-mutilation, 111
self-psychology [Kohut], 39
self-reflection, 19, 76, 77, 175
self-transparency, 55, 56
Sellars, W., 51
sequential specification, 208, 209–210
sexuality, infantile, 87
Shakespeare, W., 31, 33
Shapin, S., 225
Shapiro, D. A., 170, 179, 180
Sigmund-Freud-Institut (Frankfurt), 19, 24, 25, 74, 76, 115, 117
significance vs. meaning [Ricoeur], 169
Silberer, H., 93
Silberstein, E., 82
silence, 211, 217, 218
Simon, H., 138
Simoni, H., 19
Skolnikoff, A., 19, 235
slips of the tongue, 15
Sloan, W. W. J., 171, 179
Smith, J., 167
Society for Free Psychoanalytic Research, 89
Solms, M., xvi, 19, 40, 184–206, 236, 237
Solomon, L., 151
Sophocles, 31
spatial thinking, 203
Sperber, D., 146
Spillius, E. Bott, 38
Spitz, R. A., xxi, 42
splitting, 123
Stalin, J., 61
Starobinski, J., 30
Steele, H., 129
Steele, M., 129

Steiner, R., 10
Stekel, W., 89
Stepansky, P. E., 89
Stern, D., 32, 42, 64
Stiles, W. B., 169, 170–172, 174, 179, 180
Stoller, R. J., 20
Stolorow, R., 64
Stone, M., 186
Strauss, L. V., 236
Stricker, S., 83
structuring reflection vs. structured reflection, 119
Stuhr, U., 19, 231, 232, 235
sublimation, 224
suicide, 159
Sulloway, F., 82, 88
superego, 142
supervision, generalized, xix
Swales, P., 32
symbolization, 203
Symposium on the Unconscious and Science (UNESCO, March 1988), 33
syndrome(s)
  analysis, 195, 198, 199, 205, 206
  clinical, concept of, 187
  syndrome method, 188, 189

Target, M., xvi, 19, 22, 129, 149–167, 232
Taylor, D., 18
texts, in qualitative research, 168
Theunissen, M., 67
thing presentations vs. word presentations, 77
thinking:
  concrete or repetitive, 213
  disturbed/disorganized, 213
Thom, R., 43
Thomä, H., 3, 14, 19, 78
Thomas, S., 233
three box model [Sandler & Sandler], 142, 145
topographic model of mind, 66, 142
topographic regression, 203
Toulmin, S. E., 11, 47, 48, 52, 54, 55, 127
transcendental philosophy, 67
transference, 68, 173, 218, 234, 236
  Bakthin's concept of responsive understanding, 172
  changing nature of, 155
  communication, 215
  concept of, 40, 121, 131
    Argelander on, 75
    and intersubjectivity, 69
    understanding of, 113–124
  conflict [case study], 211
  –countertransference process, 68, 79, 131, 213, 214
    interpretation of, 64
  development of, research on, 103
  dialogical patterns in, 173
  hermeneutic concept of [Loch], 72–74
  interpretation, 102
    research on, 107
  in latency period, study of, 100
  libidinal, 215
  negative, 133, 220
  neurosis, 103
  object, third party beyond [Bakhtin], 172
  processes, investigation of, 19
  related to countertransference, 29
  repetition in, 177
  and repetition of past, 67
  role of in therapy, 68, 205
  sexual, towards analyst, 157, 158, 161
  significance of, 75, 77, 111
  stuck, 218
  thought- [*Gedankenübertragung*], 94
  unconscious processes shown in, research on, 15
transformation cycles, 208, 216, 219
transitional object, 42
transitional phenomenon, 42
trauma:
  concept of, research on, 115–117
  recognized but not treated in analysis, role of, 162–163
traumatized people, clinical work with, 111, 168–183
Traverso, C., 155, 167
treatment efficacy, research on, 98–100

Trendelenburg, F. A., 47
triangulation, concept of, infant studies on, 19
Truax, C. B., 235
truth:
  absolute, 61
  coherence theory of, 60
  historical, concept of, 42
  and truthfulness, 58–62
  universal, 61

Ulm research team, 19
unconscious, the:
  dynamic, 121
    interpretation of, 150
  Lorenzer on, 78
  timelessness of, 42
unconscious assumption, 36
unity of reason, 15
  vs. plurality of sciences, 45–62
University of Heidelberg, Department for Psychosomatic Medicine, 66
Urribarri, F., 38
Uruguayan Psychoanalytic Association, 130

validation, 18, 207, 209
  expert, 21
  pragmatic, 170
van Eemeren, F. H., 127
Varela, F., 43
Varvin, S., xvi, 20, 168–183, 169
Viennese Psychoanalytic Society, 89
  Minutes of, 88, 89
visual mental imagery, 203
Von Foerster, H., 43
von Klitzing, K., 19
von Zeppelin, I., 20, 22
Vygotsky, L. S., 143–146

Wainberg, S., 27
Waldron, S., 19, 235
Wallerstein, R., 3, 10, 18, 32, 36, 151, 223
Weber, M., 235
"Wednesday Meetings" ["*Mittwochsgesellschaft*"], 10
Weizsäcker, C. F. von, 51
Weizsäcker, V. von, 67
Wernicke, C., 188, 191
Westenberger-Breuer, H., 233
Wetzel, D., 233
Whitehead, A. N., 50, 52, 53
Whittle, P., 41
Widlöcher, D. H., xvii, xix–xxiv, 4, 39, 95, 97
Williams, B., 60, 61
Wilson, D., 146
Winnicott, D. W., 30, 37, 40, 42, 127
Winson, J., 186
Wolff, A., 232
word presentations vs. thing presentations, 77
work of negative [Green], 218

Zeppelin, I. von, 234
"zone of proximal development" [Vygotsky], 144
Zueler, M., 186